*Routes to
the Executive Suite*

Routes to the Executive Suite

EUGENE EMERSON JENNINGS

Professor of Management
Graduate School of Business Administration
Michigan State University

McGRAW-HILL BOOK COMPANY

New York   St. Louis   San Francisco   Düsseldorf   Johannesburg
Kuala Lumpur   London   Mexico   Montreal   New Delhi
Panama   Rio de Janeiro   Singapore   Sydney   Toronto

SPONSORING EDITOR   Dale L. Dutton
DIRECTOR OF PRODUCTION   Stephen J. Boldish
EDITING SUPERVISOR   Carolyn Nagy
DESIGNER   Naomi Auerbach
EDITING AND PRODUCTION STAFF   Gretlyn Blau,
   Teresa F. Leaden, George E. Oechsner

ROUTES TO THE EXECUTIVE SUITE

07-032445-X

1234567890 VBVB 754321

To my son, Chip

Preface

SUCCESS IS AN UNSTABLE ROMANCE with change and tradition. No
one understands this marriage of opposites better than the new
business elite of America. Their emergence into full view of corporate watchers occurred largely in the decade of the sixties. Then,
the traditional formula of ladder climbing that had been carefully
refined and practiced during the first half of the century was defied
by men with new ideas about how to make it big in the business
world.

This book is the fourth of a series planned for the purpose of
describing rather than prescribing the strategy and psychology of the
mobile executive. The previously published books, *Executives in
Crisis* and *Executive Success*, represent information drawn from
the authors' experiences during the last twenty years of counseling
corporate executives in career difficulties. The *Mobile Manager* was
a brief attempt to describe the general qualities of the executive
who will inherit the future. This book, *Routes to the Executive
Suite*, presents more precisely both the strategies of success and the

career crises of mobile executives largely produced by the relatively sudden change from the time-honored traditions of success to the risk-taking and venturous tactics and ploys of the new executive.

The title, *Routes to the Executive Suite,* is no gratuitous expression. The main idea in this book is that the route taken to the top greatly determines how the executive will behave. Two men transported over different routes will manage differently. This premise is valid not only because the two men will be different before they commence their arduous journey but also because the wise corporation will put them on different paths to bring out their differences. If the routes make a difference, the corporation can systematically vary the routes to produce divergent and improved qualities and styles of managerial behavior. The size and number of corporations practicing this concept of systematically developing top executives are sufficiently large that one can assume the decade of the seventies will see mobility become a widely accepted tool of management. As corporations rise to this higher stage of management expertise, greater numbers of executives and young aspirants to the executive suite will encounter the dilemma posed by the inertia of tradition that dictates corporations should manage their careers as opposed to the drive for independence that demands self-determination of career paths. We can see that individualism is not the opposite of conformity in the careers and lives of mobile executives. Rather, it is the constant effort of the executive to reconcile the demands of corporate organization with his need for isolation. Individualism today constitutes a form of corporate existence. In a society rapidly becoming totally organized, there are few viable alternatives outside. With nowhere to fly the mobile executives fly within. The men in this book have become the individualists of the corporate world!

The author wishes to acknowledge his indebtedness to many corporations and executives who sponsored and supported his research efforts. Since many corporations are continuing their sponsorship and wish to maintain anonymity, they will not be listed. However, two corporations during the latter part of the forties helped the author to launch his investigation and he wishes to thank Deere & Company and Monsanto Company. The author was greatly helped by several leaves of absence granted by Michigan

State University. Through the years the Graduate School of Business Administration and the department of management have contributed a great deal to this study.

Most of all, the author wants to express his deep appreciation to his wife, Marilynne, who has been his constant companion, secretary, typist, and loyal critic during these twenty years of research.

The book is dedicated to Chip, who has grown into manhood while sharing his father and mother with their study.

Eugene E. Jennings
Okemos, Michigan

Contents

*Routes to
the Executive Suite*

CHAPTER ONE

Winners and Losers

WHAT IS THE EXECUTIVE SUCCESS GAME all about? Any number can play and the rules are made up as the game develops increasingly skilled players. The essential ingredients are a top job to be filled and two or more contenders for it. The winner may come from within or without and is always covered with glory and awarded opportunity. The losers have many options, including retirement, ceremonial new duties, or a switch to another company in hopes of winning a new game. Given a second chance, the colossal failure may emerge a spectacular success overnight and move at flank speed through the corporate maze. Or he may have to quit again and again and job-hop his way among a half dozen companies, grounded to moving horizontally through the American dream.

At the top, careers are broken in ways not possible at lower levels. The arena is relatively small and circumscribed, containing only a few players who must cooperate to compete and compete to cooperate. The high frequency of interaction on a face-to-face basis promotes a degree of realism that pierces the contrived facades of insecure men. Here stereotypes fade under the pressure of intimate circumstance. Few may fake, bluff, and feign with the immunity granted by anonymity to the masses of less perceptive and clever middle- and lower-level managers. Individuality flourishes and ambition becomes finely honed by the drive for perfection. No one, including the president, can arbitrarily use his authority, because at the top it is not so much a matter of superior over subordinates as of mind over minds. In this climate of collegiality, experience is no substitute for mental alertness; glad-handing has little therapeutic value for displacing disappointment; and legitimacy of rights offers little defense for incompetency. The game is played by professionals who have come a long way and who continue the struggle to replace or displace even after the appointment of a new chief. Staying at the top represents a feat no less difficult than getting there to begin with. The question "Who's in charge here?" is never permanently settled. Men and the logic of the corporation's circumstances may be grossly mismatched. The right man may be ahead of the circumstances or he may be behind. Others may want his job worse than he wants to keep it. Or, as a chief, the president may be less capable of controlling his highly spirited charges than he was of excelling as a competing peer. The commonly shared drive to become superordinate perpetually compromises the grace of loyal subordination. The president resides more precariously in the executive suite than any other member because he symbolizes what the whole executive success game is all about. For one reason or another, the chief executive may fail to match his corporate mountain. To the cliché "nothing succeeds like success" must be added the fact that "nothing fails like success." Initial success fails to guarantee ultimate victory, regardless of the level of corporate endeavor, and it fails to provide skills for coping with defeat.

The rules of the success game, being contrivances of human ambition, are extracted from one immutable risk: Winning and losing are derivatives of each other. When success attends some, failure engulfs others. The promotion of one man is a "put down" of at least one other person and often several. Mobility creates immobility. Although the executive is no beast of prey, his organizational circumstances dictate that from the many only a few may be chosen. The

nature of the apex that caps a steeply sloping pyramid below prescribes that the higher men climb, the greater the chance of losing.
This ultimate risk may be compounded through error, inexperi-
ence, and miscalculation.

The men who survive this most hazardous and tortuous experience may appear larger than life. But they are more like representatives of life. Executives have the common desire to prove to
themselves that they are capable of winning. In this sense they are
no different from professional athletes, politicians, lawyers, and
many other players whose games inevitably produce winners and
losers. The executive suite attracts and develops men who enjoy the
give and take of minds jockeying for control and respect. Since
childhood, they have been bred to be winners. Their parents raised
them to go farther and do better than they themselves did. Success
was not simply getting ahead, it was getting ahead of others. In
their sports activities the winner's code was drummed into them so
that they realized that the sop "After all, it's really how well you
played the game" is meant to soften the blow to the loser. There is
still nothing like winning. Even their decisions to go to college or
to drop out and go to work were influenced by a winning strategy.
When they started their climb up the corporate ladder, few knew
exactly how to get to the top. Many acted on blind faith, impulse,
and instinct. But a little experience and familiarity with the corporate maze, including a few promotions, eventually gave direction
and discipline to the raw desire to succeed.

They set their sights to be among the select few at the top of the
corporation. As they gain the vision necessary to see the men in the
executive suite, they take full measure of themselves; and if they decide that they can do it, they will not be happy until they achieve
their goal. Their decisions to nominate themselves for places at the
top are not made suddenly, as when a nagging problem suddenly
gives way to a breakthrough solution. Rather, they acquire their
success orientations gradually in the course of several years, as momentum gathers with each step up the ladder. Once they reach the
executive suite or perhaps even sooner, they focus upon the president's office. To go part of the way when the game is to go all the
way is to become an incomplete man. To lose for not trying is as

foreign to them as to substitute trying hard for winning. Now, as the self-appointed candidate for the presidency places himself in the arena of ultimate success, he contains within his posture a whole lifetime of momentum that cannot be easily turned back even if he chooses. Executives who see themselves as being presidents someday may not be dissuaded from their course except by the logic that they have won or lost. And then, long after they have retired from the arena, the losers may not have accepted the score as final. Each may rationalize that he did not really want the presidency anyway, that it is a man-killer, that he was forced into bidding for it by his friends and supporters, or that he had too many outside interests that conflicted with giving the job its total due. His effort to rationalize is his way of managing disappointment. He must become in fantasy the man he could not become in reality: a winner.

This struggle, which often evokes both noisy desperation and quiet horror among its participants, is not an effort merely to succeed physically or materially. Charles Darwin believed that the first law of life is self-preservation. The jungle he referred to was physical in nature. Among executives the task is not physical survival. They labor in a broader area of discontent. The jungle, if that is the correct word, is characteristically psychological, and the struggle is to survive emotionally. The preservation and enhancement of one's identity or ego can better explain the cast of mobile executives in the pages to follow. The rewards most real to the men who emerge victorious at the top lie close to the very center of psychological fulfillment. The demands of self-respect beg the loser to manage his disappointments and the winner at the top to wisely manage his opportunities. We shall observe how losers and winners evolve their respective strategies. To do so, we shall have to step behind the formal life that represents the enterprise of business and observe the new rules that govern the eminently human journey to the corporate summit.

The executive suite represents for many executives the ultimate arena for testing their capacity to master men. The formality of business enterprise offers an elaborate facade for their strategies of winning and managing their disappointments. But what game has not this double life? The baseball player has his stadium, the politician his congress, and the lawyer his courtroom. These players formally present themselves to their audiences in the name of sports, representative government, and human justice respectively. They have their screens and veils which serve to professionalize their public contributions. While playing the formal versions of their roles, they engage with varying degrees of "savvy" in the informal realities of their games.

For example, the vindictive chatter and aggressive humor that professional football players exchange across the lines during a heated game may be unheard and unseen by the spectator. But it is every bit as real to the athlete as the public version of the game itself. Likewise, the professional eye may perceive the byplay among trial lawyers in their courtroom that escapes the notice of the untrained eye. In both cases, the professional players will agree that the informal side of their games and the public version represent two sides of the same coin. Because these roles are integral to each other, the participants' ability to win depends on their ability to play their formal and informal roles expertly.

In this regard, the big business executive is no different. While attempting to make lasting contributions to the efficiency and effectiveness of corporate enterprise, he is playing the informal game of personal success. Some men overindulge themselves in the practice of achieving and exercising influence. They are often labeled "political." A few are unable to grasp the subtleties of the struggle and may be strangely naïve. Still others selectively perceive only the informal modes of executive life. These cynics stand apart from the winner who attempts to see things as they are. The winner's sense of reality tells him that men press upon their corporations the stamps of their private ambitions and personal desires.

Executives use corporations as much as corporations use the executives' managerial talents. The executive may succeed over others because of his superior contribution to corporate success. Or his corporation may succeed because he achieved superiority over his peers. Who succeeds whom bears directly and simultaneously upon corporate and individual success. The game of winning may be played in an extremely low key with no apparent fighting front because of the masterly way in which sophisticated players attempt to serve their corporations and themselves. But who wins and loses and their strategies of succeeding or of managing disappointments cannot be separated from the formal enterprise of business.

All this is part of the reality of the sophisticated players. Traditional wisdom still prescribes that corporate success and personal winning be interdependent. Getting the right men into the top jobs is a prime necessity. Being a human enterprise, the selection of a new chieftain is subject to error, incompetency, caprice, and whim. Primal instincts, cultural stereotypes, popular opinion, self-interested nomination and sponsorship, and the vices and specialties of politics may all be inextricably woven together in the format by which a new president is selected. The attempt to fit the right man into the top job, while at best an approximation, produces severe hazards and risk for everyone. Behind the projecting of the firm's future goals and needs and a candidate's experience and skills, silent, implicit tests are always invoked for which he must receive excellent marks. Although these hidden persuasions of what constitutes the right man inhere in every format of the selection process today, they are radically different from those that were utilized in the past.

When industry was dominated by many small firms built by entrepreneurs who owned their companies or substantial portions of them, the tycoons naturally believed that ownership was the chief basis for assuring responsible decision making. Who could take better care of their firms than those who owned them? But entrepreneurs who singly dominated their corporations as personal fiefdoms often proved more able to build firms from scratch than to manage them effectively. As corporations became extremely large and public ownership replaced private ownership, the loyalty test became the next prerequisite for assuring that the man at the top would put the profitability of his firm ahead of all other considerations.

This change in the game was a takeoff from the owner's strong emphasis on the loyalty of his subordinates as a test of their promotability. This test, which was originally secondary to the ownership attitude, became primary with the passing of the entrepreneur. The man with corporate fealty acted as if he were a proprietor. For this reason, the loyalty theme grew to a test because it seemed to be capable of producing responsible corporate management. Actually, any decision rule was better than none at all, and we know now that a bad test for selecting top men will work if it is uniformly believed in and applied by all member firms of an industry. Be that as it may, the executive suite represented the last and most intensive trial for the aspiring president. Here his motives and character were most carefully tested and scrutinized. The kind of experiences he had acquired, the men for whom he had worked, his posture and style with superiors and subordinates, his appearance and idiosyncrasies, and his respect for and use of authority represented the vital concerns of his sponsors who nominated him to the highest office. But above all was the belief that only a man in whose heart reverberated total loyalty to the corporation, bordering on passionate affection, could be trusted to put his corporation ahead of all things, including himself.

Loyalty has remained an implicit test in many large corporations to this day. However, it has proved to be fickle and deluding for several reasons, among which is the fact that loyalty may be too easily simulated or feigned by those most desirous of winning. The display of corporate fealty taps human skills that are uniformly distributed among people in general. It cannot be trusted because the ingenuity of the players may enable them to simulate it. But more importantly, the selecting of aggressively loyal executives places inordinate coercion behind the attempt to produce loyal men at lower levels of the corporation. Demanding loyal minds becomes essentially producing obedient minds. The virtues of creativity and spontaneity are not carefully promoted and are cast aside or crowded out of the personality spectrum. For example, the subordinate who attempts to learn the boss's job proves threatening to him if the only place the superior has to go is down or out. Fast learners have to be discouraged in an immobile organization.

The kind of personality that deferred to superiors and expected the same from subordinates appeared logical at the time when business enterprise and the economy were relatively static, moving fretfully from the peaks of economic growth to the valleys of depression or recession. The rebel wanted to make decisions but was unwanted because he did not respect custom, convention, and practice, the foremost among which was the principle of corporate fealty. Rebels were driven out, and from the waves of men slowly ascending to the executive suite evolved cadres of antiseptic personalities. Since this human base from which presidents were selected comprised both enthusiastic actors and true believers of the loyalty ethic, the executive had only to ply his tools of conforming and obeying with better skill and subtlety. The ways in which the game was personally and uniquely contrived showed that not all imagination and creativity had been exhausted during the lengthy, plodding climb to the top.

But then all this that had been expounded as conventional wisdom failed to produce the intended effects under a massive barrage of forces for change and growth. The economy of the decade of the fifties gradually burst from its traditionally uneven, ambulating stride into first a sprint and then a gallop into what finally has become a race of thoroughbreds. In the throes of technological explosion, exponential rates of change, and unheralded economic affluence, the sixties required flexible, mobile men if voids and gluts were not to evolve to dampen the economic spiral. The mobile types came forth as expected, but few predicted that they would in turn spawn a degree of mobility that would drastically change the whole game of winning.

By the mid-sixties, it became apparent that these mobile types were greatly accelerating the very economy that spawned them. Mobility contributed to economic growth and economic growth increased mobility rates. In other words, mobility was both a cause and a consequence of economic growth. Nowhere was this relation between the economic function and mobility of men more clearly demonstrated than in the ranks of men in the five hundred largest industrial corporations. These few, large corporations contributed annually 70 percent of the manufacturing product and 30 percent of the gross national product. The fastest-growing corporations among the members of this most exclusive club incurred the highest mobility rates in their managers and executives.[1] As their ingress

---

[1] Executives are men in the executive suite at the top of the corporation and managers are below them in the developmental stages of middle and lower management.

rates rose, so did the rates by which they lost managers and executives to other firms. Also, to accommodate the demands of growth, the corporations had to move young men prematurely into high-level executive positions. Then the unexpected happened. As the age levels of men at the top declined, the rates of egress of executives increased among both older and younger men. This condition evolved among most of the large industrial corporations. But among the spectacular growth firms, the egress rates increased most dramatically. Finding their growth demands exceeding their ability to produce talented executives from within, corporations had to import more men, which caused their egress rates to increase. It seemed that whatever they did, the rates at which men moved increased.

Furthermore, the rates of mobility among growth corporations affected those with lower growth rates. The more executives moved within growth corporations, the more others moved away from nongrowth firms. The more they moved among firms, the greater the pressure exerted upon any one firm, growth or nongrowth, to move men within. Interfirm mobility affected intrafirm mobility because both were part and parcel of a condition in which the growth of the economy exceeded the population base of available talent. Corporations that could not get and keep their required share and quality of executive talent suffered disastrously at the hands of incompetent men. A growth economy proved to be as destructive to marginally managed firms as it was propitious to their well-managed cousins. In such circumstances, not to grow was to die. The already big corporations had no choice but to grow, since growth firms had the best chance of attracting, developing, and keeping their required share of the scarce supply of managerial and executive talent.

The lack of an effective growth strategy was a sure-fire formula for managerial mediocrity for still another reason. Corporations that did not grow could not sustain a high level of internal mobility. Mobility involves more than the mere movement of warm bodies to the top. The practice of internal mobility involves the immense task of ensuring the survival and development of superior talent. For this reason, mobility was of crucial value because of the additional competency that is generated for the corporation. Nothing reflected an effective growth strategy more than a well-managed mobility program for breeding superior types of executives. The corporation had to grow to produce superior executives who, in turn, represented the chief source for future corporate growth.

Few men thought at the midcentury mark that corporations would devise strategies of growth partly to get and keep talented manpower. In the context of the decade of the fifties, which called for more manpower to produce corporate growth, the reversal that developed in the sixties (i.e., more growth to produce better management) would have seemed to be akin to the tail wagging the dog. Furthermore, the acutely diminished manpower base that will plague corporations in the seventies will force them to perfect their strategies of manpower growth. A rewording of the conundrum in *Through the Looking-Glass* affords the dictum that "The corporation must grow managerially just to stand still economically."

We have just begun to see the beginnings of mobility among industrial managers and executives. They already represent one of the most, if not the most mobile (geographically and hierarchically alike) segments of our population. At least one out of five executives moves each year geographically, as does one out of four managers. In a period of twenty years, the future president moves geographically at least six times and sometimes as many as ten. For every geographical move, the mobile executive will move about three times within the corporation. He will move laterally at least once for every two upward moves and move out of his technical or functional area at least once for every three moves of any type. The probability of more geographical moves increases with the number of hierarchical moves, and conversely the probability of moving hierarchically increases with geographical movement. Mobility patterns uniformly reveal that moving up means moving about. And this pattern is not about to suddenly expire. The growing emphasis upon international business has already produced an increase in the total hierarchical and geographical distances that the future president will be expected to move. For the mobile executive, the relevant question is not whether he will move but when and where he will move next. Mobility has blurred the classical lines of managerial succession to the point that one may ask, "Who's in charge here?" In the five-year period between 1959 and 1964, of the combined total of 1,890 officers in 41 large, well-known corporations, 83 percent had either changed their positions or were new names added to management. At American Telephone & Telegraph Co., 13 new names were added to the officership ranks among 23 top positions; at Aluminum Co. of America, the ratio of new to old was 18 to 25; at American Radiator & Standard Sanitary Corp., 16 to 24; at Armour & Co., 17 to 27; at Bendix Corp., 30 to 52; at Borg-Warner Corp., 17 to 30; at Chrysler Corp., 17 to 27; at General Dynamics Corp., 15 to 21; at General Electric, 20 to 40; and at General Motors Corp., 17 to 40. Between 1961 and 1966, over 70 percent of the officers changed positions. Allis Chalmers Mfg. Co. had 80 percent; American Can Co., 84 percent; Celanese Corp. had 86 percent; National Gypsum Co., 79 percent; Polaroid Corp., 75 percent; Xerox Corp., 87 percent; and Westinghouse Electric Corp., 78 percent. For every two new officers, at least one other left for another organization. In 1962 to 1967, 12 new officers were appointed at Allied Chemical Corporation and 5 executives left; General Mills had 15 new officers and 18 egressors; Litton Industries Inc., 15 and 7; Douglas Aircraft Co., Inc., 10 and 8; Caterpillar Tractor Co., 12 and 9; Sperry Rand Corp., 10 and 4; Union Carbide Corp., 12 and 8; and Westinghouse Electric Corp., 22 and 12. The average time that presidents occupied their offices was reduced almost two full years during this period of time to where, by 1968, it was a little over four years. Who was ahead of whom—and behind—appeared as uncertain as the game of musical chairs, and as unpredictable.

Growth and mobility wreaked havoc with conventional wisdom. The sedate, cloistered atmosphere of the executive suite at times bordered on chaos as men chafed under the onslaught of new pressures and circumstances. The question of who was the right man and what was the logic of the corporation's situation became obfuscated by the frenzied efforts to keep on top or ahead of the booming economy. The corporation was riding a tiger that was capable of devouring its insecure rider if he fell off.

Not all rode the tiger well. Almost two hundred of the five hundred largest corporations (by assets) that started the midcentury had by the late sixties failed to keep their prized standing in the exclusive club. In 1968 alone, there were eight corporations in the five hundred group that were forcibly taken over or forced to seek refuge in the stronger arms of congenial partners. Most of these congenial partners welcomed the marriage because they could not grow fast enough by means of their own internal resources and native acumen. The vast majority of corporations that failed to meet the challenge of change and growth had been traditionally managed by executives who started at the bottom or near bottom of their firms and went to the top. It was not coincidental that corporations that shouted the loudest for men to risk and innovate had perfected in theory and fact the practice of promoting their most loyal natives from within. To stave off defeat, their boards often brought in outsiders, of whom some lacked the capacity to successfully counter the inbreeding and inertia. Nevertheless, it was common to replace the whole corps of top executives with a mix of outsiders and young native executives who had the flexibility, imagination, and spontaneity to adapt to and promote change.

The turbulent years of growth and mobility forced corporations to examine carefully the advantages and liabilities of aggressively practicing the several aspects of the loyalty ethic described in the chapter to follow. Such severe scrutiny brought an end to unmitigated acceptance of the loyalty test by many corporations. The importing into executive suites and presidential offices of large numbers of outsiders and the rapid mobility of young executives within the firm "demysticized" the self-sacrificing company man. He became an obvious anachronism. The career-centered executive arrived, and his competency became the test of his future capability to honor the interests of the corporate community. Today few executives own substantial amounts of corporate stock and fewer than the public at large would suspect have strong, passionate ties to their corporations.

The sixties were a most unconventional, disconcerting, and confusing decade. They marked the end of the loyalty era and the beginning of the career-centered period; in any given executive suite there was a hodgepodge of company loyalists who contrived to settle for what they had and to conserve their gains and outsiders who put their careers and the strong desire to increase their competency on the line. In such an emerging, unsettled environment, men were often evaluated simultaneously by both new and old tests. If they flunked one of them, they could be passed on the other. Almost any basis could be obtained for his nomination if the executive was well-sponsored. Even then, if he flunked all the tests, he could still be promoted provided that others did equally poorly or worse. Not a few aspiring executives were dazed, if not shocked, by the sudden changes in the success game. So much were they disoriented that the key question of the decade of the sixties was: What is the route to the executive suite? The loyal company executive thought he knew, as did the outsider, and if either one was the mobile type, he was vulnerable to being "in" one day and "out" the next. In this game where winners create losers, nothing was as certain as the possibility that the "other" would be promoted.

During the turmoil and strife of the wild sixties, a unifying theme could be found that made the decade more rational than it appeared. It had to do with the attempt to systematically breed talented, competent executives who had not the lethal defects of the loyalty ethic. This effort was at first predicated on the dire need of growth corporations to move available talent as rapidly as new jobs opened up or men were transferred out of old jobs. Men were moved around and up in spectacular numbers. Not a few criss-crossed the functions of marketing, manufacturing, sales, finance, and engineering. It became evident that the movement of men up, down, across, and over was creating a different base of personnel from which executives and presidents were to be selected. Something new and old was at work in the stream of executive activity.

The movement of men was not new. Not even the wide ranging of men from one function or division to another was entirely new to corporate enterprise, although its degree was unprecedented. Nor was it new that the paths that men took to get to the top affected the mix of talents and skills that they brought to bear upon corporate and personal success. It has always been implicitly understood that the routes to the top affected the postures and dispositions of the men who used them. But the route performed a secondary function. Far more important than the route traveled were the inborn personality characteristics and dispositions that experience tended

/to call selectively into expression and that work perfected. In other /words, men at the top were born at the top in the sense that they would have gotten there regardless of the route that transported them. The real route was to be genetically favored at birth by a successful personality. The implicit sign of such high birth was the capacity to work hard and dutifully in the service of the larger cause of corporate success.

But the new wisdom acknowledged that routes to the top can produce a contribution that far exceeds anything that may be attributed to personality. What tradition presumed to be human nature came to be seen as only a minor part of human potentiality. The corporate environment had traditionally selected only a few of the potential qualities and skills that could be utilized in the managerial effort. In effect, the way the corporation was organized and managed screened out those who had different potentials for development and dampened and discouraged the development of unique qualities. The corporation committed a self-fulfilling prophecy. For example, the slow movement of men to the top did not require men with ability to quickly assimilate experiences. Fast learning was discouraged, and fast learners were admonished that perfection was more important than speed. Or, as another example, decision making was not fostered because the number of options was severely restricted by a monolithic authority system. Since only one man—the chief executive officer—made decisions, no one needed to be trained in decision making and no one learned to excel in thinking for himself.

However, the potential ability to assimilate experiences and to make self-determined decisions was more widely shared among people than the typical corporation desired and traditional wisdom decreed. A wider range of the individual's capacity or endowment could be developed and brought to bear upon corporate effort. Thus, the winners who went to the top were not necessarily the most talented and the losers left behind were not necessarily those that were destined to lose anyhow. A drastic change in the rules of the game of winning and losing effected vast changes in the kinds of men who won and their strategies of winning. The way in which men moved to the top became decisive in producing the right men at the top. The route taken was a kind of school for future executives.

In this view, there is nothing inherently predictive of managerial expertise. No one at birth or even at the age of majority will exhibit the set of qualities that are necessary for winning. Such a set is unknown. During the decade of the fifties, psychologists descended (or ascended, depending upon the reader's point of view) upon corporations in search of those qualities that would predict executive success. The search has failed to isolate one trait or set of qualities that scientifically predicts executive expertise and mobility to the top in advance of the fact. And if these well-intentioned scientists had a chance to discover this fountain of executive effectiveness, they lost their propitious moment when, in the sixties, many corporations opened up the middle-management sluices to allow men of different and more varied skills and abilities to go to the executive suite.

The deemphasis of personality and the growing emphasis upon performance and competency has made the search for personality traits and dispositions seem trivial and irrelevant. And while it is not possible yet to predict who precisely will pick up all the marbles on election day and what precisely will be the new president's formal program of action, he will have been shaped less by the loyalty ethic than by the fact of mobility.

Stated succinctly, mobility has drastically increased the tempo of winning and losing. While one can go up faster and slip behind faster than ever before, the same individual can go quietly from being "in" to "out" and another may rebound faster from defeat. Mobility places a premium upon individuality, independence, and self-assertiveness. Aspirants to the top must rely upon their individual resources. They must manage their careers. In pitting themselves against the corporate universe around them, their risks will soar if they lack a strategy of winning. The unusual feature about the executive success game is the large number who do not play to win but who really want to win. Their implicit model of the game is comparable to the tradition whereby men of God received their call to the ministry. This rule of nomination by higher authority prohibits choosing the optimal strategy of winning. Today the winner more often than not practices the strategy of self-nomination. He aggressively maximizes the opportunities available to him within and without the corporation and becomes as much a partner to the promotion act as the corporation itself. In him we can see that success is no longer a one-sided game in which the outcome is solely contingent upon the arbitrary judgments of the corporation.

The decade of the fifties produced a transitional period in which executives both utilized and mocked the "call by higher authority" rule. While this practice was formally held inviolable, it proved amenable to craft and prudence. By 1970 many corporations made the new rule explicit. The individual had as much responsibility as the corporation for determining his worth and promotability. In the companies that did not make the rule explicit, it became implicit by the fact that so many winners were produced by the self-nomination strategy. Today, the wise corporation has ceded to the ablest members what it rightly insists on for itself: the right to maximum choice and mobility. This trend of understanding and recognizing the drive for individual self-development and self-determination is not about to suddenly revert to the traditional one-sided game. It has behind it the force of a new generation liberated by unprecedented affluence and national growth. Mobile executives and aspirants now undergird the entire economic structure. This novel switch in the game of success emanated from the craft and daring of men who realized their essential worth. They not only played a different game, they won because they changed the rules. Of course, real-world events are probabilities, but the odds and risks may be substantially reduced if a generation of men can determine the rules by which they play the game. Unfortunately, through ignorance or incapacity, many still play by the old rules of waiting for the call from their corporate deities. They wait and wait, never attempting to skillfully extract success from a two-sided model of the executive success game. Many grow too old to quit yet are too young to retire.

Success today has become extremely complicated. The internal rules governing the members of and aspirants to the top call for new theories, attitudes, and skills. The answer to the perennial question "What makes a winner?" will today necessarily acknowledge that skill has replaced effort. One who expects to reach the top must perform to gain nomination by his superiors for bigger jobs. He must also nominate himself for higher positions and use his options to go elsewhere when he cannot move ahead in his present job. He must manage his career for maximum effect and his strategy must take account of the basic routes to the executive suite. These routes largely determine who has the best chance of succeeding. These probabilities may guide decisions about whether to make one move or another.

Lest he have the impression that this information will produce an instant winner, the author acknowledges that a lot of slippage occurs between knowing a winning strategy and practicing it effectively. This slippage can be great enough to produce a loser. Nevertheless, knowing routes and their probabilities helps to make logic prevail over impulse, to allow the aspirant to think more than one move in advance, to take account of the likely moves of his opponents, and to avoid loss of career time by sitting and watching as the corporation dictates all the moves. The inherent risks of succeeding and failing by means other than those that ensue from one's own coordinates may be greatly reduced. Then, too, in a broader sense, career management allows each individual to assume personal responsibility for determining the style of life to which he privately aspires. By selecting routes, he chooses his future. By this means the individual rather than the corporation assumes the driver's seat. In conclusion, the engine of success today is competency, which is fueled by mobility. The mobile executive has mounted the success ethic on wheels and drives with the self-confidence and self-determination of a man who knows where he is going, what the costs and payoffs are, and what to do if he reaches a dead end. The success game has been joined by sophisticated players who are raising the facade which masks the double life of the corporate executive. Shorn of its duplicity, the struggle to succeed becomes both in appearance and fact a game of chance with known probabilities that indicate risks and with basic rules that require skill and mastery for their wise implementation.

CHAPTER TWO

The Inside Route

THE MEN WHO ARE STANDING IN LITTLE CLUTCHES, moving quickly here and there in the walnut-paneled boardroom, left their executive suites only moments before to attend this very important meeting. The personification of the end product of the whole complex success game is about to appear. Glancing furtively at the door, these men wait for the newly appointed president and chief executive officer to convene the first official meeting of his administrative staff. Their new leader belongs to a distinct managerial elite—an elite made up of men who mature in one company with the conviction that they will eventually be in charge. For them the presidency is the top rung of the corporate ladder, the final proving ground of their ability to command men. The new president enters the boardroom, nodding, turning, and greeting as he makes his way to his chair at the front of the precisely polished, large, oval conference table. His mind momentarily flashes back to the day, some forty years ago, when he graduated from college and joined this corporation as an engineer. He can almost smell the oil, the chief product of this giant corporation, to which he was the first of a group of educated men to apply the science of thermal cracking. After that, it was climbing, climbing, slowly but surely; becoming general superintendent, head of a division ten years later, president of a subsidiary, then going to corporate staff as vice-president, executive vice-president, and now finally reaching the prestigious-looking president's chair. Dressed in sober blue with a perky little yellow carnation pinned to his lapel, he commences to lead his directors, who are full-time executives in the corporation or predecessors who have helped to groom him for this final test of his maturity.

The ascension of a new president occurs frequently during any given year in the boardrooms of the big industrial corporations. The chief executive could be Monroe Rathbone of Standard Oil Co. (New Jersey), Frederic T. Donner of General Motors, Frederick Kappel of American Telephone & Telegraph, or Lawrence Litchfield, Jr., of Alcoa. The corporation's product may not be oil, the president's background may not be engineering, but he will probably be a college graduate. Regardless of what distinguishes him from other presidents of great corporations, he is similar in a very special way. He is an insider—a one-company man who has spent all or most of his career in a single corporation. If he worked for another company, it was during the early phase of his career and at lower rungs of the corporate ladder. Fred J. Borch started in General Electric's lamp division immediately after graduation from Western Reserve University in 1931. Thirty-two years later, Borch at age fifty-three became president of General Electric Co. Edward J. Bock chose the inside route to the top of Monsanto Company. In 1945, armed with a master's degree from Iowa State College, he went to work for Monsanto and became president twenty-seven years later.

Borch and Bock represent the traditional type of business executive. They took the conventional route that starts at the bottom and extends directly to the top. While appearing straight, it is deceptively long and requires time, a whole career in fact. The corporation is a biological experience. Youth enters at the base of the pyramid and old men emerge at the apex. From aging they presumably gain the necessary experiences that produce competency. They must vertically traverse the whole corporate hierarchy. This total immersion requires that they put their careers in the hands of a single company. No one not duly baptized an insider can expect to occupy the seat of ultimate authority. This constitutes the principal rule of the conventional style of the success game.

The conventional route represents a formula for success that has deep roots in the historic character of America. Since earliest times, two themes have struggled for dominance in the minds of men. One theme advises the young man to "go west"—it tells him that the grass is greener on the other side, that if he delays success will pass by, and that failure is misspent opportunity. The other theme admonishes him to settle down, to grow deep roots, to become somebody of consequence. During the Depression of the thirties the latter theme achieved ascendancy in the minds of most of those who later, in the fifties, went to the top. As children they were taught that after completing their schooling they should get a job with a good, secure company that would not pass out of existence overnight as so many had during the dark days of this greatest of all economic catastrophies. For that matter, getting and retaining a job with any organization, large or small, was a feat of no mean repute. In such a situation of scarcity, with more men than jobs, even the college graduate expected to start at the very bottom in work that would be menial even to the high school dropout. He was prepared to work hard, to overearn his rewards, to be grateful for whatever advances and opportunities came his way, and to always show deference and respect to his corporate benefactors The last to be put out in the street were those men who showed great devotion to duty and company.

Traditionally, young people are expected to think that a job, like a marriage, is supposed to be "till death do us part." Once the courtship has been consummated by a vow of fealty, it is a mark against the aspiring executive's character to leave the firm voluntarily or involuntarily. After he once places his fate in its hands, he cannot disavow his loyalty with immunity. No one needs an excuse for staying, but everyone needs to explain leaving. Staying symbolizes strong character, endurance, and reliability; leaving suggests weakness, cowardliness, and unreliability. The quitter does not know what he wants; the stayer knows who he is and where he wants to go. In other words, the men who leave are "quitters," and no one respects a quitter. As one confirmed insider replied when asked why he did not parlay his reputation into a better job at another company: "Suppose they found out that I was using them for selfish reasons. I don't think you can play games and win. I think that the word will get around that you are unreliable and insincere —a job hopper."

The decade of the sixties had more than its share of retirements of executives who were young and impressionable men during the Depression years. In 1967, for example, they included Austin T. Cushman, sixty-five years of age, chairman of the board and a thirty-five-year career man in Sears Roebuck and Co.; Frederick R. Kappel, sixty-four, chairman of the board of American Telephone & Telegraph and a forty-two-year career man; Leslie B. Worthington, president of United States Steel Corp., with forty years in his company; Frederic G. Donner, sixty-five, chairman and a thirty-five-year man with General Motors. These corporate insiders could not understand or appreciate the growing horde of quitters among the executives in the five- and six-figure salary brackets. They believed that an executive had a loyalty to the corporation that overrode advantages to be gained by quitting.

A former chairman of the board of General Motors remarked that a corporation could not be well-served by men who placed their careers ahead of their corporation. He could not understand or forgive the executives who quit General Motors because they were bypassed or felt grievously offended by some unthinking superior. He suggested that the admittedly lopsided fealty of the executive to his corporation in the first half of the century had been balanced in the second half by the practices of many corporations that assured the executive of financial security. He believed that corporations should not fire an executive who had given the best years of his life and remained steadfastly loyal to his firm. And he felt that for this reason executives should be even less concerned with job opportunities elsewhere. They had a responsibility to be more loyal now that the company assured them financial security.

The insider believes that men who are strangers to the corporation should not be allowed to occupy an office in the executive suite. Charles G. Mortimer of General Foods Corp. believed that only those men who are ready to "marry" the company and never divorce it can succeed to the top. It is wrong not to promote from within because it is unfair to those who place their fate solely in the hands of a single company. Furthermore, it is bad management to import strangers. Monroe J. Rathbone took the inside route to the presidency of the giant Standard Oil Co. (New Jersey). He subscribed to his corporation's traditional beliefs that an outsider, no matter how able, could not be effective any more than an internist would make a good pediatrician. The insider is preferred to the outsider because of his maximum training and indoctrination in the particular affairs and practices of the company and industry.

With this attitude, the future president starts his career. Small increments of well-earned pay raises and slow, plodding upward advances reinforce his attitude of settling down in the company and forgoing the ventures and risks of mobility. He immobilizes himself to gain upward mobility. This form of winning demands concentrated living. His whole lifestyle has to be responsive to the regimen of hard work that includes long hours and meticulous attention to detail. He arranges his private life to maintain and enhance his corporate existence. Family life has to be sacrificed, friends and acquaintances chosen for career value, and community activity engaged in for instrumental purposes. Because he moves his family to areas where his corporate colleagues live, his wife interrelates almost exclusively with company wives. Cliques and intimate circles serve to insulate the company wife from noncompany people. The carefully circumscribed private life creates varying degrees of xenophobia. The stranger includes anyone outside the company or from a lower level in the company or without the proper manners and graces, apparel, and address. Feared or disrespected the most is anyone who actually lives a private life apart from the closed circle of company friends. The ingroup prospers on intimacy, not privacy; which means that no one has any secrets and everyone has to contribute gracious amounts of scuttlebut and rumor. Life becomes a huge goldfish bowl. In this sense, the insider wraps up his whole life in corporate affairs. He becomes a one-worlder, or, to put it differently, his whole world becomes his company.

The inside route has become the most popular route to the top. Even during the mobile decade of the sixties, almost three of every five presidents who were not founders or favored by birth or marriage took the conventional route to the top. But it is no longer the fastest or safest route, nor the most glamorous or exciting. Nevertheless, many aspirants to the top are plying the insider's formula. It is today better understood why they do. They arrive from childhood with great concern for being protected, unthreatened, safe. This concern extends through all levels, from the individual's personality through family, community, nation, and even the world. Driven by safety concerns, he seeks a route to success that produces stable conditions. There stands the large corporation, a symbol of both security and success. By joining and belonging to it, he adopts the dominant value of the insider's success game; win-lose. This means that he will not risk a little to win a lot. To do so is to court failure, and a little of that is too much.

Of course, some executives' dominant need is to avoid failure. While doing nothing wrong, they do very little well. They are the "Mr. Cleans" who occasionally receive promotions because they have nothing against them. Still others may pursue success with reckless abandon. However, the strategy that traditionally produced the largest number of presidents in the fifties involved doing the common routines well and avoiding excellence in the unusual. They work to achieve success and to avoid failure. Whenever the insider gets a promotion he will tuck it safely under his belt and commence to work patiently for the next, being careful not to endanger what he has already gained. Loyalty to company becomes the chief instrument for achieving success while avoiding any fear of losing. The candidate's behavior comprises the trilogy of hard work, abject subordination to superiors, and respect for the corporate community. This is the loyalty ethic. Seen through the eyes of a believer, the corporation appears as a tightly enclosed arena in which success and security go together when and if a rigid set of corporate rules and norms is followed carefully.

The first of these prescriptions for success without insecurity requires that superiors and subordinates be basically work-oriented and that managers be promoted to vacant positions. The relationship between work and promotion follows the traditional logic that the one necessarily precedes the other. Hard work undergirds the whole promotion program, and advancement becomes more a reward after the fact than an incentive to achieve the fact. Few superiors so indoctrinated realize that a promotion may be the cause of high performance. Even if they realize this possibility, they do not apply it because of their inability to extract a promotion for a deserving subordinate and, more importantly, to receive a promotion for themselves for developing a promotable subordinate. Because superiors are not placed under the gun to produce future presidents, they often leave positions to less effective subordinates.

This work rule helps subordinates as employees and superiors as corporate representatives. Work is delegated in such a fashion that routine assignments go to subordinates and major assignments are reserved for superiors, with the result that the gap between the two is carefully maintained. Superiors deserve promotions and subordinates are awarded them. The amount of development that a manager receives largely depends upon the willingness of his superior to vary his work assignments. New assignments are relatively routine in nature and are held to a minimum consistent with work efficiency.

It is said that this work-oriented environment attracts and produces achievement-directed men. Many studies affirm that the executive typically seeks interesting and challenging tasks and attempts to perform them with skill and dispatch, and that his efforts may eventually be rewarded by upward mobility. The steps up the corporate ladder represent increasing degrees of challenge. Presumably, if work became more interesting with each step down the ladder, the executive would work to descend rather than ascend. The direction of mobility is not important as long as it provides jobs and satisfies the executive's achievement needs. The fun is not in mobility; the fun is in doing things right and efficiently. Since upward mobility is slow and lateral movements are practically unheard of, the insider learns to wait patiently. Meanwhile, he perfects his work routines and takes great pride in a job well done. His office gives him his sense of identity. The picture with which he associates in his mind is that of an executive about fifty years of age with his coat off, leaning over a desk with a pencil in hand, making some kind of draft or memo.

More basic still is the rule that executives can manage only what is thoroughly known to them. The executive sees the corporation as a system of organized experiences. Each managerial level in the hierarchy forms a layer of knowledge tied to the layers above and below it. To comprehend one level of management the executive must master the layers of knowledge below it. To understand the whole corporation sufficiently to manage it, he must pass through all or most of the levels of management below the presidency. At the top the insider believes in running the whole corporation. His style of managing is felt throughout the length and breadth of the corporation. He is not comfortable with the idea of having the top man run the executive group while the executive group runs the corporation. Nor does it occur to him that the knowledge required of a foreman and that required of an executive are unrelated but that the skills of the two men may be very similar. The insider has little respect for the idea that a good manager can run almost anything.

The insider observes carefully the logic of the organization chart. The pyramiding of men on top of men that he believes assures work efficiency becomes the end of human development. The processes of learning become tailored to the rungs of the corporate ladder. Alien to the insider is the thought that a young man fresh out of school makes a better corporate executive if he shortens the lengthy climb through middle-management ranks. Few realize that, by staying too long in lower levels of management, skills or dispositions can be learned that make for poor execution of high-level positions. The insider's mentality develops from an unnatural coercion of the learning processes. His mind is a product of an organizational structure that emphasizes getting work done rather than developing talented people. Executives are born, not made; and the loyalty test (hard work, subservience to superiors, respect for the company's character) is the chief instrument for identifying the future executive. The men who scale the corporate ladder are ipso facto the most talented and deserving; thus, superiors find rather than breed executives, and on this premise pivots the insider's dream of making it.

However, given the facts of mobility, the insider's formula for success has less semblance to reality today than it did a decade ago. The consequence of such change is that the aspirant working the conventional route today will go through an agonizing reappraisal of his formula, and during this time he may shed his naïve faith in the lessons of the past. A close study of this reappraisal process among insiders caught in the mobility crunch of the sixties reveals that, as entry people starting their careers, they place blind faith in the loyalty ethic as a matter of expediency and convenience rather than planning. Their formula represents a gut reaction that has not become comprehensive enough to serve as an intelligent strategy. After about five to eight years of experience and considerable familiarity with the inner workings of their corporate systems, they discover that a mobile society has brought about gaping holes in their formula. They have had to work hard to get the little mobility that they have obtained and wonder if there is not an easier way; and there is.

Once the insider is at the top of the mountain, he can always look back for the best way up. But when struggling at the halfway mark he may pause to gain perspective—only to see more mountain ahead of him than behind, with no clear signs pointing to the safest and fastest route. Middle managers will almost always acquire for varying lengths of time a sense of being lost. They will have had destroyed the notion that they had as wide-eyed young men fresh out of college that the top is just a few leaps away. They will suspect that there is a different and more efficient way to climb the upper half than the lower, but the actual skills and routes will remain vague and incomprehensible. This midmountain blurring of vision may be attended by a growing feeling of isolation and despair. It is, indeed, common to find in large industrial corporations that the most depressed and cynical group comprises the middle managers. They have come far enough to sense how much more difficult it will be to climb ahead. The fact is that what is required to take them to the middle is not what is necessary to take them to the top. Unless they are carefully coached and counseled by sponsor-type superiors, they will lose their footing; and many, if not most, do.

This period of doubting and testing the corporate system offers the individual the opportunity to gain perspective. He will observe that many achieve high scores on the loyalty test and receive few, if any, promotions. He notes the advanced ages of men above him and wonders why they did not get into the winner's circle. He may discover the possibility that he has a bad formula, but until he gets a better one he will hang on to it. What he usually does is to make additions to his formula that will better explain the separating of the men from the boys. One of these new ingredients is the often-heard notion among men halfway up the ladder that success must run in some peculiar cycle all its own, that it is caused by sunspots or some other mysterious or unmanageable force such as fortune, luck, or chance. In accounting for success, either winner or loser may allocate to fortune a huge share of responsibility, but he is probably ignorant of the complexity of his struggle, or practicing self-deception, or taking on false airs of humility, or speaking for the public ear.

The younger the executive, the more willing he is to account for the roulettelike pattern of his replacing or beating out a much older man for the presidency. Raleigh Warner, Jr., succeeded Herbert Willetts to the presidency of Socony Mobile Oil Co. An early arrival [1] at the top at the age of forty-three, Warner, attempting to explain why he was replacing sixty-five-year-old Willetts, reported, "I just happened to be in the right place at the right time." This accidental meeting of the young executive and his propitious situation never really occurred, and as an explanation the idea represents a cliché from a once-immobile world when men seldom arrived at the top until their late fifties. In that world a forty-three-year-old president was an exception, and one could turn to the principle of luck to account for the rare instances of early

---

[1] By definition, an early arrival is anyone made president of a major industrial corporation by the age of forty-six or younger and who is not related by marriage or blood to any power group in the corporation or any previous member of the executive suite.

success while still supporting the ideals of hard work and corporate loyalty for the aspiring executive below.

However, in the mobile world to be described in the following chapters, no one becomes president at age forty-three through luck. Even though the chances of becoming an early arrival are greater today, opportunities to get to the top are much greater. Men work as hard today as before to do their corporate assignments, but, in addition, they work harder to get to the top. If anything describes the new winner, it is his aggressiveness in finding and getting to the right place at the right time, and this finding of the route to the top is hardly luck. The game of the odds or gods is forced rather than merely acknowledged. The mobile executive is not a passive party to the promotion process.

The typical insider is handicapped because he believes that the anointed should never show hungry ambition to go all the way. The rule is: Never *appear* to be self-serving even though you must be to succeed. However, it is common for insiders to hide their success drive for so long that they deceive themselves. Many insiders at the top, such as Fred Borch of Monsanto, report that they never dreamed of going to the summit. When Louis K. Eilers assumed the presidency of Eastman Kodak at the advanced age of sixty, he remarked about the secret of success in this fashion: "I never thought about going ahead. These things have just happened to me." Must the reader presume that this fine amalgam of chemist and manager who succeeded in a corporation known for its excellent research and management just happened to be in front of a chair each time the music stopped? It cannot be presumed that the effort put into his many assignments did not activate the promotion process and that his rise to the top was strictly the result of a series of calls from his ultimate superiors. At best, Eilers's remarks reflect the exception to the rule.

However, few men who go all the way do not develop somewhere in their midcareers a strong identification with members of the executive suite and once in or near it do not decide to go all the way. Since tradition prohibits insiders from showing hungry ambition to go all the way, it is common for them to turn their success drive underground. But beneath their public facades the quest for challenge, power, status, and money continues to churn up the energy and discontent needed to go all the way and to avoid the pitfall of finding a more interesting job at lower levels in which to pursue self-satisfaction. The careers of mobile executives show that their ability to see the top often precedes wanting to go there. Further, seeing the top conditions their drive to go there. Some who achieve a clear view of the top decide against it, while others increase their desire to move upward. For them winning is not a sometime thing.

Belief in luck proves too impotent to direct the conscientious efforts of the midmountain executive. The next step in this period of critical self-examination involves breaking through his self-deceptions. Here he will turn upon the formula itself after discovering that the influence of hard work is more apparent than real, just as is that of luck. The work aspect of the loyalty theme lacks potency because few do not work hard who really want to succeed. Men who formulate success strategies without trying to succeed do not strongly want to succeed. In rebuttal, the questions to be asked the pious extoller of the hard-work bit are: What kind of hard work? Who will be the judge of my hard work? What happens if we disagree?

The fact of the matter is that a slight edge always prevails. The ✓ winner never works inordinately harder than the loser. The winner of an Indianapolis 500-mile race may gain five times the financial rewards of the second-place driver and may win the race by a tenth of a second, but he did not necessarily drive five times harder. In a professional golf classic, the winner may average a half stroke difference per hole over the lowest money winner, but he does not necessarily work harder. In the executive's world, evaluating men by their performances means that skill augurs more success than effort, and the differences in competence are slight at that. For this reason, the study of most mobile men in the sixties shows clearly that the application of effort does not predict upward mobility. There are more hard workers than upward mobiles. If investing energy in work was the basis of upward mobility, there would be more at the top than at the bottom. The future president leaves behind many hard workers each time he is promoted. The fact of the matter is that hard work as it is variously defined constitutes a necessary but not sufficient cause of upward mobility. It is not a route to the top.

Still, many frustrated climbers will believe that the route to the top requires a combination of luck and hard work. To exploit luck, the executive must be ready when and if the call comes; and the work theme is exploited by doing the best job in order to receive the call. Together luck and hard work seem to the naïve insider the complete answer to success. However, the manager may do his best at his job and exploit the propitious moment when the call finally comes and still be behind others on the way to the top. As one mobile executive said, "It's working smart, not hard, that pays dividends." The aspiring executive must plan his career and work his plan. We shall study in the chapters to follow the several ways that "working smart" may become a winning strategy and the various aspects of performance that produce a route to the top. Suffice it to say, an inadequate plan or strategy promoted by hard work is a sure fire formula for immobility.

Meanwhile, midmountain blurring will further turn the insider into a determined decoder. In his desperation to decipher the mysterious ways of corporate promotions, he will become more open and exposed to more conventional mythology. He will typically fall prey to the formula that orders probabilities of success to conform to the shape of the corporate pyramid. One version states that the probability of going higher relates to the width of the pyramid. Since the apex is narrower than the base, the lower the level the less probability of going to the top. This notion implies that the probability of going to the top is greater after one reaches the middle of the pyramid because relatively fewer men are positioned there than at the bottom. The aspiring executive is competing against fewer men at the middle than at the base levels. Thus, an occupant of the executive suite has a substantially greater chance of becoming chief executive officer than a middle manager. Once again, it is not the absence of facts that makes this notion invalid. Rather, it is that this idea produces an impotent strategy of winning because mobility probabilities are not based upon the number of men at the levels in question. In other words, mobility is not a function of numbers or supply. Frequently the first-level manager above the worker is heard to say, "If I can only get to become a second-level manager,

I can be on my way." Or often second-level managers remark, "The hardest thing in my life was to get a promotion out of the first level." Or another said, "We've got so many first-level managers that in this company you are nothing until you become a second-level manager." This may be true, but the indictment has more to do with poor personnel relations than mobility probability. A cursory examination of the pyramidal shape shows that the number of positions decreases with each advance up the slope. The fewer men there are above, the more difficult it is for the many below to advance upward; and this difficulty increases the higher one advances. The last step is far more improbable than the first step.

In many corporations the author found a slightly more sophisticated version of the pyramid strategy. It states that the shortest distance to the top provides the greatest chance of success. This version is a takeoff from the theme that nothing succeeds like success. Granted that one may define success for himself to be the shortest distance traveled between the starting gate and the finish line, but it is dangerous to believe that the farther one gets away from the gate the better chance he has of finishing ahead of others. We shall see that the converse is often equally valid, which leaves the aspirant with nothing. Suppose the organization was flat rather than pyramidal. The organization chart at Sears, Roebuck & Co. shows three or four levels of authority. The distance on the chart between the president in Chicago and a department manager of a Lansing, Michigan, branch store is relatively short. But there is absolutely no relationship between this distance and the distance to be traveled by the department manager who wants to become president some day. Anyone who predicates his mobility upon the organization chart will be more easily deceived by other practices even less productive of mobility.

A winning strategy must first take account of the fact that the route to the top is a function of demand and skill. The demand for managers at third or fourth levels above the worker may be growing faster than the supply of men at first and second levels. If this is the case, it will be relatively easy to move up to that level where demand is disproportionately higher than supply. This is precisely what has happened in the decade of the sixties in many growth corporations. The third and fourth levels above the worker or one or two levels below the division manager grew the fastest proportionately. These managers of managers represent the widest part of the corporate organization in terms of relative demand. Hundreds of new skills and techniques and functions have been introduced in order to manage in a rapidly changing and growing economy. Scores of new scientific and technical disciplines are coordinated through more and different managerial functions.

In the decades preceding the midcentury mark, the size of the managerial group was determined by the needs of production. Then, the greater the output of physical goods, the larger was the work force and the larger, also, the supervising force of first-level managers. A favorite comparison was the ratio of managerial expense to production expense. At the midcentury mark the ratio was approximately 30 percent compared to 10 percent at the end of the nineteenth century. In 1951, during a conference of several hundred corporation presidents that the author attended, his report about the increase in managerial expense was viewed with alarm. The general consensus was that the war and the insatiable seller's market that followed made big business flabby around the midsection. Little did these presidents suspect that the two decades of unprecedented economic growth awaiting them would make present managerial costs look puny by comparison. The ideology of managing for growth made imperative the need to excel in innovation and flexibility. Max Weys rightly observed that if the prime mission of management is to deal with change, then the size of management should be roughly proportionate to the role of innovation rather than the amount of physical output. A lively economy produced a proportionately larger middle-management force than the economy of the Depression years. Managing change created a changing management or, to put it differently, the rate of innovation and the increase in the managerial force are functions of each other.

Reduced to mobility terms, the high rate of innovation and change increases the rate of mobility to these middle-management positions. Thereafter, the apex of the pyramid above the girth closes in rapidly,[2] so that getting above middle management is far

[2] This is true even though the executive organization at the top has increased substantially.

more difficult than getting to it. One perceptive executive of a corporation that had this girth-apex asymmetry and who did make it to the top recalled, "Just when you think you are on your way, you aren't." False hopes and expectations arise from being spooked by the shape of the corporate pyramid. Further, the fastest distance between the bottom and the top is not a straight line. This was more true in the premobility era than in the decade of the sixties. The aspiring executive who has had three or more successive promotions within the same functional or technical area, such as marketing or engineering, is taking the long route to the top. He may feel mobile, but he has been spooked by the organization chart. The most mobile executives move laterally at least once for every two moves upward, and they move out of their technical or functional area at least once in every three moves. For every three moves of any type —up, lateral, within, or without their area of basic expertise—they will move at least once geographically. Few mobile executives uniformly show in their career histories less than five geographical moves in a twenty-year period, and most show seven moves or more. The probability of more geographical moves increases with the number of hierarchical moves; and, conversely, the probability of moving hierarchically increases with geographical movement.

The mobility patterns of the most mobile executives uniformly reveal that moving up also means moving about, and this pattern is not about to expire suddenly. The growing emphasis upon international business has already produced an increase in the total hierarchical and geographical distances that the mobile manager will be expected to move. For the mobile executive, the relevant question is not will he move, but when and where will he move next. He invariably takes the longer distance to the top because it is the faster route. It is faster because mobility offers greater opportunity to achieve competency. The winning strategy becomes a function of the speed of mobility, not the pyramidal distance to be traveled and the ability to quickly assimilate experiences. The men who go to the top most rapidly cover the most territory and still arrive at the top younger. Hence, the marketing manager who turns down a lateral move to the side unwittingly sidelines himself. He misperceived the route. Furthermore, he has failed to pass an implicit test far more difficult and strenuous than the loyalty ethic or the ownership interest code that preceded the era of rapid change and growth.

Men whose upward mobility is arrested halfway up the slope break down into two groups. The less discerning members are forced to behave in terms of the propitious moment. They take each job in stride and work hard, in accordance with the loyalty theme. They are unaware of the maze, its constraints and opportunities. They adjust to a reality that does exist insofar as many at their level and above have the same set of expectations about their probabilities. But there is another reality that others, who are more perceptive, utilize. They are route-bright in that they map the many constraints and opportunities with greater realism. The route-dull may live more comfortably because they are unaware of this other world that carries great risk. The difference here is a greater degree of objectivity on the part of the former group.

The route-bright are capable of testing the loyalty theme against the facts of mobility. For example, Clifford D. Siverd of American Cyanamid Company puttered around at the lower levels for long periods of time and then suddenly caught fire and roared to the top. The route-dull manager will fail to explain this not-so-rare phenomenon with his notions of loyalty. He will suspect shenanigans of an ulterior type, such as a favorable marriage or "brown-nosing," or he will explain it by appealing to luck and chance. As one middle-level insider exclaimed, "Well, you have to have a guy like Siverd now and then, it keeps the old boys on their toes." Meaning he is not "for real." However, the route-bright executive treats the Siverd phenomenon as data. He studies his corporate picture carefully and draws his own map—one that allows him to face his constraints and opportunities squarely and effectively. Let us note that any map is as good as another if the traveler does not know where he wants to go. His destination is conditional upon what he expects to find there. Some kind of mind picture of his goal makes it attractive. Thus, the route-bright manager needs to know what constitutes life at the corporate summit and, as a second basic consideration, he needs to know where the top is. In this regard, it is interesting that a map does two things for the aspiring executive: It guides his ambition and partly determines the strength of his drive. Many midmountain managers have had their ambition diluted because they unknowingly misperceived the nature of the top itself.

This pinnacle of success that attracts the ambitious many on the craggy lower slopes of the corporate Everest is a classical deception. Of course, the top legally is the few offices in the executive suite whose occupants are formally charged by the board of directors with the authority and responsibility for running the whole corporation. The chief executive personifies the tip of the corporate top. In years past, corporations were singularly dominated by strong, aggressive-minded executives who believed in using completely all the authority residing in the chief's office. Then the tip was also the top in that the distance between the chief and his subordinates involved numerous degrees of authority.

But then the problems of managing growth and change brought a rush of new presidents to the corporate top. Today, the chief executive delegates his authority to more executives who interact more frequently with him about decisions made exclusively by his predecessors. Because his subordinates are more numerous and carry more authority than ever before, the offices in the executive suite are both larger and more numerous. For example, corporate treasurers used to be back-room accountants supervising the tedious and unimaginative efforts of a few bookkeepers. Their responsibility was largely reporting (not directing, controlling, and planning); and, with their proverbial green eyeshades, treasurers could hardly be invested with the rank of corporate officers. The explosion at the top has seen the emergence of the corporate vice-president in charge of finance; and his office may have several hundred employees, including the treasurer and controller. As are many other executives around the chief executive officer, the finance officer is an active force in corporate decision making.

During the last ten years the typical headquarters staff of the largest industrial corporations has increased almost a hundredfold. These officers represent the functions of marketing, sales, manufacturing, research and development, planning, public relations, personnel, industrial relations, acquisitions, accounting, and finance. Affecting both staff and line responsibilities, the enlargement of the executive team has flanged out the corporate top. The top has become an organization within the corporation. Managing the executive organization is a task in itself. The president spends a large share of his time arbitrating disputes, establishing communication channels, motivating and inspiring critical efforts, allocating priorities, and relocating personnel within his own executive group. Even the best chief executive feels pressed between the pincerlike demands of his executive organization and those of the corporation at large. What this adds up to is that because there are more men holding down more important positions in the executive office, the top looks larger and more accessible, with more routes that supply personnel.

But the top in terms of positions on the organization chart is not necessarily the top from the standpoint of access to the tip, the chief executive position. With mobility in mind, the once-clear corporate top fades into a confused mass of uncertainties and aberrations. The top is always changing because executives move in, out, and among positions at greater speeds than before. Only the most astute observers know what and where the corporate summit is. Even men in the executive suite at times show signs of uncertainty and confusion. For example, it is common for the new breed of executive to refer to himself as "a chief among peers." Granted his authority today is broadly shared by numerous executives, but this reference to peers is more poetic than factual. The chief executive's many "peers" are not equals in their opportunities to become his successor. Few chiefs view all their immediate subordinates as equally capable of replacing them.

General Motors is proud of its fabled management in depth and boasts that any one of several executives could effectively manage the company at any given time. However, the lengthy, vigorous discussion among board members in 1967 that culminated in a one-vote plurality for Edward N. Cole over Semon Knudsen for the presidency suggests that there were differences among these two "equals." The fact of the matter is that some are more equal to the chief executive's office than others. Two or more men bearing the title "executive vice-president" may show widely divergent opportunities to become president. Likewise, some vice-presidents are nearer to the top than others.

Donald C. Burnham left General Motors in 1954 to join Westinghouse; and after a stint on the manufacturing staff, he became one of the corporation's forty-three vice-presidents. When the president and chief executive officer, Mark W. Cresap, Jr., died suddenly in 1963, Burnham was promoted over a whole bevy of vice-presidents and executive vice-presidents senior to him in position, rank, and salary. When John L. Burns was a consultant to Radio Corp. of America as a senior partner of the management consulting firm of Booz, Allen & Hamilton, he was closer to the tip than many vice-presidents, who shuddered and agonized after General David Sarnoff handpicked Burns for the presidency. So much in flux is the corporate top that the swirls and eddies created by the goings and comings among the men in motion require for interpretation a high degree of mental acrobatics.

Who is at the top and who has the greatest access to the tip is no mean question today, and the right answer can determine the aspiring executive's strategy of winning. To decipher the corporate code that holds the key to a mobile strategy, the route-bright manager divests himself of much conventional wisdom. Matters of authority, title, salary, position, and tenure are no longer reliable indicators of the corporate zenith. A beginning bench mark is the tip itself, the chief executive officer. His position is the focal point in this vortex of human movement. An incompetent executive may remain in the position of president or chairman temporarily, but he will never be in the chief executive position for long. The top below the tip is represented by the occupants of offices who have the best chance of presiding someday in the chief executive's chair. Many offices in the executive suite represent terminal positions that lead to retirement. Others may be physically distant from the chief executive's office, but their occupants may be managerially close to the corporate center.

With the corporate center represented by the chief executive and the top by those who have the best chance of becoming his successor someday, mobility takes on a different quality. The route-bright executive at midcareer attempts to discern the top and the center of the corporation. More precisely, the routes to the top to be most eagerly sought by aspirants in middle levels are those that also lead to the chief executive office. This means that the winning strategy involves knowing and getting into the routes that do not terminate below the chief executive. The potency of this strategy lies in the greater probability that the aspiring executive will become chief executive officer and as an extra dividend will get an office in the executive suite earlier in his career.

Few large, established industrial corporations do not have special routes that transport the greatest number of men to the tip. For example, in Allis-Chalmers Mfg. Co., by tradition, the chief executive job goes to men from the capital goods division. In Procter & Gamble Co., future presidents move up from marketing; and in Chas. Pfizer & Co., the tip is supplied by men from production. Marketing has been the fastest route in International Business Machines Corporation, and engineering is the fastest route at Boeing Co. The executive overseeing the Euclid division at General Motors never had the chance to go to the top that the executive had who proved his mettle in the automobile divisions. Forwood C. Wiser, Jr., president of Northeast Airlines, was an executive who could not make it at American Airlines because operations men never became chieftains. He wanted to run an airline and took off for Northeast at the first opportunity. Later he went over to Trans World Airlines.

In the steel industry there have been one or two traditional routes to the tip, but finance has not been one of these. Joel Hunter was a partner in a large national accounting firm that handled the account of Crucible Steel Corp. This fine, old-line company in the specialty steels industry was failing rapidly when the board of directors offered Hunter, a C.P.A., a vice-presidency in 1951. It elected him president three years later. Hunter was an exception in the steel industry, which has traditionally used operating and sales as the source of its top executives. The closer the fledgling manager could get to the product, the better his chances of being spotted and elevated. In 1953, Clifford Hood became president of United States Steel and brought into the office over thirty years of operating know-how—acquired largely in the wire division. When he retired, his subordinate, Walter Munford, brought to the presidency twenty-six years of operating experience largely gathered in the wire division. If Harvey Jordan had not been too old, he would have become president, as he also came from the wire division. When Munford retired, Leslie B. Worthington succeeded to the presidency and brought operating and sales experience from the steel division. Edwin Gott, vice-president of production, replaced Worthington as president. The line of succession clearly favored the executive who could get near steel and wire products in operations or sales. Hence, when Gott became chairman, he elevated Edgar B. Speer, a production man of his own stamp, to the presidency.

Sometimes the insider has a better chance of becoming head man if he is in an area or division that incurs the largest risk and produces the largest profits. In these companies, profit centers outproduce other areas in sending talent to the top. In General Motors, few presidents did not have managerial experience in the Chevrolet division, the largest and most profitable division. On the other hand, few executives who became the head of the Oldsmobile division ever became president of General Motors.

Originally, the development of inside tracks to the top did not occur from a rational consideration of how to produce executive talent. They emerged as an outgrowth of work habits. That is to say, to be recognized as capable, men had to show tangible results. Personnel and accounting men produced the least tangible products compared to manufacturing men. Later, the need for priority routes was rationalized by the rule that no one who does not know the vital functions and divisions can be expected to run a corporation. Still later, the argument arose that the men in the major functions and divisions must have respect for the top man, and that this would be more likely if the chief were one of them. Thus, men who are "like" each other fit together better and get the work done more efficiently.

However, there is another reason that accounts for inside tracks that transport men to the presidency. The insider's fear of the stranger evolved easily the norm of seeking and developing "his own kind." Insiders choose insiders for their replacements, and the chosen have same or similar qualities. The reason for this is that the insider reacts to rather than outsmarts his maze of potential rewards and penalties. A characteristic quality of his maze is the overabundance of well-defined penalties that produce negative reinforcement. By experience he becomes overly sensitive to what not to do rather than to his opportunities. He becomes shock- or constraint-sensitive. He knows what not to do and uses himself as a test case. Because he gets very few penalties, subordinates who behave as he does will not make him look bad, but will, in fact, make him look good. Hence, the principle is that "likes attract likes." As corporations moved away from an entrepreneurial base to a public orientation, the loyalty ethic gradually determined that the route the first insider took to become president should become the supply route for his future replacements. Hence, there are routes to the presidency that traditionally feed the whole executive suite. The principle of likes attracting likes directs the route-bright aspirant with a strong motivation to go to the top to get into one of these special routes. The insider is more "in" with the powers that be if he has a like background of route experience. He knows that the practice of promoting men of similar route experience breeds insiders who are more central to the chief concerns of the corporation. They are the ingroup. Lethal consequences may ensue for the insider who is typecast as a specialist in a terminal or dead-end route. From the standpoint of ever becoming a president, his probabilities are not much greater than those of an outsider. For example, Malcolm L. Denise conformed to the stereotype that many people had of a big-business executive. He was 6 feet tall, weighed 180 pounds, was precise in speech, had controlled nervousness, looked people in the eye. He could easily pass for the chief executive officer of a major industrial corporation and perhaps he could have been one, but never at Ford. As chief labor negotiator, he made a huge industrial contribution each year. When he stepped in front of a bank of bright lights and television cameras, thousands of Ford workers and millions of members of the public saw him as the corporation. But inside the Ford Company he could never become the chief executive officer because he was simply in the wrong route. There were men closer to the top positioned below him in the organization. Denise unfortunately was typecast the wrong way, which is lethal in a world of inside tracks. Literally any number of vice-presidents of General Motors had a better chance of becoming president of Ford than did Malcolm Denise. Such becomes the fate of any outside insider.

Of course, every corporation values differently the personnel or industrial relations function. Each corporation has a unique set of values about what kinds of backgrounds, skills, and competencies are required in its chief executive officer. Generally, among the largest industrial corporations, a few common patterns exist. Over 30 percent of the chief executive officers have spent five years or more in marketing and sales at some time in their careers, and a large number of senior executives of marketing each year (roughly 30 percent) jump into the chief executive office. Marketing is definitely a route to the tip, as is manufacturing. Few presidents have spent more than five years in the personnel or industrial relations function. Also, few senior executives of industrial relations ever become chief executives. Mobility patterns of chief executives quite clearly show that personnel and industrial relations are not routes to the top. In the middle sixties large numbers of finance men arrived in the corporate presidency. In the late sixties men who had experience in the international counterpart of the corporation emerged in great numbers at the top.

Today, while the routes vary more among corporations and are more numerous in most corporations, each firm still maintains priorities that determine the movement of men to the presidency. The transporting of future presidents via these priority routes serves to reinforce them as routes to the tip. A corporate personality or identity evolves from the vigorous application of the commonly shared tunnel vision of a series of presidents. The more the corporation evolves a personality, the more the personality serves to reinforce the lines of succession. Insiders who want to succeed make strategic use of the identity of the corporation. They internalize its norms, beliefs, and attitudes as a way to gain favor, recognition, and sponsorship. In turn, they find and favor subordinates who do likewise, because they make bosses look good. The inside insider, because he is in the right route and effuses loyalty to an upwardly loyal superior, covers just about every traditional possibility that assures his upward mobility.

However, insiders are vulnerable to a defect that directly ensues from their limited route experience. They usually are too inner-directed and rigid to sense relevant changes occurring outside their functions. They have tunnel vision that prohibits seeing the need to change corporate strategy when the corporation requires revitalization. Then, too, the narrow routes to the top restrict the corporation's potential for getting fresh blood into the corporate brain. The insider is trapped by his own makeup and he seldom breaks through his fixation to select a successor of different background. This aspect was not conspicuous in a relatively static economy. But the dynamics of change in the decade of the sixties made apparent this hidden defect. Boards of directors often became active participants in strategic decision making largely as a response to an emergent crisis. Men from outside the corporation or insiders from outside routes were often selected, much to the chagrin of the men on the inside tracks. Not a few vice-presidents, who tradition prescribed were the heirs apparent by virtue of their route advantage, had ultimate victory snatched away at the last moment. They suffered career stress that may be described as the crisis of the last step. Meanwhile, men at the middle of the corporate pyramid, men in need of making a final reformulation of their strategy of going to the top, became hopelessly confused by the wild convulsions in the executive suite. The question of who was in and who out appeared to these decoders below to be without any logical guidelines. Mass confusion and intense personal stress was felt by insiders who depended upon clean, clear, and rigid lines of success.

The pumping of fresh blood into the corporate arteries leading to the tip itself constitutes an interim period in which men from the outside routes and the inside will vie more intensely for position advantage. During this rerouting period, much political infighting will occur to establish the outside route as legitimate or to reaffirm the old. For example, for years the route to the top in the food processing and manufacturing industry was through the milk and dairy products division. Suddenly, from the chemicals division, a young stepbrother to the older, major division, emerged a few chief executive officers. As a result, the route to the top in such companies as General Foods favored technical men. For years the route to the top in meat processing and packing industries was through the meat operations. Then a marketing man or two moved into the position of chief executive officer. Consequently, in such companies as Swift, the routes to the top became less rigidly defined and predetermined than at any time in these companies' corporate histories.

In this rerouting period, the new route-makers will begin the familiar process of "likes attracting likes." For example, in Chas. Pfizer & Co. in 1949, John E. McKeen defied the production route by coming from a sales background. He turned the industry upside down by unheard of, unthought of, aggressive marketing strategies and tactics. Although scorned by his competition for defying traditional practice of low-pressure selling, he pirated the detail men (salesmen) necessary to build his marketing structure and transformed Pfizer from one of the smallest pharmaceutical houses in 1949 ($47 million sales) to the largest in 1964 ($300 million). His board thought well enough of him to allow him to retain the presidency when they elected him chairman. McKeen was a route-maker and he had the authority to sustain marketing as the key to the door of the executive suite. Whether he hired Ph.D.s or detail men, all were explicitly told that the key to success in Pfizer was marketing. This attitude seeped down to the managers of research departments, who looked not for geniuses but for versatile men who kept an eye to the commercial aspects of their research. McKeen's top men excelled in the skill of moving goods profitably. At age forty, John Powers, an attorney, persuaded McKeen to push Pfizer's overseas business. He was placed in charge of programs and made Pfizer the largest seller of pharmaceuticals in the whole Free World. Powers was moved into the inner circle (called "McKeen's regulars") and became one of three crucial members of the executive committee. It was no surprise that he was made president. The way to become an inside insider in Pfizer was to think of a better way or thing to market and then pursue a vigorous marketing strategy. Hence, the interim period was over when marketing displaced production as the priority route to the top. We may say that the outside insider became the inside insider.

The rerouting period was over in Allis-Chalmers Mfg. Co. when the tractor division produced its second president. The route-maker was Bill Roberts, who was the first president not to come from the capital goods division. He chose as his successor Robert Stevenson, who also started at the bottom by selling tractors. With the tractor division strongly entrenched in the corporate suite, Stevenson selected as his replacement in the presidency another tractor man, Willis Schol. But none of these tractor men proved capable of turning ailing Allis-Chalmers around, and the board had to go outside for David G. Scott. Nevertheless, the interim period was over for insiders when Stevenson succeeded Roberts and, thereby, permanently put the capital goods division behind the tractor division as the major supply route for chief executives.

There is an insider's rule that requires considerable craft and agility for its proper execution. When an occasional executive from a nonpriority or outside route breaks through and becomes president, he should reinforce this practice of promoting from that outside route by changing the corporation's strategy to affirm the need for more men of his own stamp. For example, in the middle sixties a few finance men found that their opportunities to choose their replacements from finance were unusually enlarged because they persuaded their corporations to develop strong financial strategies. When they could not persuade their boards of directors to continue the financial strategy, their successors were usually selected again from the old, more established routes. In this case, the interim period was over when the outside route failed to become reinforced as the inside route to the top.

The switching of the line of succession from one route to another is dangerous, particularly if the firm has not kept each function, area, or division well-manned by the best talents available or necessary. This failure commonly identifies firms that promote inside insiders. They do not attract talent and keep it in the functions that prove to be less strategic to the goals and needs of the corporation. A second-rate team in a function of low strategic value (outside route) may prove as disastrous to a corporation and to executives as a second-rate team in a highly valued function (inside route). To attract men of sufficient strength to an area or function, the men in that area have to be mobile or at least powerful. If the top team does not include them in their councils, the minimum condition for keeping an area or function strong is absent. However, the very fact of an inside group precludes serious consultations with the executives in the nonpriority outside routes.

A case in point is the Douglas Aircraft Company, which found itself in 1967 overwhelmed by an avalanche of orders for DC-9 jetliners. The attempt to recover from a near-disastrous series of poorly designed and marketed jetliners evolved a morass of managerial problems that included soaring costs and inadequate financial controls. It is generally acknowledged that finance represents the single most important kind of information for a business enterprise. Although Douglas imported, from Trans World Airlines, A. V. Leslie to negotiate a new line of credit and to build up the Douglas Finance Corporation, he was not kept informed enough to produce the kind of results needed by the sick corporation. The route to the top in Douglas never really included finance, whose officers, including Leslie, were tolerated but not utilized and dignified. The situation at Douglas deteriorated to the point where money had to be raised by merger with the McDonnell Company. From this merger a large amount of fresh working capital and some new management were acquired. The Douglases—Donald, Sr., and his son—who owned only 9,000 shares collectively while McDonnell owned 300,000, lost control of the firm partly because it deprecated the potential contribution of competent finance personnel. Too long mired in production and sales, the corporation lost its footing and had to be bailed out. Actually, the Douglas case illustrates more than the lack of modern management techniques of control and planning. It illustrates what can happen when only inside insiders are relied upon and outside insiders (i.e., Leslie) are endured almost as necessary evils.

The Douglas problem was further complicated by the failure of a weak bench within the aircraft division. The missile and space group under Charles R. Able was better staffed than the aircraft division headed by Jackson R. McGowen, which was five times larger in sales. When McGowen moved up, Jesse L. Jones came over from the smaller missile and space division and brought Tom Gabbert with him to be his financial manager and to help get control of costs. Now, here was a large division that should have had within it competent executive talent, but it had to be bailed out by executives from a much smaller division. In this respect the Douglas situation reflects on the ability of the division head to find and develop executive talent. This situation at Douglas illustrates also why a good team in a small division is needed, if for no other reason than to offset a weak bench in a large division. As it turned out, the team at Douglas was not up to the challenge, no matter what the mix of outside and inside insiders.

The insider fails to breed talented people in all the areas relative to business enterprise because he develops and overly relies upon a few—his own kind. When a corporation elects to the highest office a man strong in finance and accounting, as was Frederic T. Donner of General Motors, the effect is more than moving the right man into the job at the right time. A consequence is to keep alive the faith among junior executives that accounting and finance is a route to the top. That faith will help to draw and keep talented manpower. When the talent is needed, it is there; and importing is not necessary. Then an insider in an outside route can better sustain his initial victory and reinforce the new line of succession by mobility within.

Focusing upon products or an organizational area, division, or function and breeding functionally identifiable executives is both common and necessary. But tying the practice of breeding insiders to one or several of these functions, divisions, or products is essentially restricting the opportunity to spot and develop corporate talent. In the Ford Motor Co., the big Ford division got the brightest young executives, set the styling and engineering pace for the company, made the most profits, and won the hottest new cars—the Thunderbird, Falcon, and Mustang—for its product line. In the middle sixties, Henry Ford II turned his attention to the Lincoln-Mercury division, poured in more money than they blew on the Edsel, and assigned top talent to run the division in the person of Lee Iacocca. Having presided over the Ford division, Iacocca did not know where the talent was kept in the Lincoln-Mercury division and raided his former division for protégés and crucial subordinates. By the spring of 1968, men in both divisions were blatantly unhappy. Some were bypassed in the Lincoln-Mercury division by Iacocca's protégés, others in the Ford division were unhappy because they had lost the exposure and visibility [3] that attends a priority division. But the essential thing was the lack of sufficient talent to man both divisions without disturbing the managerial mix. The aspiring insider will scramble to find and stay in the inside track and thereby reinforce it by his own successes. He is apt to draw from a single route and to perpetuate the established route if he has not been in several that share a balanced talent mix.

The efforts of many corporations to establish more routes to the top and to evolve more flexible lines of succession to the tip has greatly contributed to exposing the insider's defect. The ironical result of attempts at rerouting is to turn the insider into an entrenched insider. No one shows the true colors of a confirmed insider more than the executive whose upward mobility becomes arrested at the door of the office of the president because he has suddenly acquired the wrong background and identity. The knowledge that he is not in the inside track and his decision to stay and make the most of a bad turn of fate reorients him eventually to the advantages and satisfactions inherent in his present job. He may say to himself, "I might as well enjoy it since this is it for me." In this mental state of adjusting to the logic of his condition, he occasionally is overwhelmed by periods of cynicism during which he doubts the goodness of the good life prescribed by his corporation. He may doubt that the corporation is worthy of his sacrifices, distrust the wisdom of his chief executive, and accuse others of "brownnosing" and of politicking. Between these episodes of cynicism emerge manic states in which he feels secure, comfortable, and expansive. Now he enjoys the good life as a member of the executive suite. He is proud that he has gone farther than his parents or his peer group and rationalizes that his corporation is basically a moral force in his life.

His attempt to adjust to organizational realities eventually overrides his condition of ambivalence. The time needed to adjust largely depends upon the strength of his mobility drive. A few men in the executive suite may acquire such a strong drive to become president that they cannot adjust until the very day of retirement.

[3] Exposure is the frequency with which one is seen by men above, and visibility is the frequency with which one can see men above.

Others may take less time. The adjustment period is over when they resolve the ambivalence in favor of total company identification. If this happens, the insider becomes more than an insider, he becomes a true believer. As such, he identifies more with the corporation's successes than with his own.

No one identifies with the company as strongly as the executive who stops short of total success. If the reader wants to find a company-centered man, he should not look to the president or to the first-level manager above the worker. Rather, he should look to the executive suite. It is in the men who go almost all the way that he will find the purest strain of the insider's mentality. Not even the insider who comes up the priority route with a better than even chance of becoming president exudes company-centeredness as sharply and intensely. Men who have no place to go must justify their presence somehow. Identifying with the company becomes a source of vicarious success, a justification for secondary roles, a compensation for a less than complete mobility pattern.

To understand this anomaly we must note the conditioners that transform outside insiders into strongly company-centered men. Today these conditioners are the distance traveled, the rate of mobility, the degree of disappointment, the intensity of the mobility drive, and the strength of the loyalty motive. Thus, a young, ambitious man who starts at the bottom and slowly, ploddingly goes to the executive suite to within breathing distance of the presidency and then has his upward mobility permanently arrested is apt eventually to become a true believer. If he starts at middle management, rises rapidly, and suffers no profound disappointment, he will invariably have less of the strain of company-centeredness. A person with an intense mobility drive who starts at the bottom and becomes upwardly arrested at middle management will not resolve his disappointment by producing an aggressive company attitude. In fact, middle managers are most apt to remain ambivalent. They have climbed enough to have reinforced sufficiently their mobility drives, to want and expect more mobility. But they are not near enough to the top to see the whole corporation as an entity with which to tangibly and securely identify. This insider with a strong mobility drive who faces the reality of a permanently arrested ascent achieves a partial identification with the company. He is at once a company and anticompany man. As such, he feels half in and half out of the organization. One day he commits aggression against the company and the next day feels the pangs of guilt which, in turn, produce extremely loyal and deferential behavior. There is no way he can easily resolve his ambivalence because the corporation at his level appears so impersonal and huge that he cannot embrace it, and he cannot devote himself to it if he cannot do something about his blocked route to the top. If he could apply with immunity for a transfer to relieve his blocked condition, he could better resolve his ambivalence. To whom does he safely appeal his case other than to peers of like condition? The brothers make common cause together. In the chapter entitled "Shelf-sitters," we shall take more careful note of the ambivalence of middle managers. Suffice it to say that company-centered men represent a most treacherous, divisive force in the corporation. In them we can see that the logical extension of the loyalty ethic has itself become arrested. A few middle managers are company-centered, a few are cynics, and many are ambivalent types.

Meanwhile, among insiders at the top of the corporation, the loyalty ethic has more uniformly produced company-centeredness. This is not a function of age because there are ambivalent types in middle management of comparable age. Disappointments are more real at the top because men have gone further and expect more. Also, the corporation is more real because executives must be more concerned with the whole and become involved in transactions and communications that enable them to conceptualize the corporation as a personality with which to identify. For this reason, among a few insiders at the top, the loyalty ethic may overshoot its mark to create a monster. In a man at this level the loyalty attitude may command the seat of reason. He then becomes a corporate conscience and historian. Besides knowing everything that has happened in the past, he knows what should or should not happen in the present and future. He is the repository of corporate values, beliefs, and norms. In the vernacular of the military, he "goes by the book." While rattling around in his confines, he effuses dedication to defending his company's creeds and records.

The corporate conscience attempts to serve as a gyroscope that keeps his company on an even keel in stormy weather. Because he believes in something bigger than himself, he presents himself as a heroic, self-sacrificing individual. Presidents may find him difficult to manage. As one chief executive reported who was saddled with two corporate consciences, "There is no one more difficult to manage than a true believer with a proprietary claim upon his office." Of course, presidents realize that their suggestions and directives should be carefully couched in the form of company need and welfare. Still, the corporate conscience may prove difficult to manage because he may conceive of himself as a better or final arbiter of corporate choices and differences. His respect for a superior will diminish by the degree that the latter attempts to change routine, custom, and convention.

His expression of this extreme form of loyalty to the corporation dehumanizes him. His native capacities to create, invent, and imagine become all but extinguished. While this essential flexibility to formulate self-expression atrophies, his capacity to hang loose and modify his strategies of winning diminishes equally.

The end product of attempts at self-propagation is finding the right man, ready at the right time, to take over the job of president. A strong new president represents an achievement of the highest order for the corporation and the individual. But if the complicated process of breeding superior types fails and the once strong managerial ranks grow thin in talent, the successes of the past may be completely nullified and the continuity of the firm jeopardized. The corporation may have to reach down below to fresh, untested talent, a risky but sometimes necessary venture, or bring in an outsider to resuscitate the ailing firm.

Few are the firms that have mastered the tricky process of breeding sufficient quantities of talented men. Among those that have, such as General Electric, American Telephone & Telegraph, Sears Roebuck & Co., Standard Oil Co. (New Jersey), Procter & Gamble, and General Foods, the one that stands out among its economic peers is General Motors. This industrial behemoth has no formal management training program. Yet, it is known for its fabled management in depth. In 1956 it changed one-quarter of the top executives in less than ten months, and all those who moved up came from within the corporation. A chairman retired, as did four of the twenty-nine vice-presidents. Some of the men in motion were Albert Bradley, sixty-five, chairman, with thirty-seven years in General Motors; Frederic T. Donner, fifty-four, to executive vice-president, with thirty years; Thomas Keating, sixty-two, to group executive of the automotive division, with forty years; George Russell, fifty-one, to vice-president, with twenty-nine years; Herman Lehman, fifty-six, to vice-president, with twenty-eight years; and E. T. Ragsdale, fifty-nine, to vice-president, with thirty-three years. The men below these top executives had already accumulated, on the average, twenty-eight years in General Motors. Many other companies would not survive such sweeping changes. But this process that produced its management in depth commenced over forty years ago and has acquired an inertia of its own.

In the corporation with a sharp eye to improvement that generates its own kind, of course, the inside insider literally has the edge over the outside insider. But there is no guarantee that the man who surfaces will be the most competent of those that are available within the firm. Nor is there any assurance that he will be well-backstopped by a strong second team. The first team has not always known how or wanted to identify and promote the best among the second-best. In the last two decades, many industries have been favored with rapid growth but have failed to develop sufficient management breadth and depth, particularly at levels below the top, to expand or sustain growth. Overreliance upon a second-rate team proved disastrous for many companies.

Looking back, few presidents with chief executive authority during the wild decade of the sixties will not agree that the advantages of loyal insiders were often offset by their conservative postures. For these frustrated chief executives, the struggle devolved to judiciously striking a balance between the forces of conservatism from within and change from without. And many heads of corporations simply could not stave off disaster for themselves or their corporations. They were too much the products of the system of inertia against which they hopelessly pitted themselves. What at root defeated them was the too tempting practice of likes attracting likes, of putting corporate priorities to work for them by climbing in lockstep with men above and below from the same or similar routes, with common qualities and dispositions. The routes to the presidency were too few and too tightly maintained by a small ingroup to whom an outsider was anybody who followed another route.

CHAPTER THREE

The New Route-makers

WELL-BRED EXECUTIVES represent the links in the genetic chain that carry the corporate code of inheritance. Each new generation of executives becomes in part the creation of the efforts of a preceding generation. No doubt the potential differences between the parent and the siblings may be greater than those that actually result. The reason is that the reproduction processes are carefully directed by priorities that evolve from the needs and objectives of the corporation. Men with undesirable characteristics and interests are weeded out and only the few with the right characteristics are allowed to emerge into the full light of the corporate summit. The traditional route to the top starts with the development of these few important qualities and with their perfection by a steady pattern of conscientious application. Doing these few exercises very well rather than perfecting useful idiosyncrasies serves to advance aspiring winners. The breeding processes are not perfect. Mismatches, faulty selection, and poor nourishment plague even the best-managed corporations. Incompetent men at the top are not an unusual phenomenon even in the largest corporations. Developing a superior generation of executives is as difficult as it is desirable.

In the mid-fifties many growth-minded corporations decided to make adjustments in their executive development policies and techniques. The need to manage innovation and change made the insider's mentality more apparent and less valued. Corporations realized that they should breed without inbreeding and that executives should be produced with less of the insider strain of conservatism and conformity. They attacked the problem by changing conditions in the incubation stage. Top men turned the attention of their corporations to recruiting and grooming a cadre of young aspiring executives at lower levels in the corporation. They figured that they should start with young, unblemished, hungry recruits because every ounce of effort devoted to youth in the embryonic stage would pay greater dividends than the same amount of effort applied to middle-aged insiders.

As the emerging growth cycle proved to have a durable quality, many other corporations followed suit. Some took advantage of the mistakes of the pioneers, but all would-be breeders seemed to be making as many problems for themselves as they were solving. Countermeasures were evoked, mistakes were corrected, and new policies promulgated as more talent and resources were applied to improving the quality of executive behavior. By the mid-sixties, many large industrial corporations became almost as development-conscious as they had been work-directed. But such a change of attitude was not easily sustained. Some corporations gave up and others declined in spirit to less aggressive programs of executive development. Producing superior talent became a test of the capacity of corporations to produce both talented men and profit growth. Not all knew how to achieve these twin goals, but many did succeed and the adventures of these breeder firms changed the strategy and art of winning.

The new winner may be called "the mobile executive" who defies the traditional notion that the development of executives should occur incidentally to the performance of work assignments. He does not believe that talent will automatically declare itself through application of skill and industry to work much as cream rises to the top of milk. He may grant that this "natural law" may work adequately during periods of mild economic growth, but that during long periods of sustained growth the corporation cannot wait for nature to produce adequate numbers of talented executives. Mobile executives are the progeny of corporations that had to interfere with the natural law of breeding and to rush it along by careful nudging and at times by flagrant violation of the law itself. They represent the cream that was forced to the surface by rapid shaking of the bottle. The key idea in breeding executives is the fact that most jobs can be mastered in a year and a half to two years and that from then on the executive is doing the work with a minimum effort. He does the job "out of his back pocket." However, if then he is moved to another job, masters its requirements, and is moved to still a third job, he can in a few years get more intensive training and development than the previous executive who usually stayed in any one job long after he had mastered its fundamentals. In premobility days, the insider was taught his job the way a child was taught the piano: the rule was "Practice makes perfect." He went over and over his work, each time grinding out more perfection at a tremendous cost in career time. The result of overfeeding men a stale diet was a reduced output of capable men. Executives taught by this rule were overly cautious, perfectionistic, and reserved— seldom creative and innovative. They learned to be patient, to master boredom, and to be work-oriented, but not to have initiative, the vital force in managing change.

In other words, the principle at work is that mobility creates competency. The recipient of such a program achieves experience compression. He becomes in some respects similar to the ninety-day wonder that World War II produced. The idea of taking a raw enlistee or draftee and after ninety days of intensive training commissioning him a second lieutenant seemed irresponsible to many people, particularly parents. But these ninety-day wonders made, for the most part, great contributions on the battlefield, and during the Vietnam campaign they inspired the military to transform fresh recruits into sergeants by forty days of intensive training. Likewise, the conventional belief that the aspiring executive should spend many long years in the lower levels of the corporate hierarchy was all but destroyed by the presence at the top, in large numbers, of successful, mobile executives.

The utilization of mobility to speed up the acquisition of competency has validity for a number of reasons. One factor that stands out above all others is the consensus among mobile executives that in every job there is 20 percent that counts 80 percent. By this is meant that 20 percent of any job counts for 80 percent of the training. Much of the 80 percent can be mastered easily from the transfer of knowledge that has accumulated during the previous assignments and positions. If the mobile executive is moved properly, only about 20 percent of the new job will be new to him. At this point an achievement curve in the form of a flattened S curve ($\sim$) begins to operate. President George R. Vila, who staged the successful comeback of Uniroyal, Inc., is one of many presidents who believes that in a new job the achievement curve first rises slowly as the executive learns the ropes, rises sharply as he puts the programs into practice, and then levels out. Vila attempts to catch his men at the top of the $\sim$ curve and move them on to a new challenge. This is the way he fights what he calls "occupational rigor mortis," which can happen to a corporation. The worst thing that can happen to a breeder firm is for the organization to settle into layers. So Vila keeps Uniroyal well stirred up, as do all chieftains of corporations that breed mobile executives.

The manager who can move into a position, grasp its essential uniqueness, master the new responsibilities and assignments, and then move to another job is apt to gain more competency in a shorter period of time. Time and experience are compressed. In this sense, the slower the executive moves to the top, the less he learns. The idea largely held before the sixties was that he learns most who moves the slowest. Actually, men were kept in jobs long after they learned them—they overlearned their jobs. The resultant disadvantages included loss of career time, a falling off in the learning curve, and fewer men eligible for high positions. Today, things are radically different. Promising executives are moved before they get bored and, if anything, they practice underlearning.

Rapid movement is the chief characteristic of the mobile executive. He works as hard at initiating and responding to his many moves and those of others as he does at getting his work assignments done. It is not uncommon at all for one out of every three men between the first-level manager and the division executive who are generally regarded as developmental (G.R.A.D.) to move each year. Obviously, not all make beeline moves to the top. In fact, few do. The mark of the mobile executive is that he moves as much laterally as vertically. Of course, this moving around as he moves up was not always the pattern. In premobility days, if an aspiring executive became identified as a "comer," it was because he performed well in one of several business functions; i.e., accounting, marketing, sales, production, engineering, personnel, industrial relations, finance, or law. He moved up in a single function. When he was moved out of it he ceased to be on his journey to the top.

In response to growth needs, men were moved out of their functional channels. Accounting men were moved to manufacturing, engineers to sales, and salesmen to manufacturing, etc. Now these growth corporations realize that men who stay in one functional channel all the way to the top suffer from limited route vision. Each will see the whole corporation from the view of his single functional route—with sometimes deadly results. The mobile executive who has crossed several functional routes has a much wider scope. Lee Bickford, chairman of the board of National Biscuit Co., refers to this moving of people in and out of functions as "forced generalization." It helps to produce a generalist-specialist type of attitude that identifies the mobile executive. The facts show that executives that arrived at the top in the late sixties typically spent over a third of their time outside their basic functional routes. In contrast, men left behind to sit on the lower rungs seldom spent more than one-tenth of their career time in functions outside of their primary specialty.

In addition to cross-functional mobility, there is cross-divisional mobility. The mobile executive has his vision widened by moving among several divisions of the corporation as he leapfrogs the functions. Very few men become presidents with one-division backgrounds. Nor have they come up strictly through line experiences. In premobility days, staff assignments and positions were largely terminal. They did not produce relevant experience. Consequently,

staff positions were looked down upon and their occupants were sec-
ond-class citizens to be tolerated but not utilized. Now staff assignments carry great weight. Since 1960, more and more of the men at
the top have had five or more years in staff positions. In 1969, the
vast majority of the presidents had been in staff jobs five years or
longer and over half had been eight years in staff jobs. In short, the
making of a future president involves his moving among several
functions, line and staff positions, and corporate divisions. But he
usually keeps coming back to his strong technical or functional orientation. The mobile executive's master route to the top is the
product of several routes. Doing the same thing with greater effect
and skill has become passé.

The future occupant of the executive suite must pass two severe
performance tests along the way. The first test occurs somewhere in
middle management, about three levels of management above the
worker. His subordinates are managers of managers and he is responsible for showing them how to manage managers by the way he
manages his subordinate managers. If one studies carefully men
who have had their upward mobility arrested—shelf-sitters—one
will discover that this middle-management girth comprises the largest number of men permanently passed up and passed over. They
were left behind principally because they failed to pass a test implicit in their roles at their levels. They had unbalanced technical-
managerial mixes. This mix is a state of mind that allocates energy
and time to the technical side of the job versus the managerial. All
jobs have what may be called their "technical" side. In the pattern
of the shelf-sitters, we can see too much emphasis upon the technical and not enough on the managerial. They have what may be
called a 90:10 mix, whereby they believe that 90 percent of their
problems may be solved by technical expertise, largely their own, of
course. Thus, they fail to get the benefits of the multiplier (the
word is "synergism") that comes from managing the expertises of
many others, some of whom have more than their superior. Nor do
they encourage their subordinates to manage people as managers.

The ironical characteristic of mobility is that the aspiring executive needs a 90:10 technical-managerial mix to be spotted in the
lower, nonmanagerial levels as a potential first-level manager. But if

he hangs too much on the technical side of the equation, he will get into severe trouble. Ninety:tens are poor breeders of managers, and a breeder firm will slip them out of the tracks to the top. The men who get through this risky third level of management have a more balanced technical-managerial mix, such as 50:50. They know enough about the technical side not to be "snowed" by faulty advice, to have a basis for screening relevant technical information from that which is irrelevant, but they basically consider themselves to be managers. The finest technician does not usually make the best manager unless he mentally chooses to emphasize in his managerial routines the priorities belonging to good managing. In a competitive company, wherever there are many young men being bred for future executive positions, a 50:50 mix is not sufficient. Here a 90:90 may be required. He has to excel in the technical and the managerial and cannot leave either skill to chance.

The mobile executive gives priority to managing managers without letting up on his efforts to remain technically competent. He must avoid becoming a 10:90 type of mix too. This executive with a 10:90 mix assumes that a good manager can manage anything. Many breeder firms in the fifties bred this type of manager under the auspices of professional management. General Electric used professional managers in the disastrous Phoenix operation. This rambunctious computer division failed to respond to the professional skills of many 10:90s drawn from other parts of the corporation. Finally, they acknowledged that perhaps the top men in the computer division should know something about computers and tried executives from IBM and Honeywell to rescue the ailing division. There is danger in being a 90:10 or a 10:90. But just what a happy, successful mix is is not easily described without knowing the individual and the amount of emphasis placed upon managerial excellence at his level by his corporation. Generally, a mobile executive has no mental ambivalence. He wants to keep up in both but defines himself to be a manager in the first instance and a technician second.

The mobile executive's second test will occur at the point that he is made a corporate vice-president. He may come from a division managership or a staff position in one of the divisions. Here his operating administrative mix becomes crucial. At the division level and lower he is practicing largely operating management. These are the tactical, day-to-day activities that have to do with one part of the corporation. At the corporate level he enters the arena of the whole, wherein men individually and collectively administer the overall direction and character of the firm. If he is too operational, he is too limited by one part of the whole to be an effective force in administration. No one stands out less favorably than the newly appointed corporate vice-president who cannot see the big picture and lacks the touch and sensitivity for strategic thinking. In the corporate world he is the true provincial who is mired in day-to-day detail and cannot raise his sights high enough to speak intelligently of administration matters. As in the case of a poorly balanced technical-managerial mix, a 90:10 operating-administration mix will prove to be lethal.

Lateral mobility has proved to be one of the most effective safeguards against 90:10 technical-managerial and operation-administration mixes. A second- or third-level manager with too strong a technical orientation, when moved to a function for which he has little technical qualification, must fall back upon managing. Likewise, an unbalanced organizational-administration mix will be prevented if the aspiring executive has been given staff and line experience in two or more divisions. Most of the men at the top are known by their functional identities. They are known as marketing men, or financial men, or manufacturing men, or personnel men. How they manage their functional responsibilities may vary widely, but generally they give priority to the managerial over the technical and to the administrative over the operating functions. They must know enough about the technical and operating functions to know when and how to bring their professional managerial skills to bear upon relevant problems. To know when to do what and how is the true art of managing.

In the mobile world, how the executive arrives at and departs from a new assignment is as crucial as performing the job itself. Executing well the many arrivals and departures is no mean feat. It is as big a task as doing the job itself. Mobile executives maintain that performing the task is inseparable from arriving and departing. They see arriving, performance, departing (APD) as a triad of activities that are performed each in relationship to the other. The mobile executive executes his task in such a manner as to ensure departing, and he arrives in such a manner as to expedite performance. Mobility is more than mere job performance. For instance, mobile executives claim that the best way to get a promotion is to train a good replacement. Graceful departing is essentially executing a smooth transfer of authority. Gaps in work routines and drastic shifts in managerial styles are avoided. The corporation progresses by incremental changes. Unique differences in temperament and skills that inevitably characterize the successor and the predecessor are not allowed to disturb drastically the ebb and flow of organizational activity. It is not that the mobile executive is uninnovative. Nothing could be farther from the truth. Rather, he installs new or different objectives and means in close coordination and sympathy with those of his predecessor. It is not uncommon for a departing executive to chair his staff meeting at 10 o'clock with his newly appointed successor at his side and at 11 o'clock to sit at the right hand of a superior whom he is about to replace. When the public is notified that a new president has been appointed or a senior manager elevated to a new post, chances are that the executive has been gradually performing his new responsibilities for three to nine months prior to his formal appointment. At lower levels, this lead time is less.

Successful departing relates to the condition in which the job is found by the new arrival. It does little for the departer's mobility to leave the job in worse condition than he found it, leaving his mistakes for his successor to clean up. The reason is that oftentimes he will be asked to nominate his successor. A great part of graceful departing is based upon making a proper selection and receiving support for his nomination. Executives are highly valued for their ability to spot and develop managers. In a breeder company, a good executive is one who can produce executives. The corporation will run out of executives if everyone who is promoted does not train a replacement at least as good as himself or better. The most mobile men are breeders of managerial talent. In short, departing is a basic managerial skill of the mobile executive.

The skills of graceful arriving are equally crucial to effective management. A job is necessarily made up of routine and rudimentary procedures to which previous experiences are directly applicable. Graceful arriving is performed by an exercise called "mapping." The entering executive studies intently the expectations of his new superior and those of peers and subordinates and mentally arranges his objectives in an order of priority based upon a scale of relative degrees of value. Even while he is performing his initial set of work assignments, he is mapping to find the few things that count the most. By establishing priorities, he avoids the administration of triviality. Executives are often told by their superiors to "quit handling routine and start making decisions." (They are accused of "administrivia.") Men who hear this admonition have failed to sense the inherent priorities, some of which are not explicitly revealed to them by their superior nor immediately apparent to ordinary inspection. Mapping requires a kind of extra perceptivity to the demands of the position other than those immediately apparent. The end of the executive arrival stage occurs when he has mapped the terrain sufficiently to feel confident of his priorities and then proceeds to execute accordingly. He is now in the performance stage of the APD trilogy.

One can always pick out the graceful arrivals by the manner in which they set time aside to map. They know intuitively and experientially that much of what was valued in the previous job is not valued in the new job. If the two value systems were the same, their priorities would necessarily be different. The mobile executive understands that what was important in one job may not be important in another.

The previous generation of mobile executives acted on the faith that what worked in one managerial situation usually worked in another. For example, all Secretaries of Defense before Robert S. McNamara applied this rule of thumb. They took rules of behavior from law offices and automobile companies and applied them to managing the Pentagon. In one case, the Secretary believed that what was good for his former company was good for the Pentagon. The successes of these men were indeed few. We may differ about the results of McNamara's regime, but we must admit that he changed the military establishment in such a way that it will never be the same. His first six months in office were basically a period of mapping. He asked himself what was important to the Army, where were the key forces in the Navy, who were the strong men in the Air Force. Once he had mapped his terrain and ascertained the maze of values, he then proceeded to execute his objectives. His effectiveness was largely due to how well he handled himself during these six months that marked his arrival period. His priorities were extremely sensitive to those of people he had to influence. The crucial problem in the arrival stage is not simply what is important to whom, but when it is important. Hence, the mobile executive attempts to be bright about sensing and arranging priorities.

Arriving, performing, and departing represent skills that men of action did not usually acquire as long as they saw mobility related largely to job performance. We have all seen how the first six months in office can set the tone for the whole tenure. First impressions are lasting, and replacements can come on too fast for those the executive must influence and control. Newness is to many a threat in itself because they have become accustomed to a particular set of values and priorities. New executives who gradually reveal their differences perform better. Mobile executives come on slowly, perform swiftly after achieving rapport, and depart or break gradually and cleanly. This rhythm is characterized as "style" or "panache."

Of course, there are exceptions to this rhythm of arriving, performing, departing. There is an executive whose managerial style is such that he shakes people within the first few months after his entry into a new position. He is commonly called a "stinger," and he is most useful when a department or division has settled down comfortably to setting goals and objectives below its potential. The stinger can thoroughly shake up this practice, and if he is followed by a manager with an organizational flair, the department or organization can be reorganized to a new level of performance. There are cases where the inertia of a group cannot be broken any other way. Even the rhythmic style of a mobile executive fails to achieve the effect that a stinger followed by a mobile executive can produce in tandem.

The tandem concept is becoming increasingly common today. It is a product of a mobile world. Two men with different managerial styles can more successfully move a staff than any single manager could during an equal period of time. Under certain conditions, two men who each stay two years, sharing a common set of objectives and the performance of them, will register a greater degree of success than one man who has been given the same set of objectives to be performed during a tenure of four years. Of course, the tandem principle does not always ensure superior results. Sometimes the inherent quality of the staff or objectives or the skill of the executive may exert a negative effect. But the gradual increase in the use of the tandem concept suggests that more jobs are amenable to its advantages than was once believed. This is particularly true of the tandem in which the stinger is followed by an executive with a flair for organizing.

The executive who preceded the era of mobility was depended upon to impose an entirely different set of values and priorities immediately upon his entrance to a new job. The staff that he inherited was always prepared for the worst. His first day in the job was the barometer of things to come. If things were chaotic, he was expected to correct this situation as soon as possible. The previous generation of managers came on hard and, if successful, they stayed a relatively longer time than do the mobile executives of the new generation. In a mobile organization, where bosses come and go within one-half or less of the time of their predecessors, coming on hard elevates the emotions of the staff they inherit. To sustain the advantages of rapid mobility, the rhythmic style of arriving, performing, and departing is fundamental to effective managing. The principle is clear. An executive can get more done if he plans. Premobility executives were geared to run and not map, depart, and not prepare the ground for the smooth changeover of the guard. The mobile executive is so accustomed to mobility that he is prepared to manage the performance phase. To him, managing requires mastering these skills of mobility as well.

However, rapid arrival and departure require a different set of skills than the slow pace of upward mobility that existed in premobility days. The mobile executive is mentally alert to get into a job, to learn its fundamentals quickly, and to move to another job. Of course, he has something going for him that the traditional insider did not, and this is the advantage of rapid lateral and vertical mobility. This pattern of mobility produces alertness. If there is today a single reason for disqualifying men from the upward race, it is that they are slow learners. They cannot assimilate their experiences in proportion to their mobility rates. They get ahead of their competencies; know less than they need to perform effectively. It is not common to find executives whose upward inertia propelled them one level ahead of their competency. In some cases, they were left behind to grow into a job that was ahead of their abilities. In this case they lost career time.

A mobile world implicitly favors the fast learner. He can do well the following things: First, he can learn without having to be taught, draw valid conclusions from inadequate sets of facts, react quickly to impending danger, and keep his eye on the main chance. Second, the mobile executive must be so organized emotionally that he can acknowledge the known and adjust himself to the unknown with minimum feelings of insecurity and anxiety. These two requirements exert a heavy force upon the executive's capacity to withstand stress. So much so that at least one out of every three mobile executives will wash himself out of the race rather than be taken out by others. Such a person has a low threshold of tolerating ambiguity and therefore cannot feel comfortable and mobile. He fears the next promotion or assignment and lets up on his drive and aggressiveness. Or he merely refuses a promotion. Refusing promotions has been quite commonplace, especially among some of the most loyal executives.

The practice of rapid upward mobility created a strange paradox. The more some were promoted, the more they grew tired of mobility and sought to determine for themselves the pace of their efforts. Because of an extreme shortage of talented men, some corporations were willing to let them stay where they wanted and to accord them dignity. In comparison, there were the mobile executives who could not be moved fast enough, who itched for more and who sometimes broke under the weight of too much mobility too soon. There were a large number of burned out young men who did not hold themselves back enough. Men working side by side could be classified as burned out or underutilized or rapidly become one or the other while many remained insiders, applying their skills of hard work diligently, untouched by the mobility program. The ambiguity was strongly disconcerting to many.

In spite of the many casualties, the idea of breeding superior types by putting mobility and competency back to back was highly effective in producing intended results. So much so that mobility is the chief characteristic of the competent executive today. Or, to put it differently, if the executive cannot handle the challenges and stresses of mobility, he cannot sustain or continue his drive for competency. Many an executive has had his development of competency arrested by the arrest of his upward mobility.

The study of the early arrival offers an illustration of the qualities needed by the mobile executive. To be an early arrival in the presidency, the executive must be forty-six years of age or younger, and to be a young officer below the president he must be forty years of age or younger. These men are significantly ahead of their peer group and ahead of the biomobile index that suggests they should be into their fifties. These early arrivals have two qualities: they are mobility-directed and mobility-bright. Early arrivals are motivated by the desire to achieve. But achievement is not simply performing in a position and hoping for the opportunity to perform at a higher level in the organization. To be mobility-directed, the highest form of achievement is to become and remain mobile. Mobility may not always mean vertical movement. It may just as well mean lateral movement. Nor does mobility necessarily mean position movement. It more likely means taking on new, more difficult tasks or projects in the same position. At the higher reaches of the corporation, men move through position levels more slowly but will have greater assignment mobility. In the early arrival's mind, performance is a means, not an end, and is represented by activity that was alien to the traditional insider. Performance means to arrive, to perform, to get ready for the next assignment. It means compressing time and experience. Most of all, the early arrival thrives psychologically on mobility. It brings out his best and develops the unknown or reserve strengths in him. Happiness is an alive mind engaged in a challenging assignment that augurs well for mobility.

To properly direct his mobility drive, the early arrival has a second quality: he is mobility-bright. By this we mean that he is knowledgeable about the ways of mobility. There are executives who are mobility-directed but not mobility-bright. They seek to acquire and enhance their mobility but lack the necessary wisdom. Of course, a necessary condition of mobility brightness is to be mobility-directed. But unless the executive has had rapid mobility in general and compression experience in particular, he cannot be truly knowledgeable about the mobile world. Then, too, some executives learn better than others. They experience more efficiently and draw useful principles and generalizations from their experiences. They have learned how to learn. Of all the things that they could see, they tend to see precisely those things that give maximum expression to their mobility drive. They screen out the kind of information that men less wise in the ways of mobility tend to accept. In short, the mobility drive serves as a gyroscope that keeps the early arrival on a steady course; but first the course must be set by his mobility brightness.

The mobility-bright executive knows that movement up the corporate ladder brings gradual changes in the expectations of the people with whom he must work. These changes may amount to shifts in priorities of what is valued or believed, or these changes may represent entirely new beliefs and attitudes. The differences of expectations and beliefs between two adjoining levels of executives are not as noticeable as between two levels of executives separated by one or two levels. As the executive moves through the layers of the corporation, he attempts to notice the subtle, incremental changes in his environment. In the language of the mobile executive, he maps his environment. He draws a mental picture, a map of the exact nature of his terrain. His facility to read and to map must be keenly developed in order for the mobile executive to make the necessary adjustments. He must also read and map in order to determine how best to apply his efforts to gain the greatest payoffs. Let the reader not be misled; the mobility-bright executive is not a conformist. He behaves according to the requirements of assuming initiative and becoming recognized for his results. If he conforms, it is for the purpose and to the extent of gaining the opportunities and resources to

initiate and innovate. The point is that the mobility-bright executive can see differences, differences that miss the eye of the less sensitive executive, emerge from one level to another. A careful analysis
of these differences reveals that the upper management (or executive) is different from the lower management (or manager) in a
number of ways.

First, executives [1] have more established identities than managers.
They know better who they are and feel more confident of where
they are going or what they want to do. Another way to say this is
that they are more involved in their careers and carry their responsibilities more into both their successes and failures. Whether they
are career-centered or company-centered, they bear down upon each
other in ways different from men at lower levels. They interact with
each other in the spirit of an ingroup, realizing that the concept of
face is important to all. Because authority differences among levels
of executives tend to be minimal, they tend to influence each other
by means of conversational, informal suggestions. Here it is mind
over mind and not so much superior over subordinate. What may
appear to the mobility-dull manager to be voices of trivial opposition are in fact the voices of constrained and subtle rebutting of
crucial differences, couched in an impersonal way in order to help
save face for their hearers. Successes and failures are also presented
in an impersonal way for the same reason of saving face. In all
organizations and at all levels, people find a target when things go
wrong and lay all the trouble to it, although there is less tendency
to find scapegoats at higher levels. Mobile executives are more concerned about what went wrong than who caused it to do so.

To put it in different terms, executives' mistakes are evaluated in
terms of objective consequences. To say that executives are less
petty is to hide the fact that they can become irritated by nuances
the same as managers. But they are prohibited by their sense of rapport from exposing their peers' mistakes unless these mistakes reveal
objectively provable differences in aptitude for achieving corporate
aims and goals. Also, executives are less quick to judge each other
because their decisions span longer periods of time, and what may

---

[1] Executives are men in the executive suite at the top of the corporation, and
managers are below them in the developmental stages of middle management.

initially appear to be mistakes may with time turn out to be major breakthroughs. Executives tend to use a feather-light touch with their subordinates and peers. The heavy hand of the lower positioned manager is frowned upon at high corporate levels. The terms "style" and "panache" are often used to mean the ability to say and do almost anything without antagonizing others. People tend to work better when they do not have to work at saving face.

To be mobility-bright also means to present oneself in a manner becoming to the dignity and stature of the superiors above. It means to behave as though the executive were at a higher level than his present one. For men in the arrival (top) level, it is to reveal a style that is becoming to a corporation president. The principle is that the closer he moves to the office of the president, the more an executive shows in his manners and conduct the style representative of the character of the corporation. Such executives know that they are viewed by managers below them as representative models. They attempt individually and collectively to mirror the best manners and morals of the corporation.

The mobility-bright executive knows that mobility brings high risk. Success is not measured by the distance from first-level management. He knows that the closer he gets to the top, the more likely is failure to occur. The reason is that few men arrive at the top without putting their careers on the line. The early arrival is prepared to risk his career, but he is careful to pick the right time and place. When career risk is involved, the executive realizes that if the decisions go against him, he may be removed, and if not, he will have to remove himself from the corporation to preserve his sense of dignity.

Both executives and managers incur risk to some extent every day because their decisions are based upon uncertainties. A typical decision is based upon 10 percent of the facts that would become available if the executive had twice as much time to make his decision. But these kinds of risks are not what are referred to as "career risks." The executive who makes a major contribution does so in the face of intense opposition. During the many conferences that are set up to discuss his pet project, the ball bounces back and forth between colleagues who support his idea and others who object to it.

In most cases, the deciding factor becomes the executive's sheer desire to see the program executed and his willingness to stake his whole career on the outcome. If the results fall short of what is intended, he will lose his future opportunities to be effective. At this point he will quit if he is mobility-bright.

The mobility-bright executive realizes that as he moves higher he must manage the shelf-sitter better. Shelf-sitters exist at all levels. At the higher reaches of the corporation they can be more of a problem. As one top executive reported, "You cannot afford to ignore men in the upper levels who are not going higher because they have a tenure complex. They know that they are too good for jobs below them, not good enough for jobs above them, and indispensable for jobs that match their skills." At lower levels the manager can work around shelf-sitters, but at higher levels the executive must work with and through them. To ignore them is to incur their wrath, but while they can hurt the executive they can help him much more.

The executive is measured in part by how well he can utilize shelf-sitters. There are fewer jobs at the top with more people below them. At the top, rapport forbids moving them around without regard to face, and the executive is obliged to use them. Another president said, "Anyone can manage his few crucial subordinates, but it takes a master to manage vice-presidents who are secure for life. Besides, the margins of error are narrower at the top and a bad decision can be bailed out if everyone pitches in, including shelf-sitters, to make the best of it. Here is where the shelf-sitter can make or break a program." Many executives have come to realize that the ultimate difference between success and failure often lies in the acts of shelf-sitters.

The mobility-bright executive understands how mobility brings greater logistics support. At lower levels the manager has less opportunity to commandeer the personnel, tools, and resources that are necessary to the success of his project. He is always working at the margin of inadequate supply of talent, money, and technical facilities, and hence he can be excused if errors occur that are attributable to these deficiencies. But executives are seldom in this kind of situation. They can co-opt personnel, tap hidden budgets, reorganize staff and line personnel. In other words, they can better squeeze out of the corporation the necessary logistics support. Their performances are relatively free of excuses and if they make mistakes they make them because of faulty management.

At least this is assumed to be the case in more instances than not at the executive level. Because of this, the executive has been known to steal, borrow, and trade personnel and technical resources with seemingly reckless abandon. His greater span of authority allows him to divert from a department or division logistical material to execute the mission that is currently his basic project. His superiors may not be aware of what other programs were deemphasized as long as he is successful in his critical assignment. Few executives can plead that they did not have this talent or that technical support when things go awry.

The mobility-bright executive keeps a steady eye on surplus and scarce talent and resources. These become more crucial to his success the higher he goes in the corporation. This means that he must attempt to develop and relate positively to personnel below him vertically and work well with people exposed to him laterally. His managerial successes are greatly determined by how well he reads the roster of managerial talent. If he maps poorly, he manages poorly. At the same time, he must keep exposed and maintain visibility (see Chapter 4).

The mobility-bright executive has a strong desire for visibility and exposure. He studies carefully the expectations and behavior of his superiors for the purpose of evaluating them and modeling himself after them. He prizes most highly the multilevel visibility of vertical and lateral types. He utilizes his assignments for the purpose of experimenting with the approaches of his superior to build a managerial style of his own. He is very capable of reading implicit cues and sensing minor variations in styles.

The mobility-bright executive has an equally strong desire to be exposed to superiors who are lateral and vertical to him. He has a tendency to avoid exposure when it is unrepresentative of his behavior or the behavior of his superiors. And he tends to maximize his chances of becoming exposed to the most mobile superiors. This orientation toward superiors largely determines how he selects his assignments when he is given choices. He will always go for assignments that give him high visibility and exposure even though he may suffer in salary or immediate mobility. He knows that in the long run mobility is based upon acquiring and maintaining high visibility and exposure. In particular, the mobility-bright manager is aware of the hazard of fast upward moves that are without transfer value of the lateral type. He may even turn down a promotion to accept a lateral assignment in order to avoid the possibility of becoming more mobile than mobility-wise. This is the only time he will accept the loss of career time. In short, if he wants to be mobility-bright, he must be as wise as his mobility rate requires.

The mobility-bright executive intuitively knows that movement up and around is a better indication of mobility than any other pattern of mobility. He does not discount a lateral move and does not consider a lateral assignment to be any less challenging than a promotion. Consequently, his superiors see him at his best when he is in a lateral assignment. This exposure may cause him to receive quick promotion. Contrary to what might be assumed, performance in lateral assignments can give more quality exposure than outright promotions.

The mobility-bright executive cannot be taken in by the formal organization. He is aware of job title, authority, and hierarchical position, but he views them as mere contrivances that hide more than they explain. He is prepared to see the less visible and less audible side of his superiors, chiefly their standing with their peers and superiors. He knows the signs of sponsorship and the less potent skills of evaluation and nomination. He can infer from a minimum of cues who are the centers of power, and he seeks to have high visibility and exposure with them. He will assiduously cultivate his standing and opportunities with them and seize every opportunity to learn from them. He will utilize his opportunities in the social world to size up the men who are centers of sponsorship in the corporate world. The mobility-bright executive tends to define as powerful in any organization only a few people, and these are seldom known by their formal authority, responsibility, job title, or salary. He is not enamored with the trappings of authority and salary and does not seek authority and salary. He goes for influence and power.

Mobility-bright executives notice that competition becomes more intense as they move to the top. However, the desire to cooperate increases commensurately. Executives compete to cooperate and co-operate to compete. They are intensely competitive because more people are in the arrival stage with fewer positions ahead of them. In addition, they have higher expectations because they have come farther. While they work harder to enhance their gains, they work harder to conserve the gains that they already have acquired. Executives are more cooperative because it serves to keep the competitive drive in balance and offset some of the bad effects. But equally important is the fact that the assignments of top-level executives by their very nature require more coordinative and interdependent forms of behavior. If the top group is not coordinated, the corporation is not coordinated. In this sense, the executive shows the competitive drive by his efforts to cooperate and he cooperates in order to maintain and enhance his gains. Mobility is based upon the right mixture.

The mobility-bright executive knows that as he moves up the corporate ladder, he manages and is managed by men who are more mobility-bright than men at lower levels. He knows that he enters an arena in which men's wits are the basic weapons. Their minds are honed to a fine edge, and subtle degrees of sharpness can spell the difference between success and failure. The mere presence of an individual with a superior mind gives direction to the battle. To match wits with him is a challenge in itself. The ordinary man cannot understand the challenge represented by succeeding and leaving behind men of worthy skill.

To succeed at the top requires more than getting to the top. The executive must have learned efficiently the lessons taught at middle- and lower-management levels. The middle-management levels serve to filter out the manager who cannot endure the stresses and strains of the executive life, but this screening device is not perfect. A few men may move into the executive ranks who are mobility-directed but not sufficiently mobility-bright, and some of these will cease to be mobility-directed. Early arrivals have a high degree of mobility competency, but mobile insiders need it as well. However, a mobility-directed executive may lose his drive. The stresses and strains of

mobility have dulled his appetite for more. He acquires mobility fatigue. It is evident that mobility fatigue is negative reaction to
mobility. It is likely to set in when the executive is moved too fast
to absorb the changes in his work, family, and community roles. He
simply cannot keep up in all these areas. What he does never gets
done completely or is not rewarding or is too often another person's
idea. He may do it out of a sense of duty or devotion, but he seems
to be on a hopeless treadmill.

Some executives display a low threshold for ambiguity. When
they get involved in too many activities that cannot be finished,
they lose their sense of challenge. Others can live with situations
that are always emerging, that never stand still, and enjoy it all tre-
mendously. Their span of attention is wide, and their feeling of
effectiveness is highest when they have twelve projects going at the
same time. They can mentally shift gears, pursue diverse objectives,
plan for the unexpected, and recover when the worst that can happen does happen. Yet, somehow, they always land on their feet
without any loss of equilibrium. When the word comes to abandon
one project and start a new assignment, they have no feeling of
being mistreated or cheated.

Mobility and ambiguity are near synonyms. If the threshold for
tolerating ambiguity is low to begin with or is driven down by unfortunate experiences, the call to a new assignment will arouse feelings of anxiety and dread. In a state of decreasing drive, the executive may make mistakes that could prove disastrous. These mistakes
may be caused by subtle decreases in the functioning of the senses.
For example, if X is the amount of energy required to hear, it is estimated that 4X is the amount of energy required to listen. A drop
in energy level may cause the manager to miss subtle cues that
might greatly change his behavior. When executives make mistakes,
they blame mobility—and perhaps rightly so. If they are demoted
or arrested, they may appeal to the defense mechanism of rationalization. They are often heard to say, "Oh, well, I'm glad that I'm
not going higher. The additional salary and responsibility are not
worth the cost to me." The point is usually true. In that state of
mind they will be expending energy unproductively and ineffi-

ciently. This rationalization when adhered to may actually save them from a greater degree of failure.

The corporation, however, may not fully understand the symptoms of mobility fatigue and give the manager or executive a lateral demotion or even promotion. In each of these reassignments there is a kind of mobility; and to a manager already suffering from mobility fatigue, any one change may be too much for him to absorb. A demotion is difficult enough for an executive to absorb, but if he is suffering from mobility fatigue, his overreaction to it may border on irrationality. Oddly enough, the overreaction may also occur at the point of a lateral move or promotion. The author has seen executives hand in their resignations at the point of a promotion. The shocked reaction by the superior attested to the lack of understanding of the subordinate's condition. Mobility fatigue seeks the cessation of all mobility, lateral, upward, or downward, as well as radical changes in assignments in the same position. The executive obviously needs a rest. He needs to be left alone or he will commit mistakes that meet the level of incompetency and which may ruin his future career.

The author has seen the symptoms of mobility fatigue disappear through inactivity and isolation, but only when the superior is insightful enough to inform the subordinate that he is being sidelined temporarily because he is a valuable member of the team. A good dose of inactivity and isolation may allow him to tidy up his home and community life, get back his self-confidence, and give him the desire to get going again. When his drive has returned, so will the physical energy to attend carefully to his work.

The problem is that many superiors are not trained to diagnose mobility fatigue. The mistakes that the executive may make are interpreted as incompetency. Too often the superior assumes that the executive has peaked out at the top of his ability. The word goes out that the executive is nondevelopmental and should be left alone. If the manager is left alone, he may recover and want to regain mobility which, however, may not be forthcoming because of the mistakes in diagnosis by his superiors. This presents a different problem. The executive is once again full of energy and has nowhere to release it. He finds his present job uninteresting and wants to move on to more challenging assignments. Every unit of energy expended fails to replenish itself and the executive falls into a condition called "secondary mobility fatigue." The executive grows tired of waiting for mobility.

Secondary mobility fatigue can produce disastrous results. For example, an executive regained his drive but grew impatient with his lack of mobility. He went to the superior who believed that he had peaked and asked for an explanation for his being put on a shelf. The superior, wanting to justify his judgment, denied the accusation in the usual manner, which is to face the subordinate and to say with a most serious face, "No job here is unimportant. If it were, we would have eliminated it or delegated it to someone below you." The executive received this treatment and was forced to give up his attempt to regain his mobility. What he did not know was that the superior interpreted this behavior to be further evidence that he was not capable of holding a higher position. A stalemate had been reached; the executive was desperate. He could not explain his situation to his superior who, in turn, could not explain his judgment to his subordinate. As a result, this executive left the firm shortly thereafter, and ironically enough received two quick promotions in the new firm, much to the dismay of his former superior.

There are many executives who suffer intensely from secondary mobility fatigue while they are waiting for a promotion. Meanwhile, they do not display in their present jobs qualities which can be recognized as promotable. At least one out of three arrested-mobility types reclines on a neatly prepared shelf complacently awaiting the day when he will once again be put to use. After some time, such shelf-sitters may silently vow not to expend any more energy than necessary to conserve their gains. They wait for the corporation to rescue them from their entrapment, but they will not take a hand in their own extrication. Perhaps from the standpoint of energy, this tactic is wise, since by keeping their energy in line with their opportunities they avoid severe fatigue.

Suppose, however, that the executive decides to chance the investment of huge amounts of energy in the hope that a promotion may come. One of three results is possible. The first is that he may change the superior's judgment and receive the eagerly sought promotion. In this case, everything is fine and the crisis has passed, at least temporarily. The second possibility is that, by rearranging his pattern of energy investment, he may actually come to enjoy his present position. If he does, his gamble will have paid off in the form of energy replenishment. He may become his old self again and may even get the additional bonus of a promotion. It is also possible that a promotion could be negatively received at this point. The third condition is that he will fail to receive a promotion or to increase substantially the satisfaction derived from his work. He may develop a chronic case of mobility fatigue.

The key symptom of chronic mobility fatigue is a bitter, almost vindictive attitude toward anybody or anything that smacks of change of any kind, including mobility. He becomes a confirmed reactionary and develops a philosophy that supports this kind of behavior in public. Gradually, he could evolve into an office insider who subverts the means of organization for the ends.

To prevent the burning out of capable executives, the corporation has learned a few techniques. These practices invariably involve some form of mobility. For example, the corporation has learned to keep a record of the number of moves that an executive has made in the course of a five-year period. They are particularly concerned when a hierarchical move is attended by a geographical move. The arrival, performance, departing triad occurs in both the new job and the new community. The stress is more than the arithmetic sum of the two moves—geographical and hierarchical. Much stress can be cut down by reducing the moves to one at a time. The executive who is moved geographically is given a similar assignment or position until he has adjusted himself to his new environment. Then he may be given a hierarchical move. Or he may be given a hierarchical move followed by a geographical move after he has the new position under his belt.

Another technique has been previously referred to and takes the form of changes in assignment that bring no geographical or position moves. Still another technique is to recognize the importance of gradualism. Some men can move faster than others and they must be allowed to say when they are moving too fast. In the past, the loyalty ethic prohibited the insider from saying "no" to a move. The corporation reserved the right to say "no" or "yes" to an executive. A "no" on his part was a sign of disloyalty. The consequence was that many men were burned out because of fear that if they said "no" to the corporation the corporation would say "no" to them.

We have touched on some of the ways in which mobile executives become and remain mobility-directed and what happens when they lose this drive. Executives may lose their mobility brightness too. We may illustrate this by the concept of the developmental gap and the mobility gap. Ideally, every position is developmental in that each calls forth previously acquired skills and experiences and prepares the executive for more responsible assignments. We may say that each position calls for a unique ordering of skills and experiences. Unfortunately, some executives override the unique features of a position by maintaining a style that was useful in previous positions, ignoring the differences that inhere in the new position. Executives have been known to move through several different positions without varying their managerial styles, as though they had learned nothing new. What has happened is that they have frozen the process of development to a level of high initial effectiveness. They have set their styles and they force position responsibilities to comply with them. Regardless of the number of positions they have held, they have, in effect, managed the same position several times, repeating the same experiences again and again. Style rigidity can set in easily because managing is not a fine art. There are wide tolerances of success and failure that allow for rather gross and imprecise levels of skill and development. A common saying is that a poor decision can be made to work if it is believed in. This is true of a poor managerial style that is aggressively applied.

When mobility exceeds skill development, the executive often repeats the same mistakes, carrying with him from job to job the same problems. He may even have a set procedure for handling the problem, but it is more remedial than preventive. He has learned how to minimize his difficulties. Such an oblique approach starves the executive of preventive experience and will arrest his upward mobility at levels where the tolerances that cover his problem are narrow. An executive never knows exactly when a remedial solution may become a problem itself. This is the case when a short-range solution becomes a long-range problem. The executive who is interested in sustaining his mobility will attempt to alter his style to account for the unique features of each new position. He makes full use of his development opportunities, since to him each position is a developmental one.

Every position calls for new skills in addition to ordering a unique arrangement of previously acquired skills and experiences. If the new skills that are required are radically different from those previously acquired, the executive faces a developmental gap in which his mobility is ahead of his competency. This may occur for several reasons. The first, of course, is the failure to learn from previous jobs. If we assume that he has cranked out from his previous positions all the possible skills, the second reason may be that the new position is inherently too advanced for his level of development. He may have been promoted too fast. Perhaps his sponsor made an error in judgment; he misjudged either the executive or the new position or both. Such mismatches occur frequently and, unfortunately, the executive will carry the blame for the failure that may ensue.

A third reason for a developmental gap is that the executive did not stay long enough in his previous positions to really master them. During the last decade, some executives have moved faster than they have been able to absorb their experiences, or they may not have stayed long enough to have had their performances evaluated. Mistakes from which executives learn the most are those that are not identified for as long as a year after they have occurred. It takes that long for the repercussions to set in and for evaluations to be made. As one executive said, "If you are going to make mistakes, move faster than they do." This, of course, is a dangerous policy.

The developmental gap can become a positive force in that the mobile executive may be forced to tap talent that cannot be reached by any other means. Each mobile executive has potential of which he is unaware. If he meets the crisis successfully, he is a better man in several ways. He knows better what he can do under stress and he has created new potential by transforming potential talent into actual talent. The miracle of learning is that it creates as much potential as it actualizes. Theoretically, the mobile executive is never deprived of potential but only of the opportunity to actualize it. We may then say that one way to overcome a developmental gap quickly is to throw a man in over his head and force him to sink or swim. Some learn very fast while others panic. Those that succeed receive an experiential advantage in that they have eliminated the developmental gap, sustained their mobility, and acquired a tremendous sense of self-confidence. The possibility is great that in the next job they will find a surplus of skill and confidence. It may take them less time than usual to master the next job and do it easily. In this way they have eliminated the developmental gap.

The mobility gap is an entirely different phenomenon. Here the executive has developed faster than his mobility. What he wants to do to increase his mobility is to take up some of the slack in his development. The chief reason for a mobility gap is that he experiences his positions more efficiently than most. It takes him less time to learn and control the new position and the mobility needed to sustain his developmental curve is not forthcoming. He is "hungry." Every additional day in the position causes his developmental curve to flatten out markedly. The few additional experiences cost him abnormal amounts of career time. The longer he stays immobile, the greater the mobility gap. He is overprepared for the next job because he learned the present one too quickly. In contrast to the executive with a developmental gap who has underlearned his positions, he has overlearned his job.

Overlearning may be caused by not having had exposure to evaluators. Superiors may come to expect a normal learning period that covers most subordinates. The exceptions may be missed, especially if they are obscurely positioned. Overlearning is indeed most apt to occur among executives in positions of the more routine type, with low exposure. For various reasons, an efficient learner may be put into one of these routine positions and stay far longer than other executives who learn less efficiently in more exposed positions.

One reason a fast learner may be shunted off into an obscure position is that he is a disturbing fast learner. The superior may want to reduce his exposure simply because he cannot stand his presence.

If this is the case, a most logical result usually occurs. The fast learner becomes more irritating as his exposure is reduced because he becomes bored quickly with his new assignment and because he must make a bigger noise to overcome his reduced exposure. Unless the superior realizes the essence of his situation, it may become worse. If the fast learner is given a demotion, his mobility gap will become that much larger.

In larger corporations, there are many executives who have wide mobility gaps. These are men who can perform at higher levels if they are given an opportunity. Management maintains that it is always looking for talent, but what it may not be aware of is that much needed talent lies in the most unexposed places, below executives and managers who cannot stand the irritating qualities that often belong to fast learners.

A superior who has underlearned and a subordinate who has over-learned can make an ideal match. This is true if the superior has not underlearned the skill to handle the fast learner. The problem with some mobile executives is that they move their crucial subordinates too fast because they themselves move too fast.[2] To avoid this double jeopardy, the mobile superior may latch occasionally onto an older, more experienced subordinate. Behind every mobile executive there is at least one subordinate who is eight to ten years his senior. This matching of energy and ambition with experience and deliberation represents a powerful meld, well-packed with potential mobility for both. It is a form of mobility brightness.

The consequences can be lethal if the man's mobility is ahead of his ability to assimilate and apply his experiences or if his competency is ahead of his mobility. In the former case, his reading and mapping facilities will be inadequate. In the latter case, his drive may be reduced or he may quit the corporation. The mobile executive cannot trust the corporation to keep his mobility in line with his competency and vice versa. He must assume the major responsibility for keeping his career alive and viable. This means that the mobile executive must know his true condition at all times and maneuver himself into the right situation when he has the options to

---

[2] See Chapter 7 (The Winning Couplet) for explanation of the term "crucial subordinates."

do so. To become and stay mobile the executive must direct his career as much or more than his corporation does. If he does not, he will not stay mobile. In this sense, he is clearly the master of his career and offers a final contrast to the traditional insider who places his fate solely in the hands of his corporate masters.

In conclusion, today the mobile executive has to have commitment or drive and intelligence of the real world to become effective and mobile. He has the inside track to the top. The members of the establishment still practice in one form or another the "laying on of hands," but it is more likely today than before that the anointed ones will have been to the four corners of their corporate worlds and will have less tunnel vision than the traditional insider.

CHAPTER FOUR

The Rise of
the Career Executive

By PUTTING YOUNG MEN on express routes, corporate officialdom unwittingly set in motion an incongruous set of forces that reverberated throughout the whole organization. Even the top had to be changed. No member of the executive corps escaped the unintentional consequences of changing the success game. Many loyal insiders in the executive suite who were especially good at winning the old way rejected the new ground rules that made success appear more confusing and ruthless. Or they became anxious and opportunistic in their own defense. The contest of success broke the confining, sedate boundaries set by the insider's tradition as wave after wave of youthful careerists assaulted the doors to the executive suite. Logic warned that it was only a matter of time when mobile executives would pit themselves against the bastion of central authority itself, but few predicted the size or intensity of the struggle.

In all of this rustle and hustle that sometimes bordered on frenzy and panic, the hidden effects of mobility have become awesomely real. Basically, the overriding problem today involves minimizing the effects of several opposing activities inherently generated by the objectives and unintended consequences of breeding superior men. One set of opposing forces includes the need to keep talented men, which means not to let them go if it is within the corporation's powers and to its advantage to retain them. Of course, some of the best will inevitably leave, but spokesmen for the corporation are often heard bragging that it never loses anyone that it wants to keep. Whether the executive leaves voluntarily or involuntarily, tradition prescribes that he should never be invited or permitted to return under any circumstances. Quitting is implicit disloyalty because the quitter assumes the right normally held by the corporation: namely, to determine who should stay and leave. The threat not to rehire constitutes the enforcer, and in the past it achieved widespread usefulness because, first, most of the large, dominant, established, and secure firms would not hire another's quitters; second, insiders found it difficult psychologically to leave the known for the unknown; and third, there were more men than good jobs. The enforcer put much punch behind the ability of superiors to suppress disloyalty among subordinates.

Over the course of many years of applying the policy of promotion from within, corporations have discovered that some of the best insiders will not give up their options to leave without assurance that they may stay. This we now recognize to be the expression of the insider's mentality. The enforcer helps to produce the security theme that the executive will not be thrown into the street when he is too old to successfully relocate. The fear of abandonment is one of the oldest fears among human beings and, in the variation found among insiders, one of the most powerful threats. While many corporations continue to apply the security theme, the mixture of promoting mobile executives and offering security to traditional insiders produces a set of conflicting forces.

If it is true, as a few corporations maintain, that they do not lose anyone they really want to keep, it is equally true that many stay who should leave. Unless the themes of competency and security are carefully advanced, incompetent executives will clutter up the corporate landscape with their habit of conserving their gains. Being most concerned about security and easily frightened by aggressive, competent, youthful subordinates, they will champion loyalty, which they perversely interpret to be loyalty to their persons or to the company, depending upon which form serves their personal interests best at that time.

The problem of incompetent executives hanging on by their fingernails and at the same time covered by the umbrella of corporate security raises another set of conflicts. Developing talented executives requires, among other things, mobility—which we have noted involves a pattern of moving men through related positions that provide growth experience for handling increasing degrees of responsibility. In order for mobility to work, the top has to be open or a log jam will develop. As one mobile executive remarked, "If you shake the bottle hard enough the cork will pop out." This was his way of saying that breeding talented men on a steady diet of mobility requires keeping the corporate arteries free of blocks. Accustomed to a mobile diet, young executives will not wait in a line of succession whose pace is so slow that they could face retirement before they occupy the executive suite. Speaking in mixed metaphors, one shook-up executive stated this problem succinctly: "A man with a head of steam up is not about to cool his heels in a side pocket of the corporate maze."

To keep a log jam from developing, men at the top, including the chairman and president, must keep moving themselves. Here the rub is again a carry over from tradition. Once at the top, the traditional insider will want to stay as long as he possibly can. His motives are several, including the desire for challenge, power, status, money, and security. A seldom-mentioned motive is the desire that stems uniquely from the insider's mentality: The insider does not want to go outside because he dislikes or fears the outside, and he seldom leaves the firm willingly or gracefully. His sense of identity is at stake. The men most concerned about identity are men who have nowhere to go or whose next step is out. They become overly preoccupied with what peers will think if they leave their corporations before death or mandatory retirement. In other words, when insiders are forced to go outside, the twin threats of going outside and being evaluated negatively by colleagues and peers in the business community converge to create a most intense form of anxiety.

The author has treated executives and presidents who had severe doses of this separation and identity anxiety.[1] He discovered that the conflicting force is identification of the self-image with the company—an identification that develops through several decades of hard work, loyalty, and security. The insider's self-image and company become so tightly cemented that the thought of leaving arouses feelings that border on separation anxiety.

As one insider lamented who after fourteen years as chairman was finally forced out of the company, "What will I do, where will I go? I have lived forty-nine years in the company. It has been my whole life, my soul; my reason for living my life the way I have is wrapped up in staying useful to my company. And now I must stay away, even from the board meetings. It is cruel, really cruel, terrible." For this well-known former chieftain, life seemed to stop when his umbilical cord to the company was severed. Now this attitude becomes all the more severe if the executive is eased out because of the supposed superior qualifications of youthful mobile executives. As one insider who experienced this effect of the new generation said, "I did not want to leave under any circumstances, let alone under the condition that I was too old to hold my job. I was fifty-five and in the prime of my life when the suggestion was made that I retire early. I knew what they had in mind. All around me the young men were taking over and one of them wanted my job who had twenty years more of service to the company left in him. Imagine what my friends said when they learned that a smart kid took my job."

No problem is as delicate as cutting loose a reluctant top executive. Insiders invariably face a stringent decompression period lasting as long as five years after they are shorn of their corporate attachments. Typically, they find it hard to build a new career, since a second career is alien to their one-worldness. In many cases, they gravitate to opportunities where they symbolically feel attachment to their backgrounds. Curtis N. Painter, a former insider from Armstrong Cork Co., rented a small office and set himself up as a business consultant. Ray R. Eppert, a former insider from Burroughs,

[1] See E. E. Jennings, *Executive Success*, Appleton Century Crofts, New York, 1968.

retained an office and a secretary and rose promptly at 5 A.M. each day to work in about twenty-five business and community organizations. Many companies attempt to cushion the blow by providing office space and secretarial help for departing insiders, by using them as consultants, and by calling upon them for special assignments. Courtland S. Gross received consulting fees from his former company, Lockheed, and director's fees from five other companies he served as director. Sometimes the executive has to be eased out by a slow, gradual process.

In not a few cases will the easing out be initiated by the executive himself, or at least he will be an equal party with the corporation to his gradually breaking free. In either case, few insiders can suddenly and totally leave. Elmer W. Engstrom held the presidency of RCA between 1961 and 1965. David Sarnoff, board chairman, reached down for his youthful forty-three-year-old son, Robert W. Sarnoff, to be his new president. The question was what to do with Engstrom. They decided to make him chairman of the executive committee, which at RCA is a ceremonial, secretarial duty, and to keep him on the board. On December 4, 1968, at age 67, Engstrom's contract was renegotiated providing for termination of his employment effective December 31. His new contract made him a consultant for five years at $50,000 a year, one-fifth of his former salary as an employee. Even though not an employee, he remained chairman of the executive committee. RCA apologetically explained to the stockholders that a person does not have to be an employee of the company to be chairman of the executive committee. With a strong, aggressive new management team under the direction of the two Sarnoffs, Engstrom needed RCA more than RCA needed his services. But old standbys and family friends cannot be eased out easily. As one president with a similar problem remarked, "With some of them you have to take their security blanket away by cutting off pieces of it—all the while telling them that they are needed and they have to accept each new arrangement."

The executive is fortunate if he can become meaningfully involved in another corporation while terminating his employment at his home company. Frederick R. Kappel joined American Telephone & Telegraph in 1924, fresh out of electrical engineering training at the University of Minnesota. This insider left the chairmanship in early 1967, was made board member of International Paper Co. in July, and in April, 1968, was made chairman of the newly formed executive advisory committee. Edward B. Hinman, president and chief executive officer of the world's largest paper enterprise, found Kappel to be even more valuable than he expected, and in February, 1969, asked him to become chairman of the board at a salary of $100,000 in order to participate responsibly in decisions and plans important to the development, growth, and profitability of the business. Kappel slipped easily into a very responsible position that helped greatly to fill the gnawing void created by his growing separation from American Telephone & Telegraph.

Kappel represents the problem of finding another position that holds the possibilities of command and leadership opportunity. These men who have habits of giving and taking cannot easily relocate. The other companies to which they may want to transfer their habits of leadership have their own strong chiefs who might want advice but not domination. It is hard for insiders not to present both. A chief executive who had a sorry experience with a former president reported, "You cannot put them even in an advisory role and reject their suggestions for very long or they will simply leave. I spent more time and effort graciously declining their suggestions and recommendations than in preparing my own." Another president who had had a similar experience remarked, "They are good at giving suggestions that were customs and conventions in their former corporations. But they are given with the air of finality. They think they know our problems but actually they know better their own theories and philosophy which they attempt to coerce into our way of doing business."

If there is a wide age gap between the former president and the chief executive, these problems will be magnified. In one case the president was forty-one and the new chairman and former chairman of another corporation sixty-eight. The younger executive exclaimed, "I was treated by my people as kingpin but by the new chairman as a son. He seemed to feel that I was not legitimate. It proved to be a very exasperating relationship. One day a board member to whom I went for help suggested I see the new chairman.

Then one of my own executive vice-presidents suggested to me that we go to the chairman about a problem. When this happened, it dawned upon me that the respect of my subordinates for my judgment had been whittled down to practically nothing. The chairman had to go or I would." Also, we can easily see that the marriage of an insider from one firm with one from another firm may produce considerable stress if the corporation from which the retired executive comes is much bigger and more prestigious than the one he is invited to join. Receiving the benefit of his experience without his powers of domination presents a mean exercise in imagination, diplomacy, and deftness. The urge to get *inside* again and get his hands around another corporate entity often prohibits the marriage from achieving its intended results. But if he cannot get inside another organization, he will be less likely to get completely outside his parent company.

The mobility studies show that about two-thirds of the chief executives in the largest industrial corporations during the premobility days stayed on in some capacity after they left their top posts. About half of these former chief executives stayed as chairman of finance or executive committees of the board. With such a dread of leaving the firm, the insider is fully capable of fabricating the necessary reasons to stay. He has been known to impede the development of adequate replacements, aggressively pursue a reorganization program, launch a long-overdue growth program, and generally keep himself indispensable by the way he passes out assignments and supervises their execution. The closer the insider approaches the exit door to the cold outside world, the harder he works to stay in. Gerald Phillippe, former insider president of General Electric, often said that he observed among top executives that the chairman facing imminent retirement seemed to find more problems to solve than the president who was farther away from the exit door. All of which suggests that the insider's mentality works against him as he approaches retirement. The boomerang effect of breeding insiders is that they want to stay long after they should leave.

Log jams at and near the top plague corporations going into the seventies. Insiders often arrive at the top later in life and stay longer than men who have been in several corporations. Or they arrive early and stay longer. In the past, many spent twenty or more years in the top two jobs. The average age when made president in 1961 to 1966 for hierarchs [2] of the five hundred largest industrial corporations was fifty-one, but among the twenty firms best-known for their policy of promoting strictly from within, the average age was fifty-four. For the first group, among those which drew freely from within and without, the average age was less than forty-nine. Further, the top man stayed almost 1½ times as long as his counterpart in the importer firms. It was not unusual for an executive to stay six or seven years as president and nine or ten years as chairman while keeping the chief-executive officership in each position. Under such conditions, a vice-president promoted to the presidency could become too old to be chief executive officer, and a vice-president could be forced to retire at the edge of the president's office. When one considers that the average age of the vice-president was only five years younger than the average age of the president, retirement for many vice-presidents was a greater possibility than promotion.

This is a distinct reality because of a traditional notion that to leave the top job before retirement is a sign of failure, incompetence, or weakness. It is common to give men at the top the privilege of living out their careers, and many stay until death or ill health forces tneir hands. In the premobility period, many stayed into their seventies and a few into their eighties. In this sense, a representative insider was Thomas B. McCabe, chairman of the board of Scott Paper Co., who at age seventy-five, after fifty-two years with the company, stepped aside at the end of 1968. He was made president in 1927 and chairman in 1962. But he could not entirely leave the firm. He remained a director and chairman of the executive committee. To leave his company entirely was simply beyond this highly respected executive's capability.

Another pitfall of breeding loyal company executives is that they come to act as proprietors though they lack substantive ownership. A proprietary attitude among men at the very top of large corporations allows them to feel that their companies are theirs to deal with as they deem wise. They usually have sufficient autonomy

[2] Men who were not founders: birth, marriage, or kinship elite.

from their boards of directors to back up this proprietary attitude with specific acts, among which is to stay in the firm until illness or death forces their hands. McCabe stayed so long at the top of Scott Paper Co. that eleven executives were retired before they could become president and six high-level executives simply left for more mobile situations rather than wait until the log jam cleared up. Four of these quitters eventually became presidents of corporations.

There were numerous instances of men moving up to high levels only to discover that retirement beat them to acquiring the necessary seniority before they became eligible for the top job. Sometimes the highly positioned insider waited a third of his career for promotion to the presidency. In General Motors during the period of 1961 to 1966, there were seven vice-presidents and executive vice-presidents who had to retire short of the presidency because time ran out on them. There were at least three executive vice-presidents (the rank from which presidents were usually promoted) who, if promoted to the presidency, would have had their tenure abbreviated considerably because of retirement. For this reason, they were not promoted to the office of president.

The exercise of a proprietary attitude that does not recognize the need for keeping the top open can bring lethal consequences to the corporation. A case in point was Anaconda Copper Mining Company. As of 1955, Anaconda had no mandatory retirement policy. It was up to the executives themselves to initiate their retirement. The result was superannuation. Cornelius F. Kelly, chairman and chief executive officer, was eighty years of age, and Robert Dwyer, president, was seventy. Two vice-presidents were seventy-six and seventy, three other top officers were in their mid-sixties, and only two officers were below fifty-six. During Kelly's period as chairman, two presidents died in their mid-sixties. With a relatively older set of replacements, the top officers became increasingly superannuated. The managers below the top officers became increasingly narrow and specialized in their skills and orientation and, hence, incompetent to replace their superiors. No doubt the overemphasis upon tradition helped to cause the extreme slippage of Anaconda's relative position with its chief rivals. While Anaconda gained, since 1939, an increase in revenue of about 40 percent, Kennecott and

Phelps Dodge gained about 250 and 290 percent respectively. In 1955, Anaconda's gross profit margin was about one-half that of its two competitors. In 1964, C. M. Brinkerhoff became chief executive officer at the age of sixty-three and faced the Herculean task of finding and developing youth to place the corporation in a growth pattern.

The clogging of the arteries leading to the top is entirely possible in the best of breeder companies. As stated previously, Frederick Kappel, chairman and chief executive officer of American Telephone & Telegraph, retired at sixty-five in accordance with policy. But he did not leave completely. Instead, he remained a director and chairman of the powerful executive committee, of which his erstwhile successor was a member, until he switched his interests to International Paper Co. To complicate matters, the new chairman, Haakon I. Romnes, sixty, had only five years before mandatory retirement, with part of his tenure as president devoid of the experience of chairing the powerful executive committee. The new president was two years older than the chairman, and the president of Western Electric, a wholly owned manufacturing subsidiary from which American Telephone & Telegraph often got its chief executives, would retire the same year as the board chairman Romnes. Furthermore, there were some ten other executives in the Bell System that were in similar circumstances. But Kappel hung in there and preempted opportunity for others to develop. When the top officer overstays and his potential successors are his age peers, many younger executives are deprived of their opportunity to move sequentially, in an orderly way, into a position for which they prepared. What often happens is that the superannuated executives leave all at once and the junior class takes over with less preparation than might be desirable.

However, this was not the case at United States Steel Corp. Clifford Hood, Walter Munford, Leslie Worthington, and Edwin Gott proved adequate to the president's job, but only one of them became chief executive officer. The reason was that Roger Blough stayed chairman and chief executive officer for fourteen years, longer than anyone since the legendary Albert H. Gary, the firm's first company head, who served from 1903 to 1927. In 1969, Blough retired and Gott became the only one of the four who held the final authority in his own hands. It should be mentioned that, in 1968, rumors were circulating in the steel industry that in 1963 Gott was offered the presidency of Bethlehem Steel Corp. by Chairman Edmund F. Martin. Although this rumor was denied by both Gott and Martin after Gott became chairman and chief executive officer in 1969, the wonder was that executives suffocating in the slow procession line were not enticed away. If such attempts to pirate giant United States Steel Corp. failed, it was partly because the insider's mentality was commonly shared among members of its executive suite.

In many industries, particularly those with histories of spectacular growth (as in the fields of computers and electronics), a major clogging at the top usually occasioned a steady stream of men to the outside. As a general rule, the younger, more competent executive whose route ahead was blocked was the more apt to leave. In this way, feeding young executives a steady diet of upward mobility worked against keeping them. We can now see that the breeder firm became a potential nightmare of wierdly conflicting forces pressing upon the insider to be both loyal and mobile.

The mandatory retirement policies that had flooded the corporate scene for some time helped curtail the log jams at the top. In 1961 the most common mandatory retirement age was sixty-five, but by 1969 the trend was toward sixty-three, and some corporations, including Shell Oil Company, set the age at sixty. During this period, Ralph Cordiner's voice, faint at first, grew to a shout. Cordiner, former insider and chief of General Electric, retired in 1963 at the age of sixty-three and got as far away as possible from the executive suite. With no office or secretary furnished by the company, no seat on the board, and no consulting contract, he shattered the insider's stereotype by indicting his compatriots who believed their corporations needed their wisdom. He believed that all that wisdom that retiring executives are presumed to have can get out of date fast. When a man is no longer at risk, he loses his competency. Cordiner did not buy the idea that retired chieftains had some long-term right to dignity and salary and expense accounts and company planes. He said that the fact was that these requests only showed that they just plain did not want to quit. Cordiner felt that getting out completely allowed his successors to correct his mistakes. There is much to be said for Cordiner's point of view. A favorite statement of an insider who takes over the reins from a superior who remains active in the firm is that he plans no major changes in the company's organization and policies. Why should he when he was carefully nurtured by them, and how can he when the man responsible and to whom he has a special loyalty sits observantly in the corporate wings? The insider is inhibited enough by his mentality, and the more so by the active presence of his sponsor.

When Cordiner took over, the average age of General Electric's officers was fifty-nine, but Cordiner decided to clear the deck and encouraged many to retire early to make room for younger executives. For this reason, he too retired early, which allowed his successors to expeditiously clean up the mess in the computer division. By 1969, more men were heeding Cordiner's advice and leaving their corporations ahead of the mandatory retirement age. There is a good possibility that this trend of early retirement will become widespread because of the relatively lower ages of the men moving to the top.

But mandatory retirement policies have not been the only effort exerted to unblock the log jam. Pension programs, bonus plans, stock options, and high salaries for men below the top executives help to make men independently wealthy before they get to the top. Status is better distributed by more freely passing out titles and creating new ones. Division managers become division presidents, more corporate executives become vice-presidents, vice-presidents become group vice-presidents, former presidents become vice-chairmen, and more chairmen of boards become instead chairmen of executive committees or finance committees. Companies copied Standard Oil Co. (New Jersey), American Telephone & Telegraph Co., General Motors, and E. I. du Pont de Nemours & Co. who, like the New York Yankees for many years, were wise enough to field multi-platooned teams. They detach good men or allow them to retire from operating jobs early to spend full time on what amounts to directorial "think work" without thereby weakening day-to-day company management. What this distribution of status and assignment amounts to is that men may gracefully retire, leave, or withdraw without the stigma of weakness, incompetence, or failure.

And then these many gestures and practices tend to develop a cycle of mobility that is counterproductive. With more mobility to and at the top, mobile insiders naturally set greater expectations of arriving earlier at the top. It is the fact of rapid upward mobility itself that breeds the executive whose personality centers upon enhancing and maintaining his upward mobility. This career-centered executive is the antithesis of the insider with his company-centeredness. The latter has as both a strategy and tactic the climbing of a single continuous corporate ladder. The career-centered executive has as his strategy climbing any ladder that is available to him, discriminating only with regard to the degree of opportunity that the next rung affords him to reach the higher rungs above. In any given corporation where he immediately finds himself performing executive responsibilities, his tactic is to be a good insider. In his behavior, the career-centered executive makes explicit what is implicit in the insider's ethic: that most executives are motivated by the opportunity to better themselves. Under the ethic of corporate service and loyalty, the insider merely seeks to gain personal ends. The career-centered executive puts his career squarely and openly ahead of his corporation.

By the start of the 1970s, many corporations face the inability to fulfill the expectations of mobility-bred careerists. The very things that have been established to prevent egress now enhance it. Security is not staying in the firm and going nowhere. Status is not fancy titles for administrating trivia. Stock options and bonus plans will not hold men when they are offered everywhere. Money will not hold a man's heart, especially if he has more money than he needs or wants or when he can get more elsewhere. The faster that companies bring young men along, the less chance they have of keeping them if they cannot keep the route ahead uncluttered. Many proud companies have become literally stunned by the massive flouting of corporate fealty and loyalty. They realize that the enforcer simply must go, as many conventional methods of executive development and management success have gone.

Some of the greatest corporations were caught blushing; they had to extend invitations to their quitters to come back home. Several corporations, including General Electric, developed sophisticated techniques for keeping the door open for quitters to return. The dehiring [3] process starts at the first hint that a talented executive wants to leave General Electric. If he has made up his mind to leave and has not yet found a job, General Electric will help him find it. If he does well in the new job, he may be invited to return to General Electric. This form of counseling and monitoring quitters allows the executive the faith that General Electric wants to keep him and makes it easier for him to return someday. The corporation that practices dehiring is shrewd in this endeavor because the career-centered executive understands this kind of language and is most apt to stay or to return if he leaves. Furthermore, the firm is more apt to attract talented executives because they know they can leave with immunity if things do not work out for them as planned.

The very idea of dehiring and rehiring former executives shocks the dyed-in-the-wool insider, and not all corporations recognize the value of dehiring and rehiring. Corporate pride and vanity resist getting rid of the enforcer even when it clearly has lost most of its sting. However, the trend to go to the market for talent will be sustained because as companies diversify and grow, they need new, broad-gauge talent not always available from within. Familiarity with a company through previous employment and different experiences gained at another company make for a very attractive executive. Companies cannot afford to overlook capable men regardless of the source. For these reasons, resignation and company disloyalty are no longer the equivalents they once were in the fifties. The career executive demands what the corporation rightly insists upon for itself, the right to maximum choice and immunity.

The question may be asked: Why does the top-executive group, dominated by insiders, allow these new go-go kids into their chambers? Oddly, the answer lies in the fact that more often than not it is a chief executive who sponsors and oversees the whole breeding program and who has the staying power to see that his early products reach the executive suite. Or an occasional insider who can see the

---

[3] Dehiring is helping men to relocate as a service to their personal program of self-development.

error of his ways becomes converted to the cause of mobility and recommends as his successor a mobile type. Occasionally an outsider will come in and see the new talent just below the officer core and use it to get better control of the executive organization. For example, Semon Knudsen developed in General Motors a strong breeding philosophy which he carried to Ford Motor Company as president and chief operating officer until his summary dismissal nineteen months later. General Motors has consistently produced its own leaders. This record is quite remarkable in light of the fact that, since World War II, five companies have ceased to produce autos. Ford was virtually dead at the end of the 1940s, Chrysler fell into a disastrous tailspin in the late 1950s, and American Motors has been in and out of trouble consistently. Ford, Chrysler, and American Motors were often brought out of trouble by high-level talent that was nourished elsewhere. Henry Ford II's top import who did more for pulling Ford out of trouble was a former General Motors man, Ernest Breech. The policies that men like Breech worked under represent the legacy of the management genius of Alfred P. Sloan, Jr., and his unique application of management theory derived from DuPont. This legacy forbids executives to treat subordinates strictly as work units. The job of each executive is to breed a better replacement than himself. Once men get near the division level, they are never lost track of by a monitoring system that is plied by men at the top and near top. For this reason it is not an accident that, in early 1969, within two months, four of the five General Motors auto divisions got new general managers, as did also the Fisher Body division. Lee N. Mays became general manager of Buick, John Z. DeLorean of Chevrolet, John B. Beltz of Oldsmobile, F. James McDonald of Pontiac, and Robert T. Kessler of Fisher Body division. What triggered several of these promotions was the disability leave of Donald L. Boyes, whose position as group vice-president of all car and truck sales in the United States was filled by Elliot M. Estes, and the disability leave of Phillip J. Monaghan, whose position as group vice-president in charge of body and assembly divisions was filled by Kenneth N. Scott. The Chevrolet and Pontiac posts are key proving grounds for future General Motors presidents. DeLorean was moved from Pontiac and replaced by his former subordinate, McDonald, who left Chevrolet. Kessler had been at Buick and was replaced by Mays, who had been sales manager of Chevrolet. This clearly represents movement up and around, the telltale sign of a mobile insider in a highly sophisticated breeder firm. Returning to Knudsen, his duty while at General Motors was to be a breeder. Most automobile men consider his record excellent in this respect. As do most breeders, he put men on their own after they were aware of their responsibilities. At Ford he was not in strange country. The Ford company developed a strong though inconsistent breeding program and produced many rising stars. The problem was that the foremost among them, Robert S. McNamara, who broke through to the top and could then have carried the best of the youthful wave of mobile executives with him to the executive suite, left the corporation before he could put the finishing touches on the breeding program. Now we can better appreciate Knudsen, whose practice was to keep a list, for each area of the company, of people thirty-five years old and under who had high potential. He kept a close eye on them—as on others, of course—with a view to movement. He reported, "It is very important to keep these talented executives from becoming frustrated and wanting to leave. It does not matter any longer where they start, it is important that they move about."

This problem that Knudsen alluded to bears directly upon the larger question of how the new generation finally breaks through to the top. The answer partly rests upon having sufficient numbers of high quality below the top, since they will be the logical choices for replacing the executives who retire or leave because of ill health or death. To keep mobile executives in sufficient supply and of sufficient quality requires realizing what was implicit in Knudsen's statement. Mobile executives leave in large numbers at about thirty-four to thirty-five years of age at levels commonly called middle management and at about forty to forty-five years of age at the edges of the executive suite or in the executive suite itself. The mobility studies reflect the fact that mobile executives will not wade through level after level of substandard superiors. This becomes more an exercise in handling superiors than a program of developing managerial fitness. Besides, the development of more talented executives requires that such executives be managed differently while they are at the lower and middle levels of their careers. On these lower rungs perch masses of managers who lack preparation to provide the new breed with the extra managerial and psychological care and attention they require for their continued development. Many of these men are incapable of developing superior replacements. The longer the new breed are left at lower levels, the more they acquire the traditional posture of their immobile, insider types of superiors and peers.

To prevent the undoing of the whole developmental strategy, the members at the top of the executive organization who oversee the program must follow one of several courses, of which the most popular is based upon identifying developmental talent. This most popular course in the more sophisticated breeder makes a distinction between "promotable" and "developmental." A man may be promotable to a higher job yet not capable of going the whole route. Many, of course, are capable of going to higher managerial levels but are not executive timber. All kinds are needed. Knudsen's keen eye watched for promotables and substandard performance, but his reputation represented an ability to detect the men who were prepared for the long trek to the top. What he and others at his level constantly look for are those who become generally regarded as developmental. The code word in mobility studies is G.R.A.D. A person qualifies as such in the composite opinion of many superiors and subordinates who have the necessary vision to assess his performance. A corporation is much like a school system in which expectations of student performance become established at lower levels and alert the next level of teachers to the makeup of the new class. Reputations once established create their own kind of momentum. The man generally regarded as developmental, the G.R.A.D., is not given easy tasks, nor is he protected or insulated from risk and danger. Rather, he is given exposure to positions and people who represent the grooming grounds of future executives. His assignments will be a combination of those that he needs to have under his belt as a future executive and those that represent a matching of his skill. The latter will include tough assignments because he will have acquired, as a G.R.A.D., the kind of competencies needed to execute them. Thus, his mobility pattern will show a combination of what he can do for the corporation to make it more effective and what the corporation may do for him to make him an effective future executive. At no time will both purposes be equally served. To systematically breed means to systematically move men eligible for such care and attention. But some superiors are incapable of handling the G.R.A.D. They are either incompetent to bear down upon him objectively to make sure he is not discriminated for or against, or they are emotionally incapable of extending themselves for people who have inside tracks to the top.

As Knudsen suggested, a sure-fire formula for losing G.R.A.D.s is to move them among superiors with either form of incapacity. Enough will quit because they have not been moved often enough (or because they have been moved too often) to allow a further increase in attrition rates because they have had to work with lazy or hostile minds bent upon making them immobile. Hence, it is important to identify not only the positions that are developmental to the G.R.A.D. but the superiors as well. Many of these superiors may also be mobile types, but some are promotables and a few are even immobile insiders who have adopted, through years and years of watching young men go ahead of them and prosper, the attitude of teachers. Immobile insiders with such an attitude are in great demand and in short supply. The routes that transport mobile executives represents a combination of men, positions, and assignments in various areas and divisions. Emphasis must be placed upon the plural, "routes," as no one route can possibly suffice.

Once the top becomes sufficiently reinforced by mobile executives, the whole tenor at the top becomes changed to fit their postures and styles. Through their efforts, breeding becomes more systematic, careful, and established as routine. Each mobile executive is a superior in his own right with responsibility to develop men superior to himself. The mobile executive can best practice breeding because he understands what it entails. No traditional insider can possibly duplicate the quality of experience that a mobile executive can bring to bear upon his own G.R.A.D.s.

Often corporations will announce an executive development program that aims at spotting a wave of talented men, but after they are brought to the top there are no more waves of men below because those of the first wave are not made responsible for breeding better replacements for themselves. The mobile executive proves to be a better breeder for still a second reason. He is mobile himself, which means he can more powerfully effect the future mobility of his G.R.A.D.s. To repeat an earlier point, mobile executives will not work and respect immobile superiors unless, of course, they are the teacher-coach types and are known for their ability to instruct and polish. It would be ideal to have every manager and executive a breeder, but in lieu of this improbability, the emphasis must be placed upon mobile executives assuming as their primary responsibility the breeding of superior replacements.

If the wave of mobile executives at the top contains numerous well-qualified executives and each has his developmental types below him, the emergence of a steady flow of increasingly talented executives into the executive suite will assure the corporation of the necessary human resources to sustain and enhance corporate growth and viability. We have noted how the top must be open sufficiently to curtail log jams, which represent the principal influence leading mobile executives to leave their executive suites for other corporations. In addition, the top must be fluid, or as many or more will leave. In other words, the president and chairman must leave as soon as they have made their maximum contributions and have replacements as good or better than themselves, and other members of the executive group must be moved around laterally. More specifically, a fluid top means that it is organized away from the traditional lines of functional mobility and static organization. Because of functional mobility, the products of mobility are expressions of one area or function of the corporation.

In the immobile organization, the executive group is organized by some principle or precept having little regard to the requirement of change and flexibility. Traditional insiders are fond of creating management principles, among which some involve ultimate forms of organization that provide effectiveness and efficiency because of inherent advantages in them. But, given a dynamic economy, the strategies of the corporation supersede matters of corporate identity, custom, and principles. The form of organization must conform to each new set of strategies. Strategical thinking has replaced reasoning by principles, and the form of organization that works one day may not the next and is always unique to the corporation. This means that the men at the top must be committed to innovative structuring. They have more ways to reorganize today than ever before. For example, they have accumulated much wisdom from past experience at centralization, decentralization, and recentralization programs.

In the decade of the sixties, many corporations reshuffled the members of the executive suite into new combinations as much as three times. While one corporation was centralizing, another in the same industry was decentralizing. In 1969, General Electric centralized the authority of the top group by making the president's office into the chairman's office, with the chairman the chief executive officer as well. At the same time, Westinghouse created four new subcompanies, each with its own president. While each chairman of these two competitors is a chief executive officer, the differences among these chairmen were notable and reflected the logic of each company's position. General Electric discovered that it had to cope with the effects of too much decentralization, and Westinghouse redesigned in order to manage growth in vastly expanded markets. The objective was to go from $3 billion in sales to over $4 billion. In each case, the attempt was to find the right man for limited or specific corporate objectives and strategies. Whether the firms are successful or not, they will undoubtedly change again the combination of men and their jobs.

Hence, corporations are fast becoming committed to innovative organizing. Gone are the arguments, heard during the decade of the fifties, that exalted one form of organization over another. What works well depends upon the logic of the position of the corporation at a point in time. Changing organizational structure and executive relationships involves moving men around more freely. Teams come together and later break up to form new combinations. The growth firm is always in a state of flux, and who's on first base or on second is not as crucial as whether all bases that should be are covered and that each has the best or the right man playing it.

This means that the executive group is organized not only to affect the strategies throughout the corporate system, but also to get its own tasks achieved. To put it differently, the executive organization must run the company and manage its own internal affairs as well. It is possible that the executive organization may change without any direct change in the remainder of the corporation. For example, a president may have a centralized executive organization within a decentralized corporation. It is apparent that the way the executive group and the corporation as a whole are organized bears directly upon the capacity of the firm to achieve the strategies of growth.

The study of the movement of men around and up shows that organizations must be changed to produce the superior advantages of mobile executives. Hence, it is only a matter of time before firms will put the two ideas in the same context. This means that the way in which a corporation is organized affects the production of both profits and men. In this light, we can see that the attempt to breed superior talent means that the purpose for which the corporation is organized is not simply to achieve the traditional objectives of business profits. If profits are produced at the expense of breeding talented people, the firm could fail. A hazard every bit as great awaits breeder firms that produce men at the expense of profit. The enlightened corporation knows that a successfully organized firm simultaneously produces profits and superior performers. Men and organizations that produce them must change and be amenable to further changes. The managing of a changing environment represents a far more difficult task than managing the relatively static, tradition-bound, and principle-dictated environment of the premobility era. The cliché that "the only certainty is change itself" seems almost too obvious at this point, but it is not a literary exaggeration.

Not every corporation can manage in terms of producing better men and higher profits simultaneously. The corporations that have, such as General Motors, General Electric, and IBM, to mention a very few, are often more dangerously imitated or mimicked than innovatively followed. Most attempts at breeding fall short of utilizing the inherent advantages of both mobility and organizational change. In the latter sixties, some corporations practiced mobility but did not make innovative adaptations to their organizations.

Others changed their organizational formats but did not move men into the right combinations to achieve inherent benefits. Still others moved men and occasionally changed their structures almost as though the two programs were not related. In not a few cases, the organizational changes emerged from the dictation of new strategy, and the mobility of men developed from the demands of minimizing frustration levels among the most promising mobile executives. Of course, to some extent mobility of men will be affected by organizational changes. But the desirable goal is to keep the two programs coordinated, or they will work at cross purposes.

More common were the corporations that gave up service to both. Chief executives would often mention in their speeches before financial analysts' groups that their most important asset was the young, competent management group, but few really had built a mobility program that decreased functional mobility substantially. In 1968, many chief executives of corporations in the five hundred-largest category, whose speeches before some fifty groups of financial analysts were published in the *Wall Street Transcript,* often spoke glowingly of how the average age of the division executive or the executive core or some other top group was below fifty. In only ten of these companies had the executive group referred to been on a mobility program that utilized cross-functional and cross-divisional mobility.

Likewise, lip service may be diligently paid to organization dynamics and renewal. It is common for chief executives to report that they have adopted this form of organization or that when, in fact, they have merely slipped a layer of executives in between themselves and the division manager or taken a layer of executives out. In a few cases, the moving of men creates better organizational efficiency or better executives, but in many cases the lack of coordination in the movement of men about both goals precludes cranking out the greatest value from both mobility and organization. The corporation that sometimes moves men to better achieve profitability and other times to develop executive talent will produce far more stress than if the corporation evolved a strategy and policy for simultaneously achieving both ends. Otherwise, such scenes as the following will emerge:

An executive exclaimed, "Well, here we go again. The big push is on for youth. We've all got to hand in our lists of the most capable young men in each of our divisions. Two years ago a couple of wide-eyed kids got big promotions so that the chairman could announce at the annual meeting that they had a major emphasis on youth and executive development. But, heck, after a few changes in one or two divisions, we were back at the same game of doing the job and taking our bruises."

A peer member of the executive suite reported, "We need fresh blood at the top. Here and there below we have young talent but it cannot be utilized because there is no systematic way of getting talent at the very tip. We talk a big game here, how we bring young people along rapidly, but we never see them come to the top. They simply fade away before they get up here."

It is obvious that this corporation as a whole is ill-prepared to breed executives. Let us see how the right hand is not coordinated with the left hand. The latter executive continues to speak: "This year we had quite a few rather young executives for the first time in our headquarters staff. I am one of them [age forty]. I come from the major division of the company. Two more corporate vice-presidents were my generation but they have just resigned. The reason was that the boss, our chairman, decided to have decentralization and made all of the corporate vice-presidents staff men and all the division heads fully responsible for their divisions and accountable directly to the president. He said that this reorganization was better to achieve profitability, but we know that he could not handle several of us wild ducks and cut the rug right out from under us. I am going to resign next month myself. As soon as I can make sure that several of my own men are moved into positions where they will not be hurt by the fight."

Of course, if all of the new breed leave, the top will never become reinforced sufficiently to turn the whole corporation into a breeder firm. The tragedy in this company is not that youth is not wanted, but that it is not wanted at the top nor wanted in the form that represents advantages and assets of the corporation. As the president unwittingly confessed, "We don't mind youthful executives around us here at headquarters staff as long as it is youth that fits our mold. It would be rather silly now, wouldn't it, to reorganize to fit the needs of youth?"

"Silly" is not the word for it. The corporation that wants to get the most out of its top talent mix must organize for that purpose. And as that talent mix changes because of ingress and egress of executives, the executive organization must be changed. The president continues, "I went to a seminar where I heard that the top group must be organized and then later reorganized to get the right combination of players. I laughed because this is no football game we are playing. Why should the vice-president of finance become any other than vice-president of finance? That's his specialty, as mine is production and manufacturing. The only time I will move the finance executive is when he cannot do his job, and only then. Our job here is to make money and you cannot make it by juggling the team and pulling people out of their specialties."

This attitude reflects functional mobility and the task specialization that comes with it. The president had bought an organizational principle that seemed to work in the past and that is made to work today by dint of authority and coercion. He did not realize in a practical, gut sense that a vice-president for finance should try his hand at being a group vice-president of several divisions, as did Roche at General Motors, not only because it will make him a better executive and smooth out an unbalanced technical-managerial mix but also because it will allow him to bring something new and different to the divisions in a line rather than strictly a staff program. Also, he may prove to be capable someday of running the corporation as president or chairman.

There is no way to spot a generalist-specialist before he becomes one. By not being moved to develop their talents, men will become only what their limited experiences and opportunities allow. With regard to the president's statement about profitability, he does not see the relationship between developing profits and developing men. Nor does he see that a major tool for achieving such is more than the function each executive serves but the interrelationship of these functions. Hence, the firm is not organized for producing, simultaneously, superior growth of profits *and* men.

One can feel empathy for the poor G.R.A.D. who has his upward mobility aborted because he is ahead of his time, his biomobile schedule, and because he has different qualities than those representing his ultimate superior. This type of corporation, as do many who give lip service to youth, recruits vigorously on university and college campuses. It shows to the naïve recruits facts and figures on where they can be in five and ten years. A few years later these bright, talented managers discover that what the corporation wants is conforming, conventional, slightly younger executives. The effect shatters their preconceptions and illusions and creates the feelings of defeat, rejection, and abandonment.

But the major point is that the corporation induces infinitely more stress among executives and managers. Men are moved without regard to a master program that all understand and, therefore, the movement of men is neither understood nor respected by those moved or those left behind. Estes, DeLorean, McDonald, Mays, Beltz, Scott, and Kessler may appear to the naïve public to have played musical chairs. But besides knowing what was expected of him in his new job, each of these executives knew the overall reason for which he was being moved. For example, the route to the top at Oldsmobile is through the chief engineer position. The last four general managers of the division were chief engineers, as was Beltz. However, Pontiac and Chevrolet, not Oldsmobile, are the grooming grounds for top executives in General Motors. Beltz knew this, as did Donald Burnham who left engineering at Oldsmobile to climb to the top of Westinghouse for several reasons, among which was that he knew his chances of going to the top of General Motors were very low once he was tagged an Oldsmobile executive.

Burnham showed the mobility brightness of a winner. Beltz, who at forty-three was only two years older than the total length of time his predecessor, Harold N. Metzel, had served in Oldsmobile before he retired, has a chance because of his relative youth to break this tradition and go to the top. However, he will see the possibility of a breakthrough when and if he is assigned to one of several of the priority routes, including the Chevrolet and Pontiac divisions. Meanwhile, in one sense, he knows as well as other executives favored by priority routes what his elevation to the top of a division means.

Moving men will create enough stress and strain, but to move men without a rationale of some kind will produce a stress additive that can subvert the whole breeding game. Hence, not only must the corporation breed, but it must consistently follow a rationale that becomes commonly understood. Changes in organization and talent will then be dictated by the rationale that the function of organization is to produce both profits and leaders.

Until such a breeding program becomes sustained by a continuous flow of men to the top, and to the tip itself, who are products of such programs, the corporation will be a nightmare rather than a dream for both mobile executives and traditional insiders. The gripes and grievances, frictions and factions, expectations and exasperations will inundate the executive suite. The clever hand of a capable executive team is needed to calm fears, restore pride, and encourage the depressed. Until the new game has been established and the new winners consistently emerge, the corporation will wonder if the costs of such a program can be offset by the advantages. In short, malefactors of great ambition and vested interests lurk in the executive suite and below at all levels to subvert the whole breeding program. Mobile executives will offer a test of the capacity of an executive team to manage for increased growth in profits and men—a test such as no set of traditional insiders could possibly provide.

The extent to which the top is kept fluid and open will largely determine the caliber of men that occupy the executive suite. One early arrival president of a major industrial corporation stated the case well. "If the chief executive has to stay on because even at an advanced age he is still better prepared to guide this corporation, then he has failed to breed the quality of replacements that is required in order for him to leave. He can do few things more important than to launch a well-conceived executive development program. If many or some in the wave below him are not more talented than he is, it is a reflection on his ability to manage. Why should the top man stay on interminably when there are better men below him?"

The breeding program started out to develop more imaginative and creative executives, but with the company as the foremost object of their allegiance and competencies. The program did evolve less conforming and conventional executives and managers. However, they become far more career-minded than the traditional insider. Many mobile executives had their career tendencies reinforced by going outside and using several corporations as the route to the top. This unprecedented and unexpected arrival at the top of large numbers of career-centered executives working side by side with company-centered executives provides the necessary contrast to describe the basic differences in their posture styles. We may summarize the discussion thus far developed by noting that the traditional insider was in fact a company man. Of course, not all insiders become company-centered, but those who successfully occupied an office in the executive suite were company-centered more often than not. It is not accurate to call the insider, as we know him now, an organization man. It is not the organization of the company that holds his attention, but the personality or identity of the corporation. His self-image and that of his corporation become reinforced to the extent that at the top he assumes the airs of a proprietor. He *becomes* the company. During his lengthy rise to the top, he gradually assumes a posture that is geared to maintain a steady, reliable ascent. Most of the time his behavior symbolizes sitting, standing, or bowing to his corporate circumstances. His strategy is not to rock the boat and create waves. He lives on the quiet and seeks security and opportunity with both feet firmly imbedded in the terra-corporate.

The career executive defers only to the requirements of managing a successful career. An attractive job is not something in and of itself. What counts is what the job will do for him, where it will take him, and how fast. His career extends beyond the boundaries of any single company and he fears having it prescribed by any company or institution. He finds morally and pragmatically distasteful the idea of committing a whole adult life to one business organization. As one career-centered president remarked, "No company will set a brass collar around my neck and throw away the key." This executive led his corporation through a tough growth period and then left to join another company whose challenges appealed to him more. With a third ear and eye alert to new opportunities within and without his corporation, the career-centered executive assumes a posture that girds him for momentum. He carries himself into the future with one foot in the present job while he searches for a better place to plant his other foot. He lives on the ready.

The company executive's future is circumscribed by the company boundaries. He must make the most of everything within them. And this attitude of making the most may include parlaying his achievements and leveraging within the corporation, but the threat of quitting is never explicit or implied. This would constitute an act of personal and corporate disloyalty and would abrogate his condition of trust. Without the threat and the reality of quitting, his use of leveraging within becomes more often than not politicking. While working he is also angling, fraternizing, identifying, and glad-handing. He may and often does become a great exponent of good human relations. At best, the company executive is a self-sacrificing person, and at worst he is a Machiavellian prince.

With the options of cashing in his gains at any time and parlaying them into a better job in another firm, the career-centered executive is less apt to play games. He finds the many ways that insiders put their best feet forward to be distracting and wasteful. He is more apt to quit than to conform; to switch rather than to fight. This attitude allows him to pour his energy unreservedly into the job at hand. A company is merely a point in a career path and, hence, he has the orientation of a professional person whose duty is to find the environment that will bring out his best skills and talents. He finds both opportunity and security by learning to balance on one foot. At best, he is an intensely stimulating and creative individual; at worst, he is a cold, unsentimental human being.

No two executives could be more different in their carriage habits. The company executive's relatively static posture of sticking it out through thick and thin is bizarre to the executive who believes in not losing career time. His looking out for "number one" is viewed by the company executives as disrespectful of his obligation to a company that has made him what he is. Overt behavior aimed at bettering himself without regard to the traditional insiders' codes of chivalry and fealty constitutes a naked display of self-interest, and no company can profit, let alone survive, with men in the executive suite so undedicated and insincere. Even though a company never lays down its life for another firm, the executive must not put his career ahead of his company if he expects to succeed.

In rebuttal, the career executive offers the conviction that business achieves viability and growth because of the quantity and depth of its management personnel, and that competency, not loyalty, is the most important single quality of an effective executive. The skills of a professional person are no less useful or aggressively applied by the absence of the insider's mentality. Besides, competency can be more swiftly generated if the executive is permitted to move within or without whenever he feels ready to tackle a challenge greater than his present one. Too much time is spent on trivia and routine and jobs already mastered if he has to limit his opportunities to those available within one company. With more competency, he contributes more to the economy and is more useful to himself as well. The career executive's philosophy is rooted in the conviction that he should find and use every opportunity that is legal and fair to better himself. Given this posture, he will be a more competent person in any given company than if he had less aggressively pursued his career. He is not only prepared to quit to remove insurmountable blocks to his career but he is also prepared to use leverage. It is this latter skill that is most vital to maintaining and enhancing his momentum.

In conclusion, the fifties was the last decade in which the insider's proclivity to be company-centered had unmitigated acceptance. Now, at the beginning of the seventies, he stands in juxtaposition to the career-centered executive. Today, few men in the executive suite square with these polarized versions of career- and company-centered executives. Most belong somewhere between these two poles. The trend is clearly toward becoming more career-centered.

Still, the attempt to develop capable executives goes on unabated, and the need to master the many conflicting forces involved in breeding is greater than ever. The corporation must always attempt to breed and, when necessary, to import. For this reason, the inside route is still a most powerful route to the top. Three of every five men in the executive suite have spent two-thirds or more of their careers in the same company. It must be recognized that at any given time, the aspiring executive is inside some corporation. While there, he naturally attempts to maximize his opportunities. The strategy of the new winner must be to find and get into the swiftest route to the top without acquiring the mentality of the traditional insider.

CHAPTER FIVE

The Essence of Visiposure

VISIPOSURE IS ONE of the surest routes to corporate success, a clearly marked route up the corporate mountain. The word is a combination of visibility and exposure, with visibility being the ability of the aspirant to see the top of the corporate Olympus and exposure the position of being seen by the men above. The abilities to see and copy those who can influence his career and to keep himself in view of those who might promote him are all-important to success. The manager of the Nome, Alaska branch is likely to advance far more slowly than the department manager based in New York headquarters. The Nome man may be the better of the two, but he lacks visiposure. While he works hard and hopes hard, he has something working against him, and this he senses but most likely does not know or he would not have accepted the Nome assignment in the first place.

High visiposure is to see and to be seen by the right people. To the mobile executive, the right people are those who can affect his performance and mobility. He knows that some superiors are more important to him than others and that a superior by title may not be a superior of consequence. There was a time when the vice-president was next in line for the presidency. Not so today. Multiple mergers and the increase in staff jobs have accelerated the trend of adding hordes of vice-presidents and assistants of all types to organization charts. Some companies have platoons of vice-presidents whose titles go with the man rather than stay with the position. Division heads are called "presidents" rather than "general managers." "Executive vice-president" titles are handed out without any change in the corporate setup. In the past, the titles were underestimated. Now they are ascribed to men as much as achieved by them. What all this amounts to is that men get status on top of status, and jobs that sound by title identical are not at all comparable. There still are only a very few men at any given time that are in line for the top job or have even an outside chance for it. The many other positions represent the stuff that dreams and wishes are made of. Their occupants are corporate have-nots and are not the models for the aspiring executive.

Sometimes it is better for the subordinate to be exposed to a particular member of the executive group. A recommendation for promotion by a superior held in low esteem by the powers that be may sound the death knell for the mobile executive. Power to promote, rather than title, is the engine of mobility. This means that high visiposure may come from seeing and being seen by the right superiors.

The ultimate of visiposure is for the subordinate's superior to see and be seen by the right superiors also. There is nothing quite as conducive to upward mobility as three or four levels of executives who are each hitched to rising stars. They may be in the same chain of command and serve as mobile superiors to each, or they may have high visiposure to each other because their functional responsibilities bring them together. Serial visiposure, or the ability to see and be seen by a chain of mobile superiors including one's immediate superior, is the *sine qua non* of fast upward mobility.

The basis of gaining visiposure to superiors several levels above is through the communication process. Face-to-face interaction among superiors and subordinates several levels removed from each other has augmented the decision making, planning, and control functions. The corporation is more open today, and more levels of management are in communication with each other. The indirect benefit of opening up the communication channels is that talent at lower levels is more easily and quickly discovered. Partly for this reason, more young executives have moved swiftly to the top during the last decade than before. There has always been more talent at middle and lower levels of management than men at the top have been able to see. And there have always been middle managers whose opportunities to learn and develop were restricted because of poor visibility. The emergence of a vastly more liberal communication environment has served to increase visiposure for everybody. It is now an entirely new world and the game is played with a new set of rules. In the very early period of industrial management, the emphasis was on finding and keeping the right people. Priority was placed on certain traits and qualities that produced honest, reliable, and diligent behavior. Positions created to get work done were also created to accommodate men of proper character. As the industrial organization became larger and more complicated, the emphasis gradually shifted to positions and to the functions and responsibilities that evolved from them over the years. Organization charts were utilized that were based upon a kind of inner logic about how a set of positions should be interrelated to achieve smooth, efficient organization. The traditional functions of business, manufacturing, sales, personnel, and accounting served as convenient hooks upon which to hang the several layers of positions in neat rows of decreasing degrees of authority.

As position management evolved in sophistication, the boss began to fit the right people to the right positions. Before the turn of this midcentury, executives largely operated positions. While executives moved in and out of a given position, it remained largely the same and the occupant's behavior could be predicted from the implicit or explicit job description. Only a small part of his behavior could be attributed to new or different responsibilities or duties. In this stable world, subordinates set their sights on attaining positions. At first, each man was responsible for developing himself, but when the need for superiors to take a hand in developing their subordinates came into vogue in the late fifties, superiors groomed men for positions. The decade of the sixties brought forth project managers who upset the game of men struggling to get good positions. Mobile executives were assigned, from time to time, special programs, objectives, or problems in addition to or in place of their position duties. Infiltrating position management with new and different assignments got a second impetus from the need to grow rapidly and from the special advantages of long-range planning. The projects have specific time periods and specific objectives meshed with the planning schedule. The idea of project management caught fire, and today a president may be selected less to occupy a position than to successfully execute one or several specific programs. Each year more corporations select a project president. Since 1961, the number of industrial corporations in the one hundred-largest category with project presidents has increased from eight to over fifty.

In these companies it is assumed that the mobile executive can manage the position of president or chairman. What gives the edge to him over other aspirants is that he has the skills to execute and complete the project or projects suggested by long-range planning and corporate strategy. After he completes his program, he may turn the baton over to the next man in the relay race, and so on. For this reason, the project president moves in and out of his position faster than his traditional counterpart. The average time in the position has dropped to 4.5 years in the latter part of the sixties from nearly 8 years in the early part of the fifties. Thus, the right men are fitted to the right projects or strategical programs rather than positions. We may say that instead of selecting men for their general and long-range abilities, men are today selected for their specific and immediate skills. What they can do now rather than eventually is the big difference. Of course, corporations are still looking for good men and still have their organizational charts. What has happened is that project management has been added to the other forms of management, and in many corporations the trend is to give it higher priority for the development of future executives.

Project management has created greater mobility. Today, a new president sets specific projects that will hopefully represent his tour de force. Stuart K. Hensley, the advertising-oriented president that sparked the growth boom of the Gillette Company, resigned to become president of Warner-Lambert Pharmaceutical Co. After twenty-one years with Gillette and its Toni division, he was selected to put Warner-Lambert into the toiletry business, a field where it could compete with products he helped to launch for Gillette. The common factor between Gillette and Warner-Lambert was the position of president, which Hensley held in both. What differentiated him was the project at Warner-Lambert. Literally, this objective drew him to Warner-Lambert more than the position; and he will be measured by project performance rather than position. Hensley exemplifies many men in motion in the sixties. They moved to other corporations to get more challenging assignments rather than higher, more prestigious positions. William G. Phillips became president of Glidden Co., Ltd., in 1964 and continued to run it after its merger with SCM Corporation. At forty-eight years of age, Phillips wanted more of a challenge and found it in the president's office at International Milling Company, where his number-one project was to lead a diversification program. Hensley and Phillips were two of over twenty-one presidents and chairmen who moved to other corporations in the period of 1965 to 1968. In almost all cases, what attracted them was the prospect of facing, in their new corporations, special sets of circumstances to which they felt their skills were matched. Project management has brought mobility among presidents that was unheard of in the days of position management.

As a third consideration, project presidents are made possible also because large industrial corporations, like dinosaurs, move by taking slow, precise steps. They move in highly predictable phases or cycles. For example, Harold Blanche, chief executive officer for twelve years at Celanese Corporation, rebuilt this ailing rayon and acetate company which had revenue of less than $200 million into a broadly based synthetic fibers and chemical complex with revenues of over $1 billion. It predictably developed growing pains, and when severe competition hit the fibers field a change was needed at the top. Blanche nominated John W. Brooks and gave him project number one: tightening up. He had to cut back the spending, set the right priorities, and straighten up the balance sheet without diminishing earnings growth. No matter what else he did skillfully, if he did not perform project number one, he would be judged a failure.

There is a time for growth and a time for tightening up, and it is cycles such as these that give rise to project presidents. Or a cycle may alter drastically the behavior of a president who is caught in one. C. Peter McColough, president of Xerox Corp., had to shift gears in 1968 to accommodate an increasing revenue and decreasing profits situation. In the past, he helped to push growth at the expense of being neat and tidy. But when the economics of the picture emerged full-blown, he had to set new priorities and goals and turn the organization around.

Donald Douglas, Jr., of Douglas Aircraft, was caught in a vicious cycle. The company took more orders for aircraft than it could fill at the costs estimated to make profit. This condition proved too much for the leadership of Douglas, and its directors had to seek remedy by selling the firm to McDonnell Aircraft. The difficulty at Douglas was that the problem was not caught and handled when it was still at a project stage. It grew and grew until major surgery was required. This suggests a lesson. The objective of project management is to pick off the next major problem before it becomes generalized to the condition of corporate crisis. Before Douglas could conceptualize the problem into project proportions, it had become a total tragedy. To avert total collapse, the Douglases sold out to McDonnell Aircraft. The boss, chairman James McDonnell, immediately assigned to president David L. Lewis the toughest project in the history of the aircraft business—namely, to straighten out McDonnell's new division, Douglas Aircraft. Lewis, an early arrival at the age of forty-three, then put his whole career on the line, a risk more often engendered under project management than position management.

The success of project management helped to develop the concept of the office of the president. Projects are areas to which executives devote their greatest attention by setting and attempting to achieve specific objectives and goals in a specific period of time. Defined in this way, projects can serve to be the basis of delegating authority. Several men in related positions can have their responsibilities intermingled around a project format. Thus, the chairman and president and several subordinate officers may combine their authorities and parcel out project assignments. The office of the president may be occupied by three or four executives, each with a particular slice of the corporate pie to which to apply his special skills and interests but all sharing the burden of setting and achieving corporate goals and strategy.

For example, at General Motors the office of the president was filled by Chairman James M. Roche, President Edward N. Cole, and George Russell, chairman of the finance committee, the third-most-powerful position in the corporation. Roche kept special attention on outside environmental problems, Negro employment, safety laws and safety devices, and smog and public regulations. Cole specialized in inside environmental problems excluding finance, which was Russell's special emphasis. All three shared in the duties that before were shared by two men. Each had special complementary talents and each was encouraged to act as president in his assigned field.

The concept of the office of the president has nothing to do with management by committee, which implies a vote. On the contrary, each member is to act independently while maintaining the closest communication with his associates. They have specialties and duties, being both holders of positions and assignees of projects. Thus, they have unusual authority, while the chief executive retains ultimate accountability. In Caterpillar Tractor Co. this interchangeability of parts within the whole is best dramatized. In 1954, Neumiller became the first full-time chairman and chief executive officer and named Harman Eberhard as president and William Blackie as chief operations officer. The two executives functioned as Neumiller's extensions or wings and shared responsibilities with him. All fourteen vice-presidents had access to any one of the three, depending upon when they could get something done more quickly. When they traveled they spoke for the president's office. This interchangeability opened up the sluices of mobility because more people came into contact with the top and the men who were intimate with the top few.

Largely pioneered by Chairman Birny Mason of Union Carbide,

the concept of the office of the president had been adopted by 1968 by fifty or more companies in the five hundred largest industrial corporations. These fifty included in one version or another Allis-Chalmers Mfg. Co.; Ralston Purina, Co.; Joy Mfg. Co.; Mead Corp.; Scott Paper Co.; Kaiser Aluminum; Ampex Corp.; Gulf Oil; Westinghouse; General Electric; Borden, Inc.; TRW Inc.; Boise Cascade, Corp.; Chemetron Corp.; Coca Cola; Armstrong Cork; Continental Can; W. R. Grace; and IBM. More importantly, project management and the basic idea behind it filtered down to lower-management levels where, in some of these corporations, it included first- and second-level management above the worker. So clearly is project management a major trend that few executives at the top today have not had project experience at some time in their careers. Almost all early arrivals were given and adroitly executed major projects during their careers. The sign that an executive is mobile is the number and size of his projects and not his title, position, or even salary. Men in motion have little respect for position and title. In fact, the more the executive's behavior does not conform to his position, or any position for that matter, the more likely he is to be mobile.

It is apparent that, by its very nature, project management brings high visiposure. Talent and advice may be cranked in from any point in the corporation. When the project is completed, the team will be disbanded and another team formed around another project assignment. A corporation practicing extensive project management becomes a free-forming organization with traditional notions of authority, status, decision making, and communication all thrown into a cocked hat. Superior and subordinates many levels removed see each other, which thus serves to break down the insulation that normally envelops position executives. Also, project management minimizes the exercise of serving solely the demands of the immediate superior. In the course of completing a project assignment, an executive may come under the authoritative evaluation of numerous superiors other than the one that shows up on the organization chart.

Because project management has opened wide the corporate system, the top is not as far away as it appears on the organization chart for those who draw the crucial assignments. Edward N. Cole, president of General Motors, is a case in point. In the early 1950s Charles Wilson and Harlow Curtice, president and executive vice-president respectively of General Motors, began to work with those divisions that had special problems. The major problem was the Chevrolet division, which was doing poorly in the race against Ford. The decision to turn Chevrolet around brought Thomas H. Keating to the fore as head of the largest and generally most profitable division. Wilson, seeing the market for this prime car deteriorate, said to Keating that the future of Chevrolet was so important to the General Motors high command that Keating could have anyone he wanted as long as he got the job done. Keating got his project; now he faced the question of what to do with it.

Keating immediately went for Edward Cole, who he knew by reputation had helped design the first postwar V-eight engine for Cadillac. Then, Cole had gotten the size of the engine block down to where now, with a little more ingenuity, it could be used in the lighter Chevy. Cole's project was based upon the corporate complaint that Chevrolet was too hidebound, including "too six-cylinder-minded." The nub of the turnaround was to produce an efficient and economical V-eight for the new Chevrolet. The magnitude of the task was to design the new motor in time to go into the new line of Chevrolets scheduled for production in two years. This task appeared almost insurmountable, but Cole assembled a team on the dead run, bringing over to Chevy some thirty key men from all over the corporate empire.

The result was a fantastic engine with more piston displacement than the old Chevy six, far more power and torque, greater rigidity, and 30 pounds less weight. With Wilson and Curtice taking a pointed and personal interest in the then forthcoming 1955 Chevrolet, Cole was an inordinate success. He was made division head in 1956 and was well on his way to the top. Many of the men he had assembled and who were later identified with the success of the Cole project were greatly helped in their careers. When Cole was assigned his project, Keating did not know what position to give him. This fabrication of a position and title is always the tell-tale sign of a project assignment and shows how little positions are valued relative to projects.

A growth company or a company coming out of a state of dormancy is apt to utilize project management. Al Rockwell of Rockwell Standard launched a project-management orientation shortly after taking office. It originated because there was so much to do in the beginning. The idea was to develop ways and means of achieving objectives before implementing them through specific programs. Some eighty-seven projects, ranging from a new axle plant to a computerized inventory of manpower talents, were engulfing the efforts of the Rockwell executive team. A key executive was assigned a project or two, and every month he was required to write a progress report estimating completion date, achievements to date, total estimated cost, and cost to date. A computation of all the reports was sent to each of the executives every month. This practice gave each man a corporatewide view and produced much cross fertilization. Under such circumstances, visiposure is far more acute because of the more numerous and objective means of measuring the progress of the project executive.

Project management may be practiced in many ways different from the form taken at Rockwell-Standard. Let us examine more closely the kinds of projects that may give visiposure. For the most part, early arrivals are associated with projects that produce major breakthroughs in new product lines, production techniques, or marketing. Edmund F. Martin joined Bethlehem Steel Company in 1922 and, after going through the management training program in 1924, was assigned a series of production jobs before he was given the project of remodeling the chronically deficient and inefficient integrated plant in Lackawanna, New York. The president, Arthur B. Homer, became aware of Martin's excellent performance and he brought him to headquarters as vice-president in charge of the steel division in 1958; made him president in 1960; vice-chairman in 1963; and chairman and chief executive officer in 1964. Martin became exposed by his genius in production technology.

T. A. Wilson was made president of Boeing Aircraft at age forty-seven. Halfway in his career he was assigned to the Minuteman project, which turned out to be one of the most formidable achievements in modern industrial history. First, in 1956, he directed preparation of the proposal that won Boeing Co. the assembly and test contract for Minuteman, the nation's most important missile. In 1958, he became Minuteman manager, directing assembly and testing of the complete weapon system as well as development of a major portion of the support equipment and certain sections of the missile. Because of the Minuteman's success and his contribution, he achieved high upward mobility. In 1962, he was named a Boeing vice-president and manager of the aerospace division's missile branch; in 1966, he was elected to the board of directors and made executive vice-president; and he became president in 1968. The Minuteman project involved huge amounts of capital and human resources, which made it a highly exposed project. In addition, William M. Allen, chairman, put his name on the Minuteman project. The result was that men higher up the ladder were eventually passed over by this technical and organizational genius.

Such product breakthroughs as occurred in the computer, chemical, copy machine, food, drug, auto, and aerospace industries propelled many men who were associated with the successes to the top. A representative example is Simon Askin who, as president of Tenneco Chemical, brought out a psuedosuede that became a new fad in men's and women's clothing. He was promoted to vice-chairman of the parent company, Tenneco, Inc.

Visiposure may also come to the executive who manages projects that are organizational in nature. A common project is to direct the corporation's expansion program. Bob R. Dorsey had to direct Gulf's chemical expansion program—a program that eventually put Gulf squarely in the chemical business. Leslie H. Warner was president of Automatic Electric at the time of the merger with General Telephone & Electronics in 1955. He became General's executive vice-president for manufacturing and impressed the chairman, Donald C. Power, and his board of directors by working out the assimilation of Sylvania in 1959. In 1960, he was made a director, and a year later he became president.

Visiposure may also come to the executive whose project is to consolidate after an aggressive acquisition program. Andrew W. Tarkington helped chairman Leonard McCollum of Continental Oil Co. to raise Conoco from a modest regional oil company into the ninth-largest United States oil company and a worldwide marketer of oil, gas, chemicals, plant foods, and coal. He received the reins from McCollum to consolidate the gains without letting up on the aggressive acquisition policy. Helping the top man to reorganize the firm has enabled many an aspirant to stand out from a mass of managers and executives. Robert Burns at RCA helped General Sarnoff to plan a major reorganization of the corporation, and John Logan did a similar job at Olin Mathieson Chemical Corp. Both were awarded with the top jobs of their respective firms.

Helping corporations to take organizational advantage of technological advances also gives executives visiposure. At age forty-eight, Donald Burnham was made president of Westinghouse Electric Corporation. Burnham was one of forty-five corporate vice-presidents, and the industrial products division that he headed was smaller than the consumer, electric utility, or marine divisions. In getting the presidency he passed by John K. Hodnette, his superior and executive vice-president. Although Hodnette, sixty-one, was passed over because the corporation wanted a more youthful prexy, there were other vice-presidents as young as Burnham. If Burnham's position and age were secondary to his promotion, what was primary? The answer is that in 1962, as vice-president for manufacturing, he drew the assignment of introducing automation to reduce capital spending from $70 million to $50 million. The possibility of raising the chronically depressed profit margins gave Burnham tremendous visiposure.

On the management side in general, many are well-treated who can integrate research and development, create project management, and apply systems theories and techniques to finance and manufacturing. So well-treated are those who come even close to these major advances that one becomes impressed by the extent to which a talent for innovation pays off in career success. No doubt the increased visiposure of project assignments is due to the greater inherent opportunity to be innovative. Few men reach the top without getting a leg up on their peers by the visiposure of project assignments. Innovation through the visiposure of project assignments is one of the ways. The position manager is not as well-blessed, regardless of his high performance.

Before we mistakenly deprecate the position manager, let us

hasten to add that being in the right position is still of considerable benefit. The very nature of the position may provide the needed visiposure. A good example is the position of assistant to the president, which became popular in the late 1950s and early 1960s. The position "assistant" (without the "to") in the sense of line lieutenants has existed since the beginning of time. In the corporate world, the position will denote an assistant manager or assistant stock room manager. At the top, the assistant president is usually titled "executive vice-president" or "senior vice-president." The "assistant to" represents an entirely different position. Oftentimes indefinite, the "assistant to" may have duties ranging all the way from glorified secretary to the functions of an operating executive of the company. He may be young, fresh out of college, or he may be a contemporary of the president, as was Fred W. Hoover, Jr., when he joined Continental Can in 1961 at the age of forty-three to become assistant to the president. The "assistants to" at International Telephone and Telegraph Corp. are from the outside and usually spend one-year stints before they are made high-level executives. Francis J. Dunleavy was a plant manager before he joined Geneen's bullpen for future executives to later become an executive vice-president. Richard Hodgson was kicked out as top man at Fairchild Camera & Instrument Corp. and became probably the highest paid "assistant to" in American business. His salary at Fairchild was $140,000 a year, and it was undisclosed what he received as a raise at ITT. Probably the oldest and longest-tenured "assistant to" was Harold Hellman at Corn Products. He acted as a communication filter through which every new idea had to pass, for twenty years, to several bosses.

The older outsider can best benefit by the "assistant to" assignment as his introduction to the company; and in more cases than not, he stays in the top executive ranks to make his climb. In 1953, at the age of thirty-six, Gordon Grand left the House Ways and Means Committee counselorship to become assistant to the president of Olin Mathieson. A year later he became secretary; then corporate vice-president for administration in 1955; vice-president for law and administration in 1960; member of the board in 1963; vice-chairman and executive vice-president in 1964; and president and chief executive officer in 1965. His spectacular rise to the top in twelve years lends credence to the proposition that the older the outsider, the more likely that he will become president. So much depends upon how much of the corporation's complexities he can assimilate and how long it will take others to discover him. After being spotted as a man with high potential, he will probably be groomed for the top job, as was Grand. When the insider is made "assistant to" at the age of forty or more, the cue is that he is the heir apparent. Two examples are Herbert E. Markley of Timken Roller Bearing and Joseph W. Foss of General Tire International. Both became presidents of their respective firms a short time later.

More representative of the group of "assistants to" was the bull-pen that Burlington Industries developed during its biggest growth period. While gobbling up companies right and left in the 1950s, Spencer Love, who founded Burlington Industries, made the "assistant to" position famous. Love's need for competent executives became so acute that he started the practice of hiring men fresh out of college and training them briefly by making them assistants to himself or to a senior officer. At one time he had over twelve assistants to the president. If he liked their style, he positioned them in lower levels and judged them by results. He seldom lost track of those who measured up to his high standards of performance.

In 1957, *Business Week* surveyed some three hundred corporations across the country and found that almost 70 percent had an assistant to the president.[1] In the vast majority of cases, the job and title had been created during the previous five years and the salaries ranged from $10,000 to $75,000 a year. Although not quite so common, the "assistant to" position is more popular today than a decade ago. In 1961 to 1966, more than eighteen per one hundred presidents of large industrial corporations had been, at some time in their careers, assistant to the president or chairman. Some of the "assistants to" who went on to eventually become presidents were Ralph Cordiner of General Electric, Mark Cresap of Westinghouse, Eli G. White of Endicott Johnson, K. S. Adams of Phillips Oil, Gordon Grand of Olin Mathieson, Archie E. Albright of Stauffer

---

[1] *Business Week*, Oct. 19, 1957, p. 193.

Chemical, John Phillips of R. J. Reynolds, F. Shepard Cornell of A. O. Smith Corporation, Herbert E. Markley of Timken Roller Bearing Co., G. William Miller of Textron, Andrew W. Tarkington of Conoco, and Frederick N. Schwartz of Bristol-Myers.

At American Machine & Foundry Co., four of the six operating heads in 1957 started with the company as assistant to President Morehead Patterson. In such companies as Inland Steel or U.S. Gypsum Corp., it was not at all unusual for a man to step from a high line position to the "assistant to" spot. In such cases, the "assistant to" will most likely become president eventually. In 1967, TRW, Inc., promoted Ruben F. Mettler, forty-three-year-old executive vice-president formerly in charge of TRW's systems group, to assistant to the president and made him a member of the four-man chief executive office. Previously, there were three men in the top executive group. Obviously, TRW made room for Mettler, for if he were not in line for the presidency they would not have enlarged the chief executive office.

In other companies, a promising young man on the lower supervisory levels is selected to be assistant to the president to handle routine administrative chores and learn the breadth of operations. At the end of his stint, he may return to his original level, but the company assumes the special training he got next to the heartbeat of the corporation will help him to move up fast. The facts warrant such a presumption: when forty-five former "assistants to" were compared with men of the same age and position, the "assistants to" far outnumbered their peers in occupying offices in the executive suite. Not only did more of them eventually end up as corporate vice-presidents or better, but they arrived earlier at the top (on the average of 5½ years). The "assistant to" is no terminal job. Rather, it is strongly developmental.

The "assistant to" position offers tremendous exposure regardless of the assignments that it may entail. Thomas L. Whisler, of the University of Chicago Graduate School of Business, studied "assistants to" and discovered that generally they played the role of information intermediary between the boss and the latter's subordinates for the public. He reported that the "assistant to" job is most likely to appear when the top executive is new, particularly if he is an outsider, and when the top executive runs a large hierarchy with diverse operations and a great deal of public contact.[2] These characteristics increasingly belong to large industrial corporations, which makes for an increasing supply of "assistants to."

Regardless of the exact nature of the duties and responsibilities of the "assistant to," his frequent face-to-face interaction with his superior gives him visiposure. Stanley C. Allyn, who went to the top of National Cash Register, traces his rise to a job he had as a young man clipping newspapers and keeping a scrapbook of the news of the day for John H. Patterson, then president of NCR. His duties brought him into daily contact with Patterson. He soon realized that his boss was strong on selling and decided that if he was going to make any progress with him, he would have to get into the sales department. He applied for a transfer and got Patterson's blessing, continued support, and exposure for the lengthy climb to the presidency by age forty.

A study of young "assistants to" reveals several qualities that they have learned that carry them well in their careers. One is a sense of boundary. They learn what they may do, can't do, should do, and must do. This sense of the edge beyond which the "assistant to" will abrogate his implicit contract with his chief is basic to managing any position. It is most acutely needed in the "assistant to" spot because of his physical proximity to the president and the temptation to abuse his relationship. Many career failures, regardless of level in the hierarchy, are based not upon not knowing when to do what but how much and how far. Some have failed because they did not go far enough and others because they did too much.

A sense of boundary gives one a sense of trespass and also a sense of opportunity. By seeing, in addition to his own, the boundaries to others' authority and responsibilities in the executive suite, the "assistant to" can come to know or look for the many interstices or holes through which he can thrust his efforts. He knows when to do what on his own without prior approval or checking. Some of the presidents reported that their most outstanding "assistant to" was one who did things without approval, and by his judgment and

2 *Business Week,* Sept. 10, 1960, p. 132.

results won unanimous approval. Those of whom they thought the least committed the cardinal error of upstaging their bosses, a common pitfall of those who are so close to the heartbeat. Executives who make out the best have a sense of boundary and a sense of opportunity, and these qualities when early acquired help the "assistant to" become effective in future assignments. These qualities eminently flow from visiposure.

While the position "assistant to" has high exposure because of physical proximity to the president, the senior executive of finance has high visiposure because of functional proximity. His precise responsibilities stemming from the nature of his position bring him into close contact with the chief executive officer. He and his information and judgment are too useful to overlook. And when not physically present, he is as a ghost whose formless body of precepts floats endlessly among the activities of every corporate executive. The finance man is the one member of the executive team who may know more about the company than the chief executive officer. Although often outranked by a whole squad of vice-presidents, he is becoming more qualified for the presidency than ever before. Instead of "vice-president of finance" being a position in itself, it is becoming one of the most powerful springboards to the top job. During the 1961 to 1966 period, the number of presidents with strong finance backgrounds rose from approximately 8 percent to 18 percent. In 1968, twenty-four presidents had financial backgrounds among the 100 largest industrial corporations. In 1960, the Controllers Institute of America, with some 5,000 members, had 135 members who were presidents or board chairmen. By 1968, that number had almost tripled and grew faster than the increase in membership.

The arrival of the finance executive represents a spectacular turnabout in priorities. During the pre-Depression years, the production or manufacturing man had the clearest route to the top. In the thirties and early forties, the sales and manufacturing functions shared the route. After the war, manufacturing gave way to marketing, with emphasis on finding markets and efficient means of distribution. The fall-off in the economy in 1958 started the emergence of the finance executive. The shrinking profit margins brought forth the need for more stringent financial controls. During the sixties, the finance men enjoyed a heyday of priorities because of the increase in tax problems, in corporate mergers, in acquisitions, in demand for capital, and in the use of cash for investment purposes.

During the lengthy process of becoming a stalwart figure among top decision makers, the title moved from treasurer to controller to vice-president of finance and finally to officer of the corporation and member of the policy group. Today the vice-president of finance may be over the controller's office and the treasurer's department. But he is more than these. The introduction of planning and control produced the controller. The introduction of the computer, system theory and technique, long-range planning, and a vigorous acquisition program landed the finance executive a berth in the executive suite. One former financial vice-president who went the whole route recalled that as treasurer and even controller he was kept in the jungle of accumulating, recording, and reporting facts and figures. "Not until the preparation of statements is taken away from a man can he sit back and think about the whole forest . . . think about things properly . . . so that he can set policy for the company."

What has placed the finance executive next to the big picture and its chief interpreter and adviser is the functions he performs other than planning and controlling. He may also analyze and interpret the economic situation, appraise managerial performance, negotiate acquisitions and mergers, maintain credit lines with banks, build a favorable public image for the corporation, and help determine strategy about any policies that have to do with the company's future. To recognize the larger responsibilities of the finance officer, the Controller Institute of America changed its name in 1961 to Finance Officers Institute.

The difference between controller and financial executive is real, and the mobile executive intuitively realizes this difference in going for options. For example, Robert H. Platt was invited by Frank Freimann, chairman of the board of Magnavox, to leave General Electric Credit Corporation to become treasurer. Platt was not interested because the treasurer is usually a board appointment to report rather than to recommend or control. He struck a hard bargain which impressed Freimann. He decided to go to work as vice-president for finance. He went immediately to work, keeping close watch on acquisitions and the newer plants. He complemented an aggressive acquisition policy. For his contribution, Platt was made successor to Freimann upon his death in 1968.

In some companies finance is a major route to the top. In the auto industry it has produced many stars. When, after World War I, the production men had a field day, General Motors, taking a cue from DuPont, was the first in the auto industry to introduce planning and control through the efforts and character of Donaldson Brown. Thereafter, Albert Bradley, Frederic Donner, and James G. Roche emerged at the top from financial backgrounds. In Ford the route-makers from finance were Ernest R. Breech, who had been a comptroller at General Motors, and Robert S. McNamara, who helped Arjay Miller, another finance man, to emerge after he left for the Pentagon. In Chrysler the manufacturing pattern was broken by Lynn Townsend's rise from controller to vice-president to president. Chapin came through the treasurer's office on his way to the presidency of American Motors. At Corn Products, Howard Harder became the first finance man to become chief executive in the company's history. At Container Corp. of America, the newly hired master of business administration (M.B.A.) who eventually goes to the top finds the route through the controller's office. The spell cast by finance men at Mack Trucks was finally broken when, in 1966, it hired a chief executive officer, a thorough truck man, Zenon C. R. Hansen.

And so the finance men continue their unbounded trek to the executive suite and on to the chief executive chair. Often they are working intensely on one or several priority projects, as was Harold Hammer, who came to Control Data Corp. as financial vice-president to help meet the company's growing need for credit. Not only will the finance man be seen managing projects today but he will most likely be a member of or associated with several projects directed by men to his side, above, or below him in position. But nothing makes him more visible and exposed to the whole gamut of corporate officialdom than a concept that emerged with his release from the obscurity of the back room. This is the profit center. Here the executive is measured by his return on the capital attributed to his responsibility. The profit-center position has high visiposure built into it because of the objective means for measuring performance. The exposure in the profit-center position is garnered by the degree to which the executive makes a profit on his (the corporation's) capital investment. The visibility comes about because the profit-center executive must meet with corporate officers to get approval for the size and mix of corporate financial resources. He must submit and get approval on the objectives which will guide his profit-making activity. He must periodically report financial progress or explain and account for deviation from plans. His superiors have easy access to his performance data, so that they may frequently and efficiently monitor his behavior. No one else has quite the visiposure that attends the profit-center executive—unless it is the critical-project executive.

And the finance executive is deep in the thick of it all. Because he is intimate with profit-making activity, he is used to appraise and evaluate personnel. He may have more to do with the size of bonuses to be awarded project-center executives than the personnel director. The finance position and the diverse projects that he generates and executes are loaded with visiposure. This fact is clear from the mobility findings. As long as finance men were treasurers without exposure and visibility, few went to the top. When they got out from behind their books and adding machines into the glare of corporate sunlight, they moved to the top in spectacular numbers.

One might wonder why, with all his glamour, he is not better represented at the top than marketing and manufacturing executives. The answer is that visiposure is directly related to the value placed upon the activity that proceeds from the position. And this value increases or decreases with the corporation's view of itself. This view, formulated in the form of a strategy and very sensitive to cycles and priorities, determines who from what position and background moves into the chief executive office and other offices in the executive suite. Mobility and strategy are interrelated. Strategy will call forth a new type of president and a president may call for a new strategy. The finance officer was rescued from the back room because of his ability to generate instant information and generalize it to better achieve corporate strategy. It was strategy that opened up the manufacturing route to the top, and it was strategy that brought marketing men into the limelight.

It was likewise strategy that brought a few public relations men to the top during the last two decades. But public relations has never been a strong route and is far behind manufacturing, marketing, and finance. However, a curious thing is affecting mobility in the public relations route below the senior executive level. The old public relations expert appears to be on the way out. The jovial extrovert who thinks it fun to meet people and have lunch at the business club every day but cannot read a balance sheet is in oversupply. What is needed in place of these product publicity boys and the glad-handers are financial experts who can mix with the security analysts, stockbrokers, Wall Street firms. The growth of conglomerate firms, the merger boom, and increased stress on disclosures of financial data have turned the corporate spotlight on the financial public relations expert. There simply are not enough of them around, because the corporation strategy has only lately turned to encompass these functions. In addition, as the corporation extends itself into social and community affairs via such things as minority employment, job training of dropouts, urban renewal, ghetto relations, and black capitalism, corporate community relations experts are coming into great demand. In time, the marriage of finance, public relations, and industrial relations may produce a hybrid of executive talent not presently seen on the industrial landscape. Instant mobility and visiposure may be obtained by qualified personnel who will enter these evolving positions.

All of which illustrates that the traditional functions of business are giving way to new positions. This means that functions are less relevant to mobility. This fact is best illustrated by noting the influx of men at the top who came from the international route. The international route has more bearing upon mobility than the functions involved in it. The senior executive of the international subsidiary division may be responsible for all the functions that his domestic counterpart is. What then accounts for the startling increase in the number of presidents since 1964 who have had five years or more experience in the international organization? By 1968 almost twenty-nine presidents among the one hundred largest corporations had five years' experience in the international organization. In the early 1950s such an executive was a rarity. The answer largely rests upon the fact that the president or senior executive of the international organization has moved into the executive suite. He has come closer to the corporate center because he can increase profit margins, create new markets, find new sources of supply, and fill in voids in the domestic organization. The corporation strategy has changed to place priority on foreign business. As the international executive gains visiposure, a spiraling effect may develop to give him and others behind him an inordinate amount of mobility. All of a sudden the international division may erupt with a whole host of candidates for high positions at domestic headquarters. This is precisely what has happened and what lies behind this new route to the top.

Because strategies and the caliber of men available change relatively rapidly today, the routes transporting men to the top change in speed and numbers. For years operations men could not go up in the airlines. Accountants and finance men were at best tolerated in air-frame manufacturing companies. Research men were used and abused in drug manufacturing. But the avalanche of growth and change of the last two decades brought havoc to the traditional routes. At Parke, Davis & Co., long-time boss Harry J. Loynd came through sales and built what many competitors believed was the best sales force in the industry. But he never put a priority on using research to yield a marketable drug. While others were spending twice as much, Loynd and Parke, Davis & Co. never spent more than 7 percent of sales on research and development. One can imagine the low visiposure attached to men in the laboratory who never had a chance to talk to their chief executive. But all this was changed when Dr. Austin Smith, a mild-mannered, Canadian-born physician and former head of the Pharmaceutical Manufacturers Association, was brought in from outside to head up this research-starved company. The laboratory in many drug manufacturing companies has suddenly become a hot route to the top.

A similar story unraveled in the meat-packing industry where the traditional route was through the meat-packing ranks. In 1967, Swift & Co. turned the reins over to Robert W. Reneker, the first to come from the position of sales and planning. The laboratory at Parke, Davis and the marketing and planning offices at Swift will now attract more and better men of technical and managerial talents. These once-slow and shallow routes are now becoming more populated and swift. A good man with strong mobility drive instinctively keeps away from slow routes, and in a mobile world he does not take long to detect immobility above him.

For reasons peculiar to the corporation, manufacturing may be the hot route in the immediate sense while the corporation aggressively pursues a long-run marketing strategy. Or regardless of the requirements of the corporate situation, a man may be selected because of his overriding talents. The superexecutive is rare today. However, the superexecutive usually has talents that can match the emerging strategy. Frederick R. Kappel was strong in operations at American Telephone & Telegraph, as were his two predecessors. However, Kappel, a finance man, guided AT&T through the most prodigious capital expansion and money-raising venture in its history. The strong, capable finance committee that served Kappel may partly detract from his halo as a superpresident. Even so, Kappel stands out as an exception today, when corporations place great emphasis upon closely matching the executive and the corporate situation.

Position, function, and project can be combined to make for a fast track to the top. Everything else being equal but functions, it is clear that a position in a priority function has greater visiposure than an equally ranked position in an unstrategic function. In a company in which marketing is the corporate strategy, a manager of sales may have more visiposure than a production manager. However, if that manager of production is given a project of such priority that he breaks through the corporate curtain, he will gain more visiposure than the sales manager. High performance in a relatively low-priority function must be inordinately superior to command the attention of the right people, Or, to put it differently, one must work harder when second than when first to achieve the same amount of exposure. William S. Vaughn succeeded Albert K. Chap-

man to the presidency of Eastman Kodak when the latter moved up
to chairman. This was quite a feat when you consider the fact that
Bill Vaughn came from the plastic chemical and textile side of the
business, whose unit accounted for very little of the product mix
and revenues of the total corporation and was held in low priority
generally. But Vaughn rode the wave toward diversification and
showed his fine talents in the general managership position through
which most must pass to the top.

And in a similar fashion, Augustine R. Marusi, fifty-three, came
up through the chemical division at Borden, while his fellow executive vice-president came up through dairy products. A chemical engineer, Marusi was put in charge of the chemical division in 1954
and was given the project of building it up. He exceeded Chairman
Francis R. Elliott's fondest expectation, and was rewarded with the
presidency of Borden. However, it must be acknowledged that Marusi's capturing of the helm was only partly related to the visiposure
acquired by his performance in the chemical division. The chemical
division of food and dairy producing corporations had been for
some time ascending in corporate priority. Many corporations
turned to chemicals for more of their market opportunities and
for raising their profit margins. Borden was no exception to this
change in priorities. Seen in this light, had Marusi arrived on the
scene ten years earlier, when the chemical divisions had low priority
and, hence, low visiposure, his efforts might have gone unnoticed.
Exploiting the change in priorities through high performance in a
project assignment is a fast route to the top.

All of which demonstrates that hard work is not what it appears
to be at first glance. Referring again to the international position,
the men who have sprung from it into the executive suite at corporate headquarters know the value of high performance under high
visiposure. During the last decade, the international executive had
to work at looking bad in many industries and companies. Burroughs's president, Ray W. MacDonald, got his chance to become
president because, while domestic operations were running at a
loss, his international division was a consistently big moneymaker.
Although never producing as much as a third of the revenues,
MacDonald's unit was providing the bulk of earnings and keeping

Burroughs out of the red. Few realized that while Burroughs was staking out its claim to the domestic computer market, MacDonald could sell almost anything in England and Europe, including computers. IBM, the major competitor, was slow to build its foreign markets and MacDonald, ever with a sharp eye for opportunity, exploited the void expertly. He proved that his talent was a durable commodity by turning the trick with Burroughs' profit margins. In many industries, including chemicals, farm equipment, office machines, computers, trucks, and petroleum, international executives rode the crest of an economic wave that could not help but draw attention to them and to make them look good.

As corporate presidents, they tended to place their own men in the international division from which they came. They and their replacements pushed a more aggressive international strategy. Eventually it became apparent to domestic executives that a tour of duty abroad was no longer a route leading to obscurity. Of all the factors that combined to make the international route to the top the most important was the fact that presidents who came from international performed well in most instances. They brought to the top job a larger view of the corporation that allowed for broader, more encompassing decisions and policies. Their achievements greatly strengthened the desirability of getting into the international route.

Note must be taken of the undesirability of staying in any one route too long. In the international division, men who stayed longer than ten years, regardless of their position, had less rapid upward mobility than men whose tours of duty lasted approximately five years. Even five years abroad, five years at home, and then another five-year tour overseas proved superior than ten years abroad without interruption. It is easy for an executive to get lost within the domestic organization and easier still to drop out of sight in the international organization. Here the loss of visiposure is a contributing factor. The principle is clear. The executive seeking mobility should never acquire greater distance from the top than his present position allows. The Nome phenomenon (see page 113) will work its lethal effects.

It is a fact that positions at the top or near top of newly enfranchised routes to the executive suite, such as international, are the recipients of highest visiposure. Positions halfway down and lower may still carry the very low visiposure that was formerly associated with them. A fourth-level manager in domestic marketing may carry more weight than a similarly positioned man in international marketing. The key to this oddity is the feature of mobility previously referred to as "reinforcement." This occurs if numerous executives use a given position to get to the top. By reinforcement, the position attracts aspirants from below and garners visiposure from men above who look back to these positions for men of their own stamp. Through reinforcement, a few positions may become makers of future presidents. To work its magic, reinforcement takes time, high ingress and egress of men, and high performance in and after leaving the position. In the early stages of an emerging priority division, middle- to lower-management positions will lack reinforcement while the top positions may have inordinate amounts of visiposure. Now, by going from a relatively highly reinforced domestic marketing position to a little-reinforced position in international marketing, the executive will increase his distance from the corporate top and center. A bad move of this kind could use up a lot of career time.

The facts of mobility show that the best time to go abroad is when the executive can slide into a near-top or top position in the international organization. The next-best time involves a project rather than a position. Almost always, a project brings more visiposure than a position. It involves less risk of getting lost abroad because the length of stay is not indefinite but, rather, usually depends upon the time needed to complete the project; and by taking less time the executive may expedite his return. He can better determine for himself when he may return. Such is not the case in a position assignment. The time period is open-ended, and if the executive performs well he may be kept there until he finally and vigorously protests; or the position executive may be returned in a couple of years because of poor performance, which, oddly enough, could be less detrimental to his career than ten years of adequate performance.

We have seen that poor performance or high performance is not a fact separate from the degree of exposure that attends it. Poor performance in a middle- and lower-management position that has been reinforced by the successes of men who previously held it can be traumatic and lethal. Mistakes made in the middle to lower levels of the international hierarchy may hardly affect an emerging career. Long after an executive's poor performance has been forgotten and the international division has been substantially reinforced, a management review and assessment committee, noticing that he was once in Europe (or Asia or what not), may feel disposed to give the nod to him rather than to another executive whose record reads, "strictly domestic experience." The quality of competition is never as strained as when one of two peers has more of the desired visiposure.

Which raises another rather disturbing fact. A route is a route before it becomes generally known as such. In the last two decades, during which new and unprecedented routes to the top have opened up, many executives have been ignorant of their new opportunities to snatch visiposure. For years a position in an international division was generally considered to be terminal rather than developmental to the executive's career. Literally, the division became for many corporations the dumping ground for ineffective or immobile men. Men in motion feared assignment to international because of the threat of loss of momentum. When handed their passports, not a few suspected that they had angered the corporate diety. In a mobile world, things became suddenly less certain than they once were and many took their assignments lightly or cynically, which is precisely why some did not exert that last ounce of effort that distinguishes the higher performer, that places him apart from the others. Too late did the insight that would have allowed him to correct his mistake come to the executive. In the corner of the corporate labyrinth he may be heard to protest upon being passed over by the more alert and enterprising type: "Why didn't they tell me there was more to that job in Paris than merely managing it?" A position may be more than a position; it may be a route, and in a mobile world one never knows which it is unless he tries.

Visiposure does not bring zero risk. There is nothing comparable to a mistake made under high exposure. Many an executive has discovered this fact, much to his chagrin. In late 1961, Henry Ford II decided to buy Philco in order to buy into the lucrative primary defense contractor business. He was going to use Philco to put extra cash to work and broaden the company's foothold outside the motor vehicle business. While buying Philco at a fire-sale price of less than its book value, Ford did not suspect that this major electronics firm with a $100 million defense business would become an albatross. Ford assigned Charles Beck, forty-one, director of Ford's business planning office, to negotiate and complete the acquisition. This he did with such alacrity that Ford made him president of the newly acquired subsidiary. Ambitious and driven, Beck could see that this was a chance of a lifetime. He conceived of himself as a professional manager, taking his cue from Henry Ford II himself, who believed that a good man can run anything. But Beck was headed for real trouble and apparently did not know it. He had a lethal defect; he had held staff jobs in Ford for over a decade and never really had his mettle tested against the real world of the line executive. In this sink-or-swim condition, Beck dove into the Philco mess, only to find a most degenerated, demoralized company. There was no evidence of purpose, no commitment to goals, no awareness of where the money was going, and no management team worth keeping. All but three of the top twenty-five men left before or shortly after he arrived and thus he was faced with an extreme shortage of knowledgeable people and competent executives.

Then he discovered, after instituting a financial control system, that the greatest losses came from where Ford believed the greatest profits would be—electronic computers. With divisions going off in opposite directions, staff and line responsibilities horribly blurred, Beck attempted to bring order out of chaos by bringing in several Ford men, among whom was Laurence H. Hyde, purchasing agent for Ford's international staff. Hyde started to work on the consumer products division. He restaffed and reorganized and went on an economy binge. A seven-week strike against these measures cost Philco around $5 million. Still, Beck put more money into marketing, distribution, manufacturing, control, and about every other part of the sick company. Beck and Hyde failed to produce results. In desperation and with some justification, Beck announced to

Henry Ford in Dearborn that the consumer division would be out of the red by the end of 1965. Because Beck's early estimates were badly off the mark, his latest were received with open skepticism. The men at Dearborn wanted Beck to get rid of Hyde and some wanted Beck out as well. Hyde was about as short on line experience as was Beck. But Beck panicked, a tendency common to untested executives, and refused to remove Hyde. Seeing no way to get the right men into Philco with Beck, Irving A. Duffy, the Ford group vice-president to whom Beck reported, flew to Philadelphia and removed Beck some thirty-two months after he became president of the Philco Ford subsidiary.

Perhaps Beck did not realize just how much Ford was depending upon him. Ford had high expectations for Philco, which produced high exposure. Beck was removed from a hot seat. His successor, Robert O. Fickes, failed to turn Philco around. In less than two years, Fickes was removed from the Philco presidency and the new president of Ford, Semon Knudson, brought in one of his close associates at General Motors, Robert E. Hunter. What is certain from all this is that looking down their gun barrels, Henry Ford and Semon Knudson were prepared to reward greatly the man who could get the Philco problem off Ford's back. By 1968, when Hunter took over the reins, the exact dimensions of the Philco-Ford problem were known to the business world. The top at Philco-Ford was by then a nationally exposed hot seat. The man who can produce under maximum exposure will be able to write his ticket inside Ford or outside.

An interesting bit of comparison may be found in the Autolite Division of Ford. The Electric Autolite Company was purchased before Philco for the purpose of getting Ford into the market that supplies parts to purchased cars. Autolite was a relatively well-adjusted and efficient company. Compared with Philco, the integration of Autolite with Ford was child's play. No one could get as much national or corporate recognition from managing Autolite as from managing Philco. Opportunities and problems are the two faces of visiposure.

This brings up a most critical point; a mistake is not a fact, it is the product of human evaluation. Its size is determined partly by how much is riding on the project or program. The men who move the fastest to the top seek the limelight of high exposure, and if they do well, they receive the exponential advantage of high performance under high exposure. It is natural for a man to expect a promotion when he has done a good job. But if this were to happen to every deserving executive, we would have to invert the corporate pyramid. There would be more at the top than at the bottom. The lion's share of credit should go to the men who perform well under high visiposure. For the most part, this is what happens.

The executive who wishes to become and remain mobile must exercise his options in order to get high visiposure. It was not luck that brought Beck to Philco. Many argue that had Beck been smart, he would not have accepted the Philco assignment. He stood well enough with Henry Ford that he could have requested or proposed another assignment more congenial to his skills and background. Too many executives do not aggressively use whatever options are available to them. It is no wonder that they believe that luck plays a big part in success. Luck is not as vital to success as is the aggressive manipulation and exploitation of opportunities.

The following illustration of the utilization of options to achieve visiposure is found in the book *The New Managers:* A young man named Olin Larson went to work for a large corporation in the area of control. He chose the company because control was a strong function that produced many top executives. As an assistant to Carl Pierce, a department manager in the central control group, he was given two assignments, one identified by his boss, Pierce, as routine, and the other exciting. The first was to maintain a file of reports for Martin Luce, the vice-president of control and planning. This so-called "uninteresting," doggish, routine work took one-fourth of Larson's time. But a week before, the chairman of the board had handed this file to Luce with the admonition, "This is a mess, get me a one-inch binder of essential reports that will tell me what I need to know." This assignment brought Larson in contact with Luce, and through him he acquired a sensitive understanding of the priorities of the corporation.

The other assignment was to explore the possibilities that existed for improving the company's operation by operation research (OR) techniques. OR encompasses a new orientation of professional, scientific, and managerial interests toward the application of scientific methods to the situation of organizational problems. Larson saw that because he was given a free hand, he could roam widely and make himself instantaneously known to a wide variety of people at all levels in the corporation. He did both projects very well and was next given two alternative opportunities. First, he could continue with the operation research assignment that he caused to be successfully adopted in financial controls and develop further application of analytical models to company problems. Or he could step into the job of internal costing and pricing consultant, which bore the responsibility of helping to settle interdivisional disagreements about costs divisions charged to each other for materials and components transferred between them. This second job was more centrally tied to daily operations, and it was Larson's work with Luce that showed him that experience in daily operations was the route up. Larson reasoned that continuation in OR would bring the label of technician and would not bring him as much visiposure as the consultant's job. With this in mind, Larson chose to get close to operations.[3]

The fine sensitivity of a mobile executive is seen in this case of Olin Larson. He realizes that in each job there is the possibility of visiposure, and high performance under these circumstances will bring options. When the mobile executive is given a choice of jobs, he examines carefully the potential visiposure in each and accepts the one that has the most exposure. Of course, the mobile executive must not accept an assignment that may be beyond his ability to perform well. But his intense desire to achieve and his strong sense of confidence may cause him to minimize the possibility of failure. In this sense, Beck is representative of the mobile generation. They look to gaining visiposure more than finding a job that matches their abilities. Their motto is "keep moving" and they are often heard to say, "You don't know what you can do until you try, so let's get on with it." All too often this attitude causes them to throw caution to the winds. They may say, "What good is it to know what

[3] W. R. Dill, T. L. Hilton, W. R. Reitman, *The New Managers*, Prentice-Hall, Englewood Cliffs, N.J., 1962, p. 57.

you can do if you don't know what you can't do?" Or, "What fun is it to make a slow, easy climb to the top, never once getting in over your head, if at the top you are too old to keep what you've got?" In these attitudes we can see that the mobile executive offers an interesting contrast to the organization man who delights in the pseudoscience of matching the right man to the right job. While the organization man pursues his matchmaking, the mobile executive wrestles for visiposure; and when he cannot find it within the corporation, he will get it from another firm.

In this sense, the mobile generation is a phenomenon unto itself. It does not choose the secure, safe route, stuffed with lots of plodding, working, obeying, smiling, deferring, and profuse amounts of corporate fealty. Rather, it chooses the route of medium to high risk which will never permit the comfort of pat explanations of success. Authority, salary, status, position, and rank are not easily definable. Hard work, loyalty, luck, and chance are false explanations of success that continue to be perpetrated upon a gullible public by Cassandra-like reporters of the business scene. The mobile generation knows that unqualified success in one area may bring no appreciable reward, but qualified success in another may sweep the candidate up and land him eventually in the executive office. Likewise, this generation knows that failure in the corporate corner is nothing like failure in the corporate limelight. When the rising executive feels secure, he knows something could be wrong; and when he feels insecure, he knows things are probably going as they should. He is like the Indian scout in the classic Western campfire scene who says to his companion, "Listen, it's too quiet."

CHAPTER SIX

The Sponsored
Executive

MOST CORPORATIONS ARE DOMINATED by an established ingroup whose spirit and character pervades the many ranks to condition the aspiring executive to execute and enhance the proper values, beliefs, and priorities. Few winners are not discovered by one or several of the ingroup well in advance of their elevation into top offices. After they are initially discovered, they execute a very difficult maneuver. They achieve sponsorship. Their sponsors have the capacity and willingness to vouch for, be responsible for, and answer for them in the highest councils. In most firms that promote strictly from within, sponsorship is an absolute must. To be eligible for it, the executive must have high visiposure. But sponsorship will not come automatically to him even though he has visiposure. It is in the quality of his interpersonal relationships that he achieves sponsorship. Many executives see and are seen by the right people but fail to become sponsored by a member of the ingroup. The reason is that they fail to become trusted. Corporations of mobile insiders are most apt to place an implicit value upon this quality. This emphasis flows naturally from the fear of the outsider and the in-breeding that commences at early phases in the executive's career. Surfacing at the top of an insider firm is much like the senior year of high school where all or most students have known each other since the elementary grades. Insiders become known to each other either personally or by their reputations. The vast network of committees and work groups, conferences and seminars, makes each one a known quantity. Reputations have become established generally by the time the executive emerges at the division level. The fear of jeopardizing one's chances to go all the way centers upon being careful with the authority invested in the executive's position. Careless use of authority is an unpardonable sin, and the insider has little recourse when he shows poor judgment in delegating authority to subordinates. At the division level and higher, the selection of an incompetent subordinate who makes the superior look bad should not occur because of the familiarity that develops from the breeding practices. If each man is a known quantity, then handing out assignments to the wrong subordinate is inexcusable. In the importer firm this mistake is more permissible. With men coming in and going out in greater numbers, the executive must discover talent for himself if he has not brought it with him. Mistakes in mismatching assignments and men are more forgivable. But with insiders the story is different; they have no excuse.

The consequence is that superiors and subordinates learn to accommodate each other under the same umbrella of self-protection. They mutually protect each other from bad exposure to the in-group. The author on several occasions has closely observed insiders who broke their corporate bonds to join other corporations that had a generous mixture of outsiders. They appeared to the author and the executives they joined to be extremely cautious with their superiors in contrast to outsiders who were not bred by a single corporation. The reason for the conservative reaction was that they had learned to practice the trust principle. They were accustomed to having to determine who is in and who is out. They knew that few men arrive at the top who are not trusted by someone already there and have not the blessings of the current ingroup. For that matter, few men placed in crucial assignments at any level are not trusted by their superiors. A crucial assignment is one that could affect the career of the superior—one that, if not performed well, could place the superior in a bad light with the establishment.

High performance and trust are not to be confused. A job well-done can send the boss into a panic if he suspects the subordinate's motives. Mobile insiders know well that they can maneuver their superior into an anxiety attack. They know enough not to upstage their boss if the establishment has not yet blessed the superior or the latter is known by them to be critical of the subordinate's potential for advancement. Men are judged by their ability to judge others, and a subordinate's spectacular performance must be discounted by the superior or taken credit for to preserve his reputation as a good judge of men. The point is that no one wins when high performance is not attended by a high degree of mutual trust.

It is difficult to define trust. The executive can sense that another does not trust him, but he does not know exactly the cause of the distrust. He may find reasons to justify his suspicions. Similarly, the same executive may not trust another and not know exactly why. Yet, as irrational and emotional as this factor of trust is, it has tremendous career-pulling power and represents an outstanding quality of the men on the move to the very top.

High performance and trustworthiness are among the characteristics of the executive who is most apt to be sponsored. We must next define the career point. An executive may look back on his past and see points in his career when he had everything operating in his favor but missed his opportunity. He had the right kind of superior and the kind of work that could reveal his best skills and motives. This situation constitutes a career point, and only about four or five of them occur in the life of a mobile executive. At these points many executives fail to achieve a condition of trust with their superiors because of the violation of any one of the four conditions of trust—accessibility, availability, predictability, and loyalty.

The fourth factor, loyalty, is a remnant of a premobility era and continues to be the dominant test in corporations that have failed to use internal mobility to increase competency. The application of the trust principle and the loyalty rule causes different consequences to occur in a career. The executive may be trusted without effusing the loyalty theme; or he may be trusted because he does not have fierce loyalty. Loyalty is characterized by showing faithfulness to vows, allegiances, and obligations. Trust is the confident expectation of something. Thus, two evil men may trust each other but may not be loyal to each other. In the executive world, trust is a very private condition between two people, while loyalty can extend to embrace groups, organizations, and corporate identities. In this context of meaning, one cannot trust a corporation but one may be loyal to it. The loyalty rule as practiced traditionally was responsible for insiders becoming dedicated to their corporations. While loyalty is an act that can be easily simulated, trust cannot be easily faked. It is less predicated on intentions and more on consequences. These differences may appear slight and artificial, but the fact of the matter is that the new winner intuitively understands that these differences can make and break careers.

Keeping in mind that trust is the confident expectation of something, the first condition of trust is accessibility. The accessible executive is one who takes in ideas easily and gives them out freely. Think of a friend and you will see a man who values your ideas. He may ultimately disagree, but he will first roll the idea around in his mind and give it a chance to appear worthy. He does not ridicule your ideas. The opposite of an accessible mind is a closed mind. The subordinate who thinks more highly of his own ideas than those of his superiors never receives trust. His closed mind is also seen in his unwillingness to share his ideas and information with others. One can always sense when someone is holding out. He is suspect; his motives are evaluated as selfish when in fact he may be rather shy.

It must be stated that the trusted executive does not necessarily always agree with his superior. Mobility has broken down the yes-man phenomenon that identified the loyal insider. The minimum requirement of trust today is that the subordinate respect new and different ideas enough to think them through carefully and energetically. Screening them out after careful deliberation enhances the creativity of both superior and subordinate. Mutual respect will grow from the necessity to disagree because of the overpowering force of cold logic. Radical disagreement may exist between the two, but it is never over the legitimacy of new ideas and the sincerity of the subordinate.

The second condition of trust is availability. The principle is that the executive who thinks more highly of his own job than of his superior's does not receive trust. A good illustration of this comes from a personal experience. An executive declined the customary invitation to lunch with the author during a day-long interview because the president of the corporation was in a difficult board-of-directors meeting. The author inquired if the president had asked the executive to stay in case he was needed. The executive said that this was not the case but that he had learned to be available at certain times in case his superior sent down for information or suggestions. He said that he had learned that it was wise to anticipate his superior, who had come to rely upon him. This executive was his trailer as far back as when he was a production supervisor and the president was plant manager. It is an unwritten rule that executives should be attentive to their superiors. A superior should never have to be the first to inform a subordinate of the former's problem. A perceptive subordinate should be able to put clues together and not be taken by surprise. The superior who can rely upon a subordinate to be alert and informed will not always have to start his briefing from scratch. A trusted executive has a wide span of attention that allows him to attend to many problems beyond those that confront him directly.

There are some executives who cannot monitor their superiors. Their cognitive faculties are not developed enough to attend to two activities at the same time. There are other executives who operate under the mistaken assumption that if their superiors need them, they will be told, at which time they show little ability to offer the boss advice. Perceptiveness and rapport constitute a form of charismatic reaction that the traditional insider practices assiduously to make his boss feel that he knows everything. The executive who, in using good judgment, makes himself available to the superior's needs and problems at the strategically proper time comes a long way toward meeting the condition of trust as mobile executives conceive of it today. Of course, the executive must be careful not to reveal an overzealous attitude of wanting to move into the superior's territory or of usurping his authority. One of the unspoken expectations that superiors have of subordinates is the prevention of major mistakes if it is within the province of the subordinates to do so. The executive has absolutely no defense if he fails to correct the superior when the latter suspects that the former had information better than his own. The subordinate may plead that his advice was not asked for, but his failure to protect his superior will certainly not augur trust. The trusted executive serves as his superior's third eye and third ear and never assumes that his superior's needs will be made explicit. In fact, he feels that it is his job to tell the boss what the boss's problems are as much as it is the boss's responsibility to report his problems. This free interchange defies conventional standards of conduct between superior and subordinate, and when it is practiced the two parties are in a relationship of trust. Where this practice cannot exist is where the two parties cannot mutually trust each other. Then they must act as superior and subordinate.

The third condition of trust is predictability. This word does not refer to being able to second-guess the daily habits and hours of a subordinate. Predictability means that the subordinate will always handle delicate administrative circumstances with good judgment and thoroughness. An illustration of predictability is the case of a chairman of the board of directors whose trusted executive, the president, was not at the board meeting to defend himself. An outside board member asked why the president (who was absent) had made a particular decision. The chairman's reply was essentially that the president made decisions based on facts, and that when the facts of this particular case were known, the reasons for the decision would be clear. Predictability means the assumption that the president would always make his decisions based upon fact and, even though the superior might look at the same facts and arrive at a different decision, he could defend the decision to his authorities because it was logical. The minimum condition of trust in the sense of predictability is that the superior can defend and justify a subordinate's decision and that he is confident that this will always be possible. Note that predictability is not anticipating the boss's mind and making decisions that conform to his expectations. The hobgoblin of traditional insiders was to make a decision different from that which the boss would make. They were trained to react to people more than to events and facts and their logical relationship. They were more people-minded than event-minded, more yes-men than decision makers. Predictability today is reacting to the force of managerial situations rather than personality.

The last condition of trust is loyalty—personal loyalty. Organizational loyalty may be important, but it does not carry the career-pulling power of personal loyalty. It is still wise to never trust a crucial responsibility to a subordinate who will sacrifice others for selfish gain or for abstract principles. Principles that cause superiors to be sacrificed may serve the conscience of a subordinate but hardly the career plans of a superior. The executive lives in an eminently human world; if he is smart, he will treat his superior as a human first and an executive second. That is to say, he can follow principle and go to the top of the corporation as long as he remembers that there is a vast difference between an executive who will readily expose his superior's errors and one who will reluctantly do so only after it becomes clear that others will not personally benefit by such disclosures.

To a large extent a trusted executive fulfills all four conditions of trust: accessibility, availability, predictability, and loyalty. These conditions are severe and exert a dominant influence upon the nature of the superior–subordinate relationship. Mobility has decreased the value of loyalty and increased the value of the other three. The reason is that the rapid movement of men geographically and hierarchically prohibits keeping track of their motives. The necessity of working for many superiors in a shorter career cycle makes more important the relationship to any given superior than to the company's entity. In premobility days the traditional insider moved up slowly in one route and usually upon the heels of another. His loyalty could be better assessed and was measured usually by a very limited set of superiors. Today the mobile executive who moves to the far corner of the corporation is presumed to be loyal or he would not have made the move. In addition, it is what the subordinate can do to augment the effectiveness of the superior that counts more than his personal respect for the boss. While personal and company loyalty are less active ingredients, in every trust relationship one of the other three will be more pronounced, and which one will be more crucial depends upon the makeup of both superior and subordinate. The mobile executive will experience many different sets and will acquire a code of behavior that implicitly manifests deftness in all four qualities of trust.

Trust in one form or another operates most acutely at levels where the responsibilities are more encompassing and critical to the executive career, but it operates to a certain extent at all managerial levels. The reason is that trust is a vital condition where control of the behavior of the executive is minimal. If the superior can control the subordinate's behavior completely, he will not have to rely upon trust. Likewise, executives who cannot trust others usually attempt to overcontrol them. They substitute control for trust. This is commonly seen in the style of the traditional insider. Today, mobile executives find great advantage in giving subordinates wide latitude, and they derive great gains from the creativity that usually ensues. This cannot be done for all subordinates as some will inevitably misuse their freedom, but controls will be minimized when there is opportunity to invest trust. The more the executive is trusted, the more opportunity he has to make decisions based upon his own choices. The more opportunity he has to develop his powers of self-expression, the better his chance of bringing fresh and unique approaches to his work and that of his superiors. The more valuable the executive is, the more trustworthy he will become.

Men who move to the top have reputations. They have become known because they have done things differently and have kept their superiors' support. This is possible largely because their superiors trusted them and did not have to control them strictly. Perhaps it will always be easier to appear and act bright when the authority environment is supportive. In any case, trust must be earned, and the degree of trust that binds a superior and his subordinate is the rare blending of the compatible drives and emotions of two or more people who need and support each other. Together they can do more than could the same number of people whose solidarity is more formal or mechanical, as it was under the loyalty ethic.

At least this is the form that trust assumes under ideal conditions.

These conditions obtain most appropriately among men at the top. In the executive suite, the trust game is played with extremely fine skill and subtlety, and for the most part it produces consequences that are constructive and conducive to running a smooth executive organization. At lower levels, the picture may change drastically. Here the trust principle is involved as much or more, but the interpersonal skills of the executives are less refined. Sometimes hairy scenes emerge. Examples of jealousy, rivalry, and distrust are not uncommon. Without a steady influx of outsiders and an outgo of quitters, the struggle can take on institutionalized proportions. Divisions have been known to perpetuate a mode of infighting from one generation of executives to another. But with mobility and importing, the distrust condition can be restricted to interpersonal relations between superior and subordinate.

If not carefully managed, the trust principle can exert a telling effect upon internal mobility. Careers can be made and broken because actions are launched without proper degrees of trust. For example, the art of rescuing the superior is indeed hazardous under any conditions, but when the motives of the subordinate are suspected by the superiors, it is fraught with peril. Yet the subordinate must rescue his superior or he can never be completely on top of his responsibility and the events that unpredictably attend the management function. The executive must spread his efforts over great stretches of activity. He often must leave undone seemingly trivial matters which later take on great importance. Every superior expects to be rescued from errors of an embarrassing type that ensue from acts of omission or commission.

Among mobile insiders who sit as superiors and subordinates under a common umbrella of mutual protection, there are three kinds of rescue. In preventive rescue the subordinate keeps the boss from going over an approaching administrative precipice. He holds him back from trouble. In the remedial rescue he lowers a ladder and helps him out of a hole. He bails or backs him out, perhaps taking the blame. In the camouflage he erases his superior's errors, he covers for the boss. In rescuing the boss the subordinate cannot help but misuse his authority and sometimes that of his superior. He has his neck way out and the boss can choose to cut it off. Most bosses are sensitive to usurpation of their authority. Rescuing can become usurpation if the subordinate is seen through the eyes of a distrusting superior.

The trusted executive's life is not easy. Financial security is easier to attain than emotional comfort. The executive is playing a deadly game. It may be called "double or nothing"—those who have, get. Once an executive is recognized by the ingroup, it is hard for him to get out. But once he gets out, it is terribly hard to get back in. Trust tends to minimize or excuse bad performance. In fact, the chief way to determine if an executive is in or out is by how his mistakes are evaluated by the ingroup in general and his sponsor in particular. In this regard, there are four grades of executives. The trusted executive for the most part has his mistakes underevaluated. If not, there are two mistakes for which his superior is accountable. There is the subordinate's ineffective performance and the superior's mistake for assigning him the project. In a competitive industry, there is also the time lost to the competition in the market. For this reason, trusted executives may not even make mistakes. The second grade of executive is one who has made a few mistakes intermingled with his successes. He has a spotty record and is half in and half out. We call his condition "marginal." He may be too good to go down and not good enough to go up. The ingroup has not made up its mind about his future. When he makes the same size mistake as the in type, it is overevaluated. The third grade of executive is called "vulnerable." He has one more mistake to make and then he is entirely out. Inbreeding contributes to long memories and accurate scorekeepers. When the vulnerable type makes his last mistake, he is quietly shuffled to the side and given problems that do not need to be solved. Under vulnerable conditions, it is hard to do anything right. The fourth grade of executive is the one who is recognized by the ingroup as out. He may be seen but not heard; he has no presence; and he is in the worst situation possible—he is an outside insider. He can do nothing right and no one much cares if he does anything right. He is avoided by mobile executives like a plague.

What this means is that a mistake is not a fact no matter how well-represented it may be on charts or computer tapes. A mistake is a product of human evaluation. One man's mistake is another man's error. The distinction here is not irrelevant. An error is the result of human frailty. To err is human. A mistake is the consequence of incompetency, and trusted executives make errors, the other grades of executives make mistakes. When the trusted executive makes his error, it is discounted by his sponsor as a lesson, part of his training and development. But when a marginal executive makes mistakes, he must fully absorb the consequences by means of his own emotional resources. No arm goes around his shoulders and no words are spoken to show continued support.

Corporations complain that not enough executives are willing to take risks. Cordiner at General Electric was amazed by the large number of younger executives who were given a chance at high positions and asked to be passed by. He had cleared away much of the deadwood and encouraged others to step aside or retire gracefully. With the route wide open, young mobile insiders just did not want to stick their necks out. The reason was that Cordiner had removed many of these executives' superiors who were their sponsors and in whom they had trust and confidence. Without their protective umbrellas, these young executives feared the worst: that their errors would not receive the human touch of a supportive sponsor. As one of these executives remarked, "I had moved up three levels with my boss. We knew each other, trusted one another, and mutually protected each other. I always knew that if I did my best, he was prepared to shield my errors. He was suddenly moved to one side in Cordiner's huge shake-out. I was asked to take over a division, a jump of one level above my former superior. I would be under a group vice-president that I knew was out to prove that my superior and the division I was to inherit was mismanaged. I didn't see how I could look good if I had no one in the councils of authority to stand up for me. I decided, as did others in similar situations, that only a fool would put his career on the line under such conditions. I was right, because a year after I quit General Electric, the whole division was overhauled, and the man who took the job I was offered has not been heard from since." This executive would be rated wise by the mobile executive's standards. He was offered a risky opportunity that required sponsorship in the highest reaches of the corporation. He had no one to vouch, plead, or speak for him. He was strictly on his own in a world where men cannot survive on their own.

Although the essential condition for achieving sponsorship is to be trusted, trust will not garner sponsorship except from superiors who are capable of sponsoring, and not all are; only one of four sets of superiors can sponsor. The first set are known as "evaluators." They are all superiors, lateral and vertical, who have the necessary visibility to evaluate the executive's performance. The principle is that the broader the base of evaluators, the better the chance of mobility, lateral and upward. To get this broad base of evaluators, the executive must move laterally as he moves up. His position must carry many project assignments and task-force assignments that call for working with peers, subordinates, and superiors in many areas outside of his chain of command. An executive may not know all of his evaluators, but they may be able to know him or his results without his knowing them. We must mention this possibility because exposure and visibility may not be equal. Because the mobile executive never knows who his evaluators are, he must always act as though each superior may be evaluating him.

The second set of superiors are known as "nominators." They are evaluators who stand well enough with their peers and superiors to be asked to nominate men for promotions. Not all evaluators are nominators, and generally only a few superiors are viewed as being blessed with the rare capacity to spot promising and promotable talent. Many executives do not stand well enough even to nominate their successors, but those who excel at developing highly talented subordinates are more apt to have nominating power. Executives who stand well with their superiors and with superiors and peers in positions lateral to them are also apt to have nominating powers.

The higher placed executives usually have nominating powers. Even so, there are some who have this capacity to a greater degree than others. Powers of nomination are achieved and are usually a sign of the individual's standing with his lateral and vertical superiors. The powers are sources of much pride, and men feel gratified by being "in" on promotions as a basic psychic reward. But more importantly, powers of nomination are critical sources of influence.

When an executive has these powers, he can help to determine the managerial mix of the organization without being visibly known. The powers can be utilized to dispense patronage and ensure the building of a secure base of support below and to the side of the executive. Also, powers of nomination help to create a supportive environment for the executive.

Yet, powers of nomination are fickle. They can be lost by merely picking a loser. Executives who are "in" on promotion decisions are very careful not to abuse or misuse their powers. To be certain of their choices, the nominators must have visibility of the men who are eligible for promotions. They must have wide lateral and downward visibility of managers at the side and below. If a superior has been moved laterally frequently, he may have the wide visibility necessary to spot new talent. His nominating powers are greatly enhanced the more he knows the rising young men in positions lateral to him. It is true that an executive who can spot a rare find in some nook or cranny of the corporation has his powers of nomination increased geometrically; but he must not be wrong. His powers of nomination decrease in direct relation to the magnitude of the errors of his nominee. All of which suggests that the greater his powers of nomination, the more reluctant he is to use them. It is the young, inexperienced executive who is quick to nominate and to regret his decision later.

The power of nomination is precariously based upon understanding clearly the problems of superiors. Executives who have visibility to superiors can assess the qualities that they look for in promotees, qualities that will solve their problems and increase their effectiveness. If the nominator does not know these problems, he will select men who are not acceptable. Powers of nomination may decrease in direct relation to the number of nominees who are not acceptable. The mobile executive is more apt not to recommend if he is unsure of what is acceptable. One way to gain this vital information is to listen attentively to the formal and informal remarks that essentially approve of or reject executives' performances. Another way is to watch the men who are promoted for the clues as to their success. The direct approach is to ask the superior what his requirements for the position are. Executives who have retained their powers of nomination never give a recommendation blindly. It is better to ask for information, even if the request is resented, than to receive a rejection to a nomination. Superiors will forget the probing questions if the choice proves to be good, but they will never forget the recommendation that was rejected. A rejection is an indication to the superior that the executive is not aware of what is going on. Such an impression detracts from his future opportunity to nominate because it detracts from his trustworthiness.

The third set of superiors are known as "sponsors." They are nominators who are different in one major respect. They stand so well with the authority set that the latter will think twice before the sponsor's recommendations are rejected. This seldom happens and, in fact, their recommendations are taken so seriously that they are not solicited in an aura of doubt. Notice that the word "solicited" is used here rather than "asked for" or "demanded." The lower the executive, the fewer his powers of nomination and the more his recommendations will be demanded. The sponsor does not *have* to offer his wisdom, but when it is offered, it cannot be gracefully rejected. The principle is that the sponsor will not give advice if it is not properly solicited, if it will not be followed explicitly, and if he cannot be certain of his source of information. When his recommendations are given, they are couched in language that is suggestive and permissive. The recipient is made to feel that he is free to accept or reject it, but in reality he does not dare reject it. The recipient receives the command as though it were gratuitous advice. Although this gives him face, he is stuck with the nominee whether he likes it or not.

The executives who have this critical power of sponsorship are few. Unlike nominators, sponsors may be utilized by their superiors, peers, and subordinates in lateral and vertical positions. The real test of sponsorship is the number of people outside of the sponsor's chain of command who are promoted because of his recommendation.

The fourth set of superiors are known as "promoters." They are executives who have the authority to place people. Evaluators, nominators, and sponsors do not have the formal responsibility to select and promote except in their own areas of authority. Today, the higher-placed executive relies upon sponsors and nominators to help him make his decisions. Few promotions occur at levels above middle management without careful examination of the views of nominators and sponsors, who may be anywhere in the corporation. Of course, advice of the latter may be used in ways other than the actual soliciting of nominations. That is to say, sponsors may be asked to identify critical skills and experiences that serve as a basis of selection. The next step may be to gain information from a broad base of evaluators. Gradually, nominators are plugged into the process and, finally, sponsors may be asked whenever it is proper and necessary to do so. The latter may be asked to confirm a decision, but only when it is understood that they already concur.

An executive may have the authority to promote in his own area or department, but to his superior he may simply be an evaluator of executives who are peers to him. Not all promoters serve as evaluators, nominators, or sponsors to superiors in lateral and vertical positions. When an executive is delegated the authority to promote, he enters the first stage of this process that may lead to his someday becoming a prestigious sponsor. As one who must promote people within his chain of command, he learns the tricky skill of spotting talent and performance. As he excels in his own department, he becomes recognized as a source of evaluations and nominations to other executives above and at his side. With each successive round of success, he grows in stature, but the leap to sponsorship is the largest of all. To become a sponsor, the manager must have a tremendous performance reputation; he must himself be trusted and excel in managerial skills. So valued is his reputation and skill that his presence cannot be avoided. His reputation for high performance and his skill for nominating winners combine to give him a formidable appearance. His power to influence promotions is far greater than his authority to promote. In this sense, he is basically a sponsor and, secondly, a promoter. The sponsor is all four types of executive wrapped into one man.

The selection and placing of highly positioned executives is a rather lengthy and exhaustive process that is not taken lightly by any one of these four types. The care with which promotions are made is easily demonstrated in the resulting gains, among which is the opportunity to determine the kind of environment in which the executive will live. In the corporate drama of managerial activity unfold the scenes of evaluation, nomination, sponsorship, and promotion, revealing executives here and there in formal and informal situations. It is a never-ending process that consumes vast amounts of the time and energy of great numbers of executives. It offers opportunity for many and bestows status upon a few. To be included in the selection and placement process offers a central challenge to the mobile executive.

Sponsors understand trust because trust once gave them sponsorship. Hence, they are apt to be careful about whom they trust. But they are vulnerable to trusting someone. The reason is that the corporation is a vast communication medium in which information competes with information in an endless array of variety and with varying degrees of intensity. In this medium, everyone fights against being bowled over by excessive information. Men at all levels have screening devices based upon priorities that identify relevant information and filter out the mass of irrelevant information. If we consider each executive an information source and receiver, then some executives know better than others how to send and screen information. They achieve penetration of the screens that superiors have devised to protect themselves against information saturation. Executives become exposed, and once exposed they maintain their priority over others with their superiors. By skill and deft maneuvering, they may even become sponsors. The mobile executive knows not only how to draw the attention of superiors successfully but also how to screen the information that superiors release in their behavior and results. He treats with greater priority the information given off by men with powers of nomination and sponsorship. In other words, the root activity of becoming trusted by a sponsor is high interactional frequency on a face-to-face basis. There literally is no substitute for having a face-to-face relationship with a sponsor and for obtaining this advantage frequently. Barriers of communication are dropped and both superior and subordinate are free to say anything with immunity. They are credible to one another. Trust begins to emerge, which in turn increases face-to-face interaction.

When an executive group lacks face-to-face communication, mobility is not unpredictable. Who will succeed whom and when is a question that can be as well answered by the throw of the dice. The reason is that there is little opportunity for trust to develop to separate the men from the boys. Comparing C. R. Smith of American Airlines and W. A. Patterson of United Airlines will serve to illustrate this point. During almost all of the twenty-six years that United and American were competing, Smith and Patterson were at the helms. They were the same age, had strong accounting backgrounds, and had been pilots and aviation roustabouts. But their differences were of the kind that made a difference to their corporations and to their subordinates, whose opportunities were so closely enmeshed in their superiors' successes and mistakes. C. R. Smith, a tall, blunt, excessively formal man, controlled his company by means of a stream of terse memoranda that he typed out himself. As one executive who left American for a better job at Northeast reported, "When you have done wrong he will let you know in the fewest words what he thinks of you. His memo is always taken personally." Inability to swing to face-to-face interaction largely accounted for the huge turnover at American while Smith was boss. According to one executive who became president of another airline, "He overcontrolled because he could not trust, he could not trust because he could never get to know us as individuals . . . human beings. Misinterpretation was the principle rather than the exception. From him I discovered that if you can get to know somebody personally, you can better trust him and then you don't have to control him as much." Four men besides this executive left to become presidents of other airlines, and close to twenty became vice-presidents. Many found top jobs elsewhere.

In contrast, "Pat" Patterson of United was short, relaxed, tactful, and easily approached. He relied on face-to-face meetings and trips to keep in touch with his executives. United's swinging door seldom swung to let executives out. For example, in 1961 its twenty-five vice-presidents averaged more than eighteen years in the company. The fact that few left while Patterson was in charge is all the more remarkable in light of the vast executive turnover that almost all airline companies experienced during the last two decades. But given the large turnover of airline executives, American produced more than its share of dropouts and United considerably less. What Patterson had to learn to do was to augment the verbal with the written and what Smith failed to do was to augment the written with the verbal. During the sixties, United slowly closed the market gap with American to where, by 1963, it appeared ready to overtake the industry leader. No telling what American might have become if it could have kept its executive talent. For this reason, American Airlines may rightly be dubbed the "might have been" airline and United the "friendly skies."

A classic example of how poor communication can affect executive mobility is found in the Hughes Aircraft Company. This company, founded by Howard Hughes in 1932 as an outlet for his obsession with flying, became a revolving door for extremely talented executives, scientists, and engineers because Hughes never personally visited this subsidiary of Hughes Tool Co. Hughes had long been known for his aversion to face-to-face interaction, and his executives were not able to get approval for projects and programs fast enough. They never really knew what he expected of them. Decision making was like a dozen blind men feeling various parts of the pachyderm. He kept them informed through written memos, personal representatives, and occasional telephone calls. While Hughes Aircraft was making aircraft, custom building and modifying planes for its absent proprietor to fly, the effects of low face-to-face interaction were minimal. By 1953, Hughes Aircraft was a crucial supplier of military hardware. The executives' inability to contact their elusive boss and interference from several of his potentates from the parent Hughes Tool Co. caused a big blow-up, with over eighty top scientists, engineers, and executives walking out.

The Pentagon was so shocked by this 1953 exodus of talent from a critical defense supplier that Secretary of the Air Force Harold Talbot bluntly told Hughes, "You've made a hell of a mess of a great property. As long as I am Secretary of the Air Force you're not going to get another dollar of new business."[1] Finally, under this extreme type of pressure, Hughes acted first by liberating Hughes Aircraft from Hughes Tool Co. and bringing in Lawrence

---

[1] *Fortune,* April, 1968, p. 103.

A. Hyland, one of the inventors of radar. The choice was fortunate because Hughes had no intention of changing his phantomlike managerial style. Hyland, fifty-four, was much older than the young Turks who left and carried a relaxed, informal, and easygoing air about him. With more than forty valuable patents behind him, he was not easily intimidated or made to feel insecure.

Further, he did not need definite, firm guidelines and directives from on high. He learned to signal and receive signals from Hughes by a kind of semaphore system. He wrote memos, and when he got no return message, he assumed that he had been given consent. Hyland sent these written memos to Hughes Productions, which was a relay station for messages that came in from all over the vast Hughes empire.

This unorthodox relationship between superior and subordinate was effective to the extent that the revolving-door problem all but disappeared. But the damage to Hughes Aircraft could not be undone. In the mass exodus of the summer and fall of 1953, Charles B. Thornton, Roy Ash, and others left to build Litton Industries; Harry Singleton headed up Teledyne; Simon Ramo and Dean Wooldrige founded Ramo and Wooldrige Corporation (later to merge with Thompson Products into TRW, Inc.), and many others left to found or head up corporations. Having not set foot on the property in years, Hughes was not aware of what Hughes Aircraft could have become had he had face-to-face interaction with these great entrepreneurial and innovative minds that had turned away from him.

The advent of the computer decidedly rearranged the affairs of corporate executives and managers and forced the use of more face-to-face communication. Computerized information systems gathered, organized, processed, and retrieved information so swiftly and efficiently that top management became more able to know everything important that happened as soon as it happened. The problem became one not of getting information to the top but of keeping useless information from swamping the top. No matter how decentralized organizationally, the corporation found itself acting more and more centralized as the mass of largely useless information came to the top. In many cases, the solution was to find a means of evaluating the information qualitatively before it got to the top. This could be done only if division heads and corporate executives continually exchanged their opinions about priorities and values. Achieving this sense of understanding called for maintaining, if not enhancing, the emphasis on face-to-face meetings. The more instant information was made available, the more executives crisscrossed to communicate personally and informally. And because computers and technicians did more of the paper work for them, they had more time to discuss the relevance and merit of the visual messages. Computers have not decreased face-to-face involvement but rather enhanced meaningful interaction. They have raised face-to-face communication to a higher plane of quality and intensity. In contrast to C. R. Smith, who penned his own memos, the executive today reads and writes less and talks more. He gets around to more and different people in varying levels of management in the course of a week. Evaluative or qualitative information is for him far more critical than descriptive or quantitative information.

The greatest product of these face-to-face settings is to get to know and be able to judge individual performance and worth. When John Cole was technical vice-president of the Fibers Division of Allied Chemical Corporation, it became apparent that the attempt to marry nylon to polyester was producing a fabric inferior to both. He was about to abandon the effort until Ian Twilley, a determined English chemist on his staff, pleaded for sixty more days. Cole explained, "You can read all the research reports you want, but sometimes you can look a man in the eyes and be convinced he can do it." Twilley got more time and the impossible was accomplished. After Allied's new fiber source was successfully marketed, Cole was elevated to the presidency of the division. Cole found his man, and together they prospered.

The process of being discovered as trustworthy and of becoming sponsored comes from the advantages of face-to-face contacts. They give feedback that cannot come any other way. The executive sees himself as his superiors see him, in a perspective that has value regardless of its degree of validity. The mobile executive needs a view of himself from every angle. After studying the careers of hundreds of executives, the author cannot hold back the suggestion that upward mobility is largely based upon having both a wide-angle and in-depth picture not only of the corporation but of oneself as an executive. The two views are complementary and reinforcing. A paucity of self-views is detrimental to corporate success. Opening the communication channels between sponsor and subordinate under conditions of trust does more than allow for a broader decision base. It enables executives to gain both a broader and more detailed picture of themselves. And this enriched self-image allows the opportunity to correct behavior and to compensate for weaknesses. Both techniques are crucial to mobility.

For example, many executives fail to get their share of mobility because the feedback necessary to correct their performances comes too late. Long after their critical difficulty they discover their conditions or their mistakes. The principle is that the higher one goes in the corporation, the more one must base his decisions upon inadequate facts. If he can take into his confidence a sponsor whose facts help to supplement his own, he stands to win more often. And if he has frequent interaction with a sponsor who has a broader picture by which to assess his facts, the executive has a distinct advantage. Even with the sponsor's help, the executive must still base his decisions on a fraction of the facts that could be available if he had twice as long to make the decision. What he needs after making the decision is feedback that will tell him when something is going wrong and how to correct for errors.

Face-to-face interactions with a sponsor give him another great edge. We have seen that a mistake is not a naked fact. It is an event that needs to be and will be evaluated by the one who is ultimately responsible. An executive may become aware through stringent financial reports that his division's investment in computers may not bring a return for five years when he had planned for a return in two years. But the question is: How big a mistake is it? Only those who must evaluate his performance can give him the answer.

Only from the intimacy that frequent face-to-face interaction engenders can the executive get some bench mark of his degree of failure. For that matter, an estimate of his degree of success can be reliably obtained only by this means. Few executives who lack frequent face-to-face interaction with highly positioned superiors fully understand their relative net worth to the corporation. It is also a fact that frequent face-to-face interaction ceases if the executive does not have a high net worth. The marginal executive never has ready access to a sponsor executive officer. He lacks this most important source of instant feedback or receives it secondhand with all the defects of distortion, elaboration, and coloration that go with less secure or less articulate intermediaries. The cliché "getting it from the horse's mouth" is never more appropriate.

The executive lives in a human labyrinth in which he attempts to receive cheese and to avoid shocks. Rewards and punishments come in many forms, sometimes subtly, other times directly, in combinations that defy the imagination. By moving in the corporate maze, the executive learns what constitutes effective behavior. From rewards and punishments, skills, precepts, and beliefs are reinforced or extinguished. Through the years the executive builds a mental picture of himself that includes his strengths and weaknesses. Through direct and indirect feedback from friendly sponsors, he acquires a notion of what he can and cannot do. The more authoritative and direct the feedback, the better his self-understanding. Men who know who they are can better determine what they can become. The executive who understands himself makes fewer mistakes because he is on his guard to compensate for his inferiority. This is done by selecting the right men to fill his team slots and overcome his weaknesses. On this basis, many an executive with little or no background in a particular area or function has achieved spectacular results. The key is that they know their own weaknesses. Frederick Kappel of American Telephone and Telegraph knew very little about finance, but his adroit use of the finance committee and informal hounding of the men who did know helped him to lead the corporation through one of the largest capital financing programs in its history.

Most presidents have had sponsors in their lives—men who gave them inordinate amounts of guidance and counsel. From these sponsors, the executives garnered much of the insight, skills, and support needed to be nominated to succeed them. It is not that they become perfectly whole in the eyes of their superiors. Rather they achieve predictability, one of the four conditions of trust discussed in the first part of this chapter. The central concern of the sponsor who must nominate his successor is what the subordinate will do when he holds the reins in his own hands. Note that he is stacking the subordinate up against a future role rather than his present role. When the sponsor learns his subordinate's strengths and weaknesses and he knows that the subordinate knows them as well, the minimum condition of predictability is present.

In conclusion, the fastest route to the top always involves frequent face-to-face interaction with sponsors and generating great amounts of insight and support from them. No one goes to the top rapidly without a sponsor. The naïve or idealistic individual may consider this fact to be political and evil. Unfortunately, such a view prevents him from learning about himself and others by conservatively engaging in the communication process. He is usually difficult to get to know, may have trouble in making himself understood, may be difficult to counsel and advise, and hence, he may be difficult to predict in a future role. He is on his own and does not have a chance. Whether he likes it or not, few insiders arrive at the top whose strengths and weaknesses are not clearly known by at least one man in the ingroup. The many formal and informal interactional settings that transpire in and out of the executive suite are the appraisal grounds for nominating and sponsoring individuals for higher positions. In a dynamic sense, these face-to-face relationships hold within them the potentiality of trust. The naïve or idealistic executive merely loses his opportunity by default and may give way to the very person he despises, the politician.

The route to the executive suite is not a concrete, permanent road which all must travel in order to get to the top but to which only a few are fortunate enough to be given the right of way. Rather the executive suite is fed by many who emerge and recede with varying degrees of swiftness and directness. But whether the individual is starting at the bottom or emerging at the new top, he must someday become trusted by a superior who has the power to sponsor. This process of discovery occurs most eminently in the manifold face-to-face settings which constitute the real environment of the corporation. In human relationships he can differentiate himself from the mass or recede into oblivion. He is, indeed, fortunate who can learn from and give support to superiors who, in turn, can bring similar capacities to bear upon their superiors.

Interacting frequently on a face-to-face basis with sponsors who do not interact frequently on a face-to-face basis with their superiors can and does create insulations and barriers to aspiring executives. All organizations have voids and gaps in human communication. Ideally, the corporation should have open and equal communication between superiors and subordinates at all levels in the organization. But if this were the case, face-to-face interaction would not be the potent force for upward mobility that it is, in fact, today. The massive introduction of committees, conferences, and meetings of all types has given more executives at all levels greater opportunity to express themselves, engage in the influence processes, defend and advance their projects and performances. The routes have become less determined by tradition and policy and more by skill and achievements. Excelling in interpersonal skills is not exactly new to the world of successful men, but it is more highly prized today than before. The mobile executive seeks these skills because they allow him to give and receive information, to help others, and to gain help from them. The communication process enhances learning and development and has greatly increased the opportunity to be sponsored. Success is a capacity to be trusted and to trust. Trust is a two-way street between the mobile subordinate and his sponsor superior. They represent the winning couplet.

CHAPTER SEVEN

The Winning Couplet

Momentum is everything. With it the aspiring executive may easily get more, but without it he must take his chances. The magic of momentum inheres in the greater opportunities that evolve from a series of well-executed performances. These opportunities, when exploited properly, produce reputations without which few men get to the top. Their reputations have preceded them in proportions that capture respect and admiration. In the industrial corporation there are the haves and the have-nots, who are distinguishable by the quality of their relationships to their superiors. It is in these relationships that momentum may begin to unfold, and with it the beginning of a swift ascent to the top.

The men on the fast track have made fine records. But they have been obliged to because they were given an extra dose of care and feeding from overly supportive bosses. Nearly all mobile executives have at least one sponsor and many have several who put them ahead of their peers. We may call the beneficiaries of this sponsorship "crucial subordinates." The facts of mobility show that the fastest route to the top is to become a crucial subordinate to a mobile superior and to keep him upwardly mobile. Behind every mobile executive is at least one crucial subordinate and often two or three. A crucial subordinate is viewed by his superior to be crucial to his managerial effectiveness. A mobile executive may have twenty or thirty subordinates reporting to him, but he always has a right hand and a left hand. They are crucial to him because he needs them about as much as or more than they need him. But all benefit from such a relationship. A mobile superior and his crucial subordinate generate a greater product than the sum of their individual efforts.

In struggling to become discovered, the executive must first become crucial. He makes his superior look good and his superior reports his subordinate's performances favorably to his boss. They both gain, because the effective executive develops effective subordinates. They both are discovered and become more permanently established. Their need for each other steadily grows as they move up the ladder. Now, with their momentum on the rise, they need only to be seen by the right people at the top, to get the right project or position, to evolve a new corporate strategy or a sudden departure from tradition or precedent, or to work under a new chief executive. Whatever it is, the corporate spotlight must focus upon them if only for the time required for identification. When that someone above beckons to the mobile superior and his crucial subordinate, the final step to the executive suite may be a leap past several layers of executives. Those bypassed and left behind, after they have calmed down, may implore, "Where did they come from?" From the heights of Olympus, looking down on this eminently human scene, one may see what few can clearly see while in the thick of the battle: two or more men interdependently related can move up faster than the same number in an orthodox superior-subordinate relationship. Success is a relationship among people.

The picking out of a crucial subordinate from a group of corporate executives is most difficult. Traditionally, a subordinate is differentiated by lesser degrees of authority and freedom, a less prestigious title, and a lower position. But not the crucial subordinate, for he may share these qualities equally with his peers. What identifies the crucial subordinate is sequential mobility; his mobile superior moves and he takes his place or goes with him. If this happens once, the event approximates coincidence. If it happens twice, the subordinate could be crucial to his superior. But if it happens three times, the superior needs the subordinate badly for maintaining his high level of effectiveness and upward mobility.

Crucial subordinates may follow one superior all the way to the top. This happened to Mark Shepherd at Texas Instruments. In 1948, at age twenty-four, Shepherd paid a call on Patrick Haggerty, thirty-four, general manager of the ASI (as it was known before it took the name Texas Instruments) laboratory and manufacturing division. Haggerty hired him as a project engineer. Then, later, as assistant chief engineer, he set up a small group of engineers to fabricate transistors, which a year and a half later became the semiconductor division. At thirty years of age, Shepherd became its manager. From Bell Laboratories, Shepherd picked up Gordon Teal, who wanted to relocate back in his home state of Texas and to build his own research organization in electronics. Under Haggerty's watchful eyes, Shepherd and Teal perfected the development of the silicon transistor, which put Texas Instruments on the map and helped it to become the largest manufacturer of semiconductors. As Haggerty moved up, so did Shepherd. When Haggerty became president in 1954, Shepherd moved up to executive vice-president. In 1967, Haggerty took over the chairmanship and Shepherd became president at the age of forty-four.

Often the crucial subordinate is hitched to his superior's rising star for five to eight years and then becomes unhitched. But during this period he will advance more swiftly than normal. Often he picks up a superior sponsor again to give him another edge on his rivals. Few presidents have not had at least one sponsor, and the majority have had two superior sponsors. Ray E. Eppert began his career as a salesman in Ogden, Utah in 1921. He came to Detroit in 1926 to become a salesman in Burroughs Corporation. There he met John Coleman, another salesman for Burroughs, and they became fast friends. As Coleman moved up, so did his friend Eppert. Coleman became president in 1946 and made Eppert marketing vice-president and executive vice-president in 1951. From 1946 until Coleman died in April, 1957, these two associates worked hand-inglove. Because they both came from sales, Coleman delegated the sales and marketing responsibility to Eppert, leaving him (Coleman) free to attend to pressing duties. Later, when he succeeded Coleman as chief executive officer, Eppert's crucial subordinate Carl E. Schnecter was made his vice-president and general manager of the big Burroughs division, where he was completely responsible for the competition and profit position of his unit. This arrangement allowed him to turn his attention to the computer division.

Another illustration may serve to show the momentum that can be generated. During the late fifties, the concentration at the top of United States Steel of men who came through the wire division was no coincidence. It all started with Clifford F. Hood, who became president of American Steel and Wire Division in 1938. At this time Steel and Wire had some of the oldest plants, some of the least profitable products, and more competition than most other United States Steel producing companies. It was sluggish, complacent, and mired in tradition. This, being one of the corporation's biggest headaches, was also one of the biggest opportunities. With Chairman Myron Taylor believing that reversing the direction of the whole company was an absolute must, this special emphasis cast an even bigger and brighter spotlight upon Hood below. He set out to concentrate on efficiency by improving both plant and management. He built volume by aggressively selling and developing products and applications the customer wanted. Hood's people helped to determine how the customer could use new and old products, and this dual effort brought him to discover research and development.

Hood left to become president, in 1950, of Carnegie Steel, the corporation's largest steelmaking subsidiary. Before he left, he placed two of his crucial subordinates in authority at Steel and Wire. They were Harvey Jordan and Walter Munford. Both were thoroughly grounded in the many programs that eventually were adopted companywide. Neither wanted to change the rules when they were obviously winning the game. Rather, they intensified and refined the programs initiated by their sponsor. Jordan succeeded to the presidency of Steel and Wire and Munford became operating vice-president. In 1953, after three years of another successful hitch, Hood moved from Carnegie-Illinois to the presidency of United States Steel, sent for Jordan, and made him his executive vice-president. Munford took over Steel and Wire. In 1956, Munford became assistant executive vice-president of operations of the parent company. Now the three, Hood, Jordan, and Munford, are once again back together. The expected happened. In 1958 Hood reorganized his executive group naming two new executive vice-presidents, and one of them was Munford. Now Jordan and Munford were at the same level and it was apparent that Munford had his momentum up when he finally overtook Jordan. Unfortunately, Jordan was the older and too close to retirement, and in 1959 Munford won the presidency when Hood retired.

During the period that Munford hit his stride at United States Steel, another crucial subordinate was arriving at the top in Bethlehem Steel Corporation, the number-two steel producer. Arthur B. Homer acquired his momentum under Eugene Grace's reign. And Homer came to the top from the least likely division, shipbuilding. Hired in 1919 in Bethlehem's shipbuilding corporation, he worked for eight years in the engineering, production, and operating ends. He accepted the position of sales manager because it was open, as few men wanted the job of selling ships. He caught the eye of vice-president Wakefield. Wakefield overlooked the shipbuilding division and made Homer his assistant vice-president. When Wakefield died in 1940, Grace appointed him vice-president and also made him a corporate director. Through Wakefield, Grace had become aware of Homer's talents. He therefore placed him in charge of Bethlehem's massive shipbuilding program during World War II. Over 1,100 ships were produced, for which Homer received the Vice-Admiral "Jerry" Laud Medal. But more importantly, he won the respect and trust of Grace. From 1940 to Grace's departure from Bethlehem, Homer was in almost daily contact with his sponsor. At the end of the war, Grace called in Homer and told him that he was the only man who met all the requirements to succeed him. Replying that he knew little about the steel business, having been confined to ships, Grace replied that they could learn it together. Homer was in the difficult position of trying to fill Grace's shoes. But he was happy to learn and to serve and Grace was pleased with his student. For a little over a decade Grace and Homer ran Bethlehem, and it came as no surprise when Homer succeeded Grace after he suffered an impairing stroke in 1957 at the age of eighty-one. By that time, Homer was moving in full stride.

For various reasons, the relationship between a crucial subordinate and his superior may be terminated. The relationship may be broken because the superior, in a new assignment, may not need the skills of his crucial subordinate. Or the crucial subordinate may get a chance for another job inside or outside of his company. There are times when terminating the relationship is injurious to one or both of the parties. Probably the classic example of both superior and subordinate losing the top prize was the tragedy at Chrysler that engulfed Lester L. Colbert and William C. Newberg in 1960. This case of a dyad that moved together for more than a decade became one of the most bizarre examples of early termination from a major corporate presidency during the last two decades. In 1954, Colbert became president and chief executive officer, replacing K. T. Keller, who moved up to chairman. Colbert inherited an ingrown management organization that was not able to change with the changing times. When Keller retired as chairman in April of 1956, Colbert became the lone pilot, with the chairmanship remaining unfilled and with no executive vice-president. He reorganized the whole company, making E. C. Row administrative vice-president and W. C. Newberg group vice-president in charge of automotive divisions.

In effect, Newberg was number-three man at Chrysler below Row and Colbert, but Colbert needed Newberg's aggressive touch and engineering know-how and had Newberg report, past his superior Row, to him, the president. A year later Newberg became executive vice-president and another year later succeeded Colbert to the presidency when the latter moved to the chairmanship. Although it took him twenty-seven years to rise from graduate of the University of Washington in 1933 to the presidency, Newberg had a meteoric rise to the top after he was first discovered by Colbert. Actually, James Zeder, engineering vice-president, was Newberg's first sponsor. Zeder discovered Newberg working under a car and encouraged him to go for two years to Chrysler Engineering Institute. Two years later

Zeder got young Newberg placed in several engineering jobs and then brought to central staff. There Newberg met Colbert, ceased being a corporate protégé, and started becoming a crucial subordinate. Colbert was always a step ahead of Newberg, and the latter succeeded him in a number of executive positions. He took Colbert's place as head of the Dodge division in 1950 when Colbert left to become vice-president of the corporation. Colbert and Newberg were a closely interlocked team and were well-known for their mutual trust and respect. But Colbert was not turning Chrysler around, and by 1959 it was in a full-fledged depression. A litiginous little stockholder named Sol Dann had made a shambles of the 1959 annual meeting and pressed to have Colbert removed. A most unfortunate set of events incurred the wrath of the whole board. It first started in 1960 with the disclosure that Newberg owned a 50 percent interest in two supplier firms. Conflict-of-interest charges were levied against Newberg, and on his sixty-fourth day in office he abruptly resigned the presidency of Chrysler Corporation under pressure from the board of directors. His exposure left a gaping hole in Colbert's defenses, and by 1961 Colbert himself was put out to pasture to the chairmanship of Chrysler Canada.

The problem of the crucial subordinate as illustrated in the Newberg case is that close identification brings a pooling of skills and liabilities. As the superior goes, so goes the subordinate, and as the subordinate comes under fire, so may the superior. He could bring defeat to the both of them, as Newberg did to Colbert. For this reason, crucial subordination is often made covert so as to minimize possible losses to both parties. In fact, the only way to really spot a crucial subordinate is by sequential mobility patterns—a superior moves and shortly after his subordinate moves too. Because their relationship is often covert, for every crucial subordinate-superior sponsor combination that is known there are probably seven or eight couplets that are not known.

It is difficult to detect a crucial subordinate who is in complementary relationship to his mobile superior. A complementary crucial subordinate tends to fill in his superior's deficiencies and to overcome his weaknesses. For example, an executive who cannot communicate easily has as his crucial subordinate a good communicator. Because he does not talk or behave as his boss does, he is less apparent. The second type of crucial subordinate is more apparent because he tends to supplement his boss by adding to his strengths and acting like his superior. Because he is similar to the boss, he is more apparent than the complementary. The supplementary crucial subordinate comes about because many superiors look for themselves in their subordinates.

The supplementary crucial subordinate functionally reinforces the boss. Thus, Coleman at Burroughs had as his crucial subordinate Ray R. Eppert who, like Coleman, came up through sales. In some cases, the supplementary type emotionally reinforces his superior in the sense that they are psychological supplements. They enjoy each other's company. The minimum prerequisite is that they reinforce each other managerially, and if they fit as well emotionally, the team will be that much more interlocked. However, this was not always the case. The autocratic manager in the premobility period always insisted that his subordinate be emotionally supplemental to him, regardless of whatever functional or managerial skills he had to offer additionally. He produced the proverbial yesman who served to please and was pleased to serve his superior. Then personality traits were the major basis of evaluating subordinates. The mobility era ushered in the evaluation of men by the consequences of their behavior. Performance over personality served to shift the focus of attention to crucial subordinates. As superiors and subordinates came to respect each other for what they could do for each other, their ability to tolerate personality ambiguities was raised. The discovery of the superiority of functional reinforcement (the contribution of the supplementary crucial subordinate) set the basis for the discovery of the complementary type. For a marketing executive to choose a finance expert to be his crucial subordinate is a logical extension of the idea of complementary crucial subordination. And if emotional supplementation is inherently bad for both superior and subordinate, perhaps emotional complementation is inherently good. The intuitive Charles B. Thornton and the logical Roy Ash of Litton Industries and the impulsive Royal Little and the reserved Rupe Thompson of Textron are examples of personality complementation.

By 1968 complementary crucial subordinates became an established prerequisite for a balanced management team. In the persons of Peter G. Peterson and Robert A. Charpie, chairman and president of Bell & Howell, respectively, we see an illustration of this trend. While Bell & Howell had developed a strong technical base, Peterson, whose strength was marketing, felt the need for a strong right-hand man in technological application. He reached over to Union Carbide to find in Charpie the complementary second half of his corporate duet.[1] The mobility studies show that the complementary crucial subordinate is the most mobile executive because project management requires a complement of skills. A project group may number twenty or more, but the central thrust will come from the project executive and two or three of his key subordinates. This team of three or four must be well-rounded to cover the whole field of critical skills. Potential contributions based on past performance and not personality traits or dispositions is the project executive's basis of selecting his crucial team members. As long as personality differences do not impede the team's efforts, they are subordinate to performance potential. The many more crucial complementary types than crucial supplementary types that dot the industrial landscape demonstrate the fact that yes-men are less mobile and effective. Two or three men who are in a complementary relationship can make a bigger impression on the corporation than the same number in a supplementary relationship. Complementary teams have larger visiposure, as do their individual members.

To find and develop complementary crucial subordinates successfully requires a knowledge of weaknesses and strengths. The mobile executive never lets anyone become crucial to him without first knowing thoroughly his subordinate's strengths and weaknesses. The higher he goes up the ladder, the greater must be his ability to judge men. One ability that definitely increases with experience is the ability to hide weaknesses and to project strengths. Knowing this, the superior must be exceedingly clever in seeing through the facades of all types that men intentionally or unintentionally establish as their best selves. But the greatest facade to be seen through is

[1] But this marriage presumably made in heaven did not last long. Within a year, Charpie quit.

his own. Some executives are incapable of frankly assessing their own weaknesses. An executive with a background in chemicals was selected to run an ailing steel firm, and he took as his crucial subordinate another chemical man. This supplementary team did not last the year. The superior did not believe that steel required an entirely different set of functional and emotional skills than those he possessed. He deprecated the idea that he should take six months after joining the firm to find and build his team. He brought in a chemical man with whom he had worked for years, because he could depend upon him. Neither he nor the crucial subordinate had, between them, the necessary skills and abilities. In fact, his crucial subordinate's supplementary skills made the superior look the more incompetent. The executive to remain mobile must discover his own weaknesses and have subordinates cover them. This executive becomes a formidable opponent to fellow aspirants to the top.

In a mobile world a man who has easy access to competency other than his own is rich. Some men do not know talent when they see it, and when they do, they lack the ability to attract talent to them. Unfortunately, they lose out in the struggle to become effective and mobile. This is no more clearly seen than when an executive moves to a strange corporation to find the reins suddenly thrust in his hands. Now he is in the driver's seat. What does he do now? At this point, having access to competent people may spell the difference between success and failure.

A case in point is Lynn Townsend at Chrysler. Many auto executives were literally amazed at Chrysler's spectacular comeback in the middle and late sixties. Townsend's story is a classic medley of visiposure, project management, and crucial subordination. For ten years Townsend was a practicing C.P.A. and partner in the accounting firm of Touche, Ross, Bailey & Smart, headquartered in Detroit. These ten years, in which he handled both Chrysler's and American's accounts, were to be the springboard for his assumption of the presidency of Chrysler. Because his professional responsibilities gave him high visiposure, he had continual contact with Colbert, the president. Townsend caustically reported unfavorably about Chrysler's costing methods, and Colbert in 1957 asked him to become controller. He was then thirty-eight years of age and knew more about the company when he started than most insiders. Townsend's analytical skills with the members was what Colbert was looking for, and a year later Townsend was made vice-president for international operations. Among other things, he negotiated the purchase of a 25 percent interest in Simca of France and met Phillip Buckminster, forty-two, who had worked as a financial analyst under Robert McNamara at Ford and came to Chrysler in 1957 to set up the Chrysler International operation in Geneva, Switzerland.

In 1960, when Edgar C. Row retired as administrative vice-president, Townsend moved into his position. At this point chairman Colbert lost his president and protégé, William C. Newberg, who had been suspended over conflict-of-interest charges. The board of directors had lost faith in Colbert and established a committee to search for a new president. The committee was headed by George C. Love, chairman of the board of Consolidated Coal Co., who was invited in 1958 by Colbert to join Chrysler's board. Meanwhile, Townsend was making the right noises as administrative vice-president. He simply and firmly began acting like a president. Ignoring long-standing internal factions and friendships, he cut overhead by relieving the payroll of more than seven thousand superfluous white collar workers. He set up stern criteria for future employment, realigned plants and consolidated Chrysler Imperial division with the Plymouth division, tightened up sales supervision, sold off two large old plants and two sizable office buildings, and closed down several other plants and supply depots. On an output of only 80 percent of car production capacity in 1961 Chrysler was able to extract a profit of $11 million largely by a reduction of costs of more than $50 million.

George Love now knew that the right man for Chrysler was in the company and dropped the search for an outside genius. But Love was more convinced than the board. In order for him to sell Townsend to them, he had to agree to become chairman of the executive committee. In 1961, at age forty-three, Townsend became president of Chrysler and Love several months later became chairman of the board. To spruce up marketing, Townsend reached over to American Motors for the services of Virgil E. Boyd, whom he got to know while Townsend was the partner in charge of the American Motors account at Touche, Ross, Bailey & Smart. Boyd was later made president when Townsend moved to chairmanship. He reached for W. Stewart Venn to help in dealer relocation problems. Phillip Buckminster, to whom he became exposed when Townsend was running international operations, was brought back from Geneva to revitalize Dodge Truck distribution and sales. He did it so well that he was made general manager of the Chrysler-Plymouth division in 1964. Byron J. Nichols was stuck behind a power block during the Colbert regime. Townsend got him unstuck and because he did a great job with the Dodge division, Townsend made him vice-president in charge of marketing. Elwood Engel, who had just completed a fantastic restyling job on the Lincoln Continental, was selected by Townsend to restyle the Chrysler lines and then became the number-two man behind Townsend as group vice-president for domestic sales and manufacturing. John J. Riccardo was first spotted as a manager in Townsend's old firm Touche, Ross, Bailey & Smart, was brought in by Townsend and eventually became Townsend's top line officer with Buckminster as his top staff man.

The turnaround at Chrysler was a prodigious undertaking. In Townsend we see an executive who had available to him talented men—known quantities. Because of visiposure made possible by being partner in charge of the Chrysler and American Motors accounts, Townsend spotted men ready for his program. He attracted them by inspiring them to give up safe, secure jobs and to join a rebellion. He jockeyed men about, tested and challenged them, moved, promoted, and demoted to finally find his team of crucial subordinates. The emphasis, of course, is on financial backgrounds. His top line officer, Riccardo, was an accountant, as was his president, Boyd.[2] His top staff officer majored in business administration with strong emphasis on accounting and finance, and his assistant, Juan H. Gilespie, thirty-five, was a twelve-year veteran in accounting and had been at Touche, Ross, Bailey & Smart before joining Chrysler. But the team is well-balanced in the skills that its members have acquired and can bring to the decision-making function.

[2] Riccardo was an accountant in his early career at General Motors Acceptance Corporation.

Never has a team with such diverse and functionally cohesive skills been assembled at the top of Chrysler.

All of which shows that the secondary objective of face-to-face communication is the building of a rich network of human relationships that may someday serve the primary purpose of creating a top-flight executive team. When a man has the ball in his hands, it is too late to start the discovery of talent process. It must be well along or the executive will not carry the ball for long. Executives are made and broken by their ability to find those very few men who, when so placed, can together produce a successful result. The fact of synergy is just as real in the affairs of men as in the field of chemistry from which the term was borrowed.

What attracts admiration is the man with momentum. Standing on his own two feet after a high-protein diet on crucial subordination, he arrives in the executive suite with every expectation of becoming president someday. He now can better make his melds with superiors, peers, and subordinates. He has been trained to be a key subordinate and knows the importance of training his own key men. He is wanted because he has more to offer than himself. He does not have to start from scratch on entering his new job and risk having his aides selected for him. He has access to talent because his very momentum makes him attractive to others aspiring to the higher reaches of the corporation. Knowing who he is and where talent can be found, he has poise, self-confidence, and carries himself into the many struggles and battles with a determination that belongs to a consistent winner.

Men who have experienced the exhilarating effects of momentum uniformly report that once they became established as winners, their options became suddenly wide open to go almost anywhere they wanted. Lee S. Bickmore, chairman of the board of National Biscuit Co., reported that when he successfully popped through his division managership, he could have been president of a dozen companies, so great were his options. But he was confident that he could maintain his momentum at Nabisco. Men with momentum have an inscrutable sense of being right and needed. Note how Townsend simply and firmly began acting as president at Chrysler while he was still Colbert's administrative vice-president. This was momentum born of the confidence that Colbert needed him as badly as he needed Colbert. Because he was right and his timing was perfect, he picked up the momentum that swept him into the president's office. But his source of momentum must not be overlooked. It was first a crucial relationship of a complementary type to Tex Colbert and later to George Love. Colbert had a strong manufacturing and engineering orientation.

William Newberg, who we noted earlier was summarily relieved of the presidency, had been a crucial subordinate for many years, but his strong engineering manufacturing background supplemented rather than complemented Colbert's style. When he left abruptly, Colbert had to move swiftly to fill the void. He knew that attacking costs was the quickest way to show change of the more visible kind, and suddenly there was Townsend, who knew more about costs and costing at Chrysler than he did. Sitting there beneath Colbert's nose was a packet of skills that perfectly complemented his own. Townsend became the man of the hour. Then he became a perfect complement to Love, who replaced Colbert as chairman of Chrysler. Love had a strong outside orientation that allowed attacking problems from an investor's point of view. In administrative circles he is generally regarded as a generalist. Townsend knew more about Chrysler than Love did, and his special skills of internal organization and control combined to make Townsend and Love into a double threat. As Mr. Inside and Mr. Outside, they together literally overwhelmed all opposition, and it is doubtful that any less of a combination could have captured control of a company that for years had been torn by internecine strife. Certainly no one man could have done it and no two men in a supplementary relationship could have done as well.

While Chrysler was being turned around by Townsend, Ray W. MacDonald was trying to turn the trick at Burroughs Corporation. Let us return to this case, because through MacDonald we can see what happens when two men meet with one losing and the other gaining momentum. The differences in determination, poise, and style were apparent when Ray R. Eppert had his power checked as president in 1964. At that time MacDonald was looking extremely good, running the international division smartly, producing the bulk revenues, and helping Burroughs out of the red. To shore up the company's sagging fortunes, a few influential Burroughs directors sponsored MacDonald for executive vice-president. For six years, while Eppert was president, this number-two spot had gone unfilled. Eppert, who rose as a supplementary subordinate to John Coleman, was slow in developing replacements. His heir apparent had been Carl E. Schnecter, who was vice-president and general manager of the big Burroughs division, but Eppert never felt disposed to move him into the line of succession. The moment MacDonald was made executive vice-president he put his momentum to work. He instituted a massive shakeup, stopped the computer drain on earnings, stressed putting electronics know-how to work revitalizing the regular line of business machines, tightened up costs and controls, and destroyed any semblance to the casual, paternalistic regime of Eppert. While MacDonald was acting like a president, Eppert, the president of record, could not check his power. He studiously avoided a showdown, probably because the board was better prepared than ever to support number-two man MacDonald. By the time MacDonald's efforts began to pay off in handsome profit margins, Eppert had been completely eclipsed. Eppert took early retirement at age sixty-four and MacDonald picked up all the pieces, including chairmanship, chief executive officer, and president.

Momentum, a combination of timely competency and authoritative sponsorship, can be defended against only by more of it. When two men meet with differences in momentum as great as those between MacDonald and Eppert, the consequences will be predictable. During the encounter, titles, positions, tenure, and even authority will become fickle and irrelevant. It was momentum that swept MacDonald and Townsend into the driver's seat and it is momentum that is the basis of mobility. The fastest route to the top is to become a crucial subordinate to a mobile superior, to keep the superior mobile, and to get out from under him if his upward mobility becomes permanently arrested. This last act must be done with care, for the upwardly mobile executive must not offend his immobilized superior, who cannot help him but who can hurt him. After all, the upward-bound executive may need him on the way down.

The crucial subordinate gains when his superior has the status of a sponsor who can offer the subordinate protection. Sometimes, however, what is a crucial skill at one level is not crucial at a higher level. If the subordinate loses his cruciality, his superior, who has the capacity to sponsor, may find a position for him in a lateral area in the firm that holds high visiposure and potential mobility. No one ever gets hurt by becoming a crucial subordinate unless he greatly disappoints his superior. He must take the high risk that accompanies high exposure.

The crucial subordinate and his superior sponsor are easily confused with a more traditional couplet, the sponsor–protégé. This pair was more common in the premobility days. Although the protégé is still frequently found in large industrial corporations, the crucial subordinate has overtaken him in number and importance. The protégé is the result of being discovered by someone several levels above who simply moves the protégé rapidly to a position immediately below him. His grooming comes from an intimate personal relationship to his mentor. Such a protégé does not usually have a crucial managerial relationship to his superior sponsor. George William Miller went from a cub lawyer with Cravath, Swaine & Moore in 1952 to president of Textron, Inc. in 1960 and chief executive officer in 1968. His sponsor was the remarkable Royal Little, a legendary figure who built the granddaddy of the conglomerates: Textron, Inc. In 1923 Royal Little persuaded his ex-boss to loan him money to start Special Yarns Corporation, and for twenty-nine years and three name changes, his company remained a textile company. During World War II he set out to build a highly integrated textile operation from synthetics to yarns to finished apparel. Through a series of stormy acquisitions he found himself with a company of $500 million in sales with products ranging from electric golf carts to helicopters. It was during one of his famous acquisitions—one that electrified the corporate world—that he discovered his protégé.

Miller was a mobility-directed and mobility-bright person. He chose law school so that he could gain visiposure that would produce an entrée to corporate management. Graduating from the University of California at Berkeley in January, 1952, at the top of his law class, he could have had the pick of almost any West Coast law firm. He chose instead a New York law firm because of the exposure and visibility that could come with a Wall Street practice. In 1954, Little attempted to take over American Woolen, got involved in a proxy fight, and retained the law firm Cravath, Swaine & Moore to represent him. Maurice T. Moore assigned Miller to help him with the case and Little, working closely with Miller, was extremely impressed by Miller. Fortunately, Little needed all kinds of talent since Textron had always been a "one-man company" and lacked depth, particularly in corporate management. In 1955 he brought in, as executive vice-president, forty-nine-year-old Rupert C. Thompson, Jr., from the Industrial National Bank of Rhode Island, and in 1956 he offered Miller a job. Miller made it clear that he had no interest in joining Textron as a lawyer and was interested only in the management side. Royal Little replied, "You come to work for the company and if you are competent, in a year I'll make you a vice-president. If you aren't, I'll fire you." With nothing to lose, Miller started as an assistant secretary on this shape-up-or-ship-out cruise and made it. A year later, he was made vice-president, then assistant to the president, and two years after that, in 1960, he was made president. Little retired at the age of sixty-four and turned the chairmanship over to Rupe Thompson. The much-abbreviated leap from lawyer to president took less than four years.

Leaps of this kind are not without precedent. They were common in the early nineteenth century and later tycoons and captains of industry were known for their protégés. Many took great pride in their ability to spot the outlines of great talent and, by grooming and disciplining, produced worthy successors. During the last two decades, corporate protégés were most commonly found in the fast-growing industries and corporations run by autocratic leaders. In this sense, Textron and Roy Little fit the pattern. Corporate protégés were usually young men ahead of themselves even before they met their sponsors. Charles Percy was groomed for the presidency of Bell & Howell by the age of twenty-eight and completed all of the chairs by thirty-four. Others, such as J. Frank Forster of Sperry Rand, whose sponsor was Harry Vickers, the founder, were spotted later and groomed longer. Or corporate protégés may start later and rush to the finish, as did Robert H. Platt, who joined Magnavox in 1963 at age forty-three and, after five years of behind-the-scenes grooming by Frank Friemann, was made president. A slightly more dramatic case of corporate grooming occurred at Chesebrough-Pond. Jerome A. Straka was executive vice-president of Colgate Palmolive Company, which bought and distributed Chesebrough's entire output of Vaseline and Vaseline hair tonic. Because he was in charge of the account, Straka had frequent dealings with Arthur B. Richardson, president of Chesebrough-Pond. Straka, restless at Colgate-Palmolive because the top appeared blocked to him, was invited by Richardson to become his executive vice-president with the understanding that he would become president in a year when Richardson moved to the chairmanship. The protégé met his sponsor's highest expectations and was made president in 1955. The grooming of Straka, while very intense for a short period of time during his tenure as executive vice-president and president, illustrates the fact that grooming may be started even after the sponsor and his protégé are at the top of the corporation.

Sometimes corporate grooming involves pairs, such as John F. Burdett and Henry Correa, who became the youngest top officers of ACF Industries in the company's history. Sometimes a pair at the top will groom a pair to replace them, as was the case at Ingersoll-Rand when William L. Wearly and D. Wayne Hallstein took the respective jobs of chairman Robert H. Johnson and president Lester C. Hopton. In 1954 Joseph Wilson, proprietor of Xerox, recruited through the services of a management consulting firm Peter McColough and John Rutledge from Lehigh Coal & Navigation Co. In 1965, McColough became president at age forty-four with John Rutledge, forty-three, backstopping him as senior marketing executive.

Probably the most famous set of corporate protégés were the "whiz kids" at Ford. Ford, which later advertised as the company with the "better idea," certainly had a bigger idea when Henry Ford II hired a package of ten young men in the late forties and placed them in a training program with the opportunity to go wherever they wanted and ask as many questions as they needed. Because they were forever bombarding the establishment at Ford with questions, they were tabbed the "quiz kids." But as they began to move to the top under the adroit grooming skills of Breech, Harder, Crusoe, and Ytema, their momentum gave them the nickname of "whiz kids." For several years the whiz kids worked together as a planning and programming group under Lewis D. Crusoe. When he set up the Ford division in 1949, their novitiate was over and intense, real-life grooming began.

Take James O. Wright as an example. He went to the new division as assistant to Crusoe, then to production as assistant general manufacturing manager, then to purchasing as assistant general purchasing agent. In these jobs the top boss was a veteran and assumed responsibility for exposing the protégé to the right ideas and techniques. In 1955, Wright was made company director of purchasing at central staff. And then a year and a half later he went back to Ford division as assistant general manager under Robert McNamara, another whiz kid, and succeeded him as boss of the Ford division when McNamara became group vice-president for cars and trucks. McNamara, with a slightly greater momentum than his team members, went on to become president of Ford, and after a year he went to the Pentagon as Secretary of Defense. When John Dykstra, who was not a whiz kid, succeeded McNamara, James Wright, forty-nine, was vice-president of the cars and trucks group and fellow whiz kid J. E. Lundy, forty-six, was controller. Arjay Miller was finance vice-president, Ben Mills was general manager of the Lincoln-Mercury division, and Charles E. Bosworth was director of purchasing for the Ford division. Arjay Miller succeeded Dykstra to the presidency. In addition to McNamara, four other whiz kids left Ford by 1959. But the whiz kids did leave their marks on Ford, and by the middle 1960s a second generation was making its way to the top.

The least-known whiz kids were about twenty young Germans who headed the Volkswagen sales-service-parts division in Germany. They were selected by Carl H. Hahn for the purpose of moving them around the American subsidiary to get them prepared for top management back home. Five, averaging thirty-five years of age, returned to top-management positions. They were Hanz Holzer, thirty-eight; Leonhard W. Jansen, thirty-five; Hans J. Henricks, thirty-five; Peter J. Spies, thirty-one; and Hans-Dieter Deiss, thirty-seven. Unlike Ford, Volkswagen successfully retained most of its corporate protégés. Their hero no doubt was the thirty-nine-year-old president of Volkswagen of America, British-born Stuart Perkins, who served as their groom.

When mobility studies in the early fifties discovered the corporate protégé, it was found that his relationship to his sponsor was initially one of emotional supplementation. The sponsor liked what he saw in his protégé. We know now that the familiar practice of traditional insiders of "likes" attracting "likes" was at work in the discovery of a protégé. The result was that the protégé was bred functionally in the image of his superior and, hence, he became both functionally and emotionally reinforcing. We must mention that only after the protégé succeeded his mentor could he become an independent center of decisions and change. At no time in the grooming process was he expected to be crucial to his mentor's managerial effectiveness to the extent that the crucial subordinate is.

Within this tradition the crucial subordinate evolved first as a version of the corporate protégé. He became emotionally and functionally reinforcing. We recognize this relationship to be supplementary. Then a twist occurred that made the relationship entirely different. Functional supplementation became more valued and emotional supplementation decreased in salience. As mobility and project management became more common, functional complementation replaced functional supplementation. Emotional reinforcement became even less valued, to the point that the crucial subordinate and his superior merely had to be compatible. In other words, they had to get along to the minimum extent of being able to discover and maximize their functional strengths and to minimize their weaknesses.

In the final stage of the development of this couplet of superiors and subordinates, notions about emotional compatibility became refined to include personality complementation. In this condition, the pair was functionally and emotionally complementary. Referring to the couplet at Textron again, Rupe Thompson came from banking and knew finance, while Royal Little, who built Textron, knew textiles and organizing for growth. Thompson's methodical pattern balanced off his superior's habit of jumping first and thinking later. The members of this famous pair were complementary to each other all the way around. Together they had what the logic of Textron's position required. It is not difficult to see how momentum may be generated for both subordinate and superior with complementary relations. Nor is it difficult to see the sizable difference that a complementary couplet can generate in the form of corporate effectiveness and momentum. The mentor–protégé dyad generates an effectiveness and momentum that depends almost entirely upon the ability of the superior. Their contributions to effectiveness and momentum are asymmetrical, and hence the advantages to the corporation are minor by comparison.

There are several other ways in which crucial subordinates and corporate protégés may be distinguished from each other. The sponsor is seldom the protégé's immediate superior at the point of discovery. Through his development as a protégé, the young trainee may be quickly drawn next to his mentor. The major exception may be found in the assistant-to-the-president type. However, here the protégé is in the anomalous condition of being next to the president physically but separated from the president by many ranks of positions. When the "assistant to" completes his novitiate, he may be sent down the ladder to a lower rung from which to commence his journey to the top. If he remains a protégé, his climb will be greatly compressed and, in a few cases, he may continue to be exposed to his sponsor in addition to performing the duties of an underling. Stanley C. Allyn of National Cash Register went down into a low position in the sales department, where he occasionally went on selling trips with Patterson, the boss. In several rapid-fire promotions he emerged from the sales department to become treasurer only ten years after he first started cutting newspaper clippings as the president's assistant. In five years he became vice-president, and in 1940 Chick Allyn succeeded to the presidency at age forty-nine. At that time the average age of men in the executive suite at National Cash Register was almost ten years greater, or fifty-nine.

A related difference is the size of the jump or leap. Crucial subordinates can go no faster than their superiors, but corporate protégés can go as fast as their mentors want them to, and then too, their relationships are different. Corporate protégés are usually involved in highly intimate and confidential relationships to their mentors. Referring to Allyn and Patterson again, this couplet went abroad together on junkets. On these trips the Allyns were always outfitted with expensive wardrobes, given ample spending money, and provided with the finest hotel suites that Patterson could buy. There was a genuine method in Patterson's seeming madness. He wanted to instill a strong drive in his protégé. He reasoned that if his salesman protégé was permitted to sample the pleasures of wealth, he would not want to remain a salesman at a low salary. Notice that the intimacy is predicated upon shaping the whole man. The superior of a crucial subordinate does not attempt to interject himself into his subordinate's private life. In complementary cases, they are not social friends at all. If anything, complementary types make a point of keeping away from each other during off hours. For them, intimacy stops at the point of managerial effectiveness, for this is their only bond.

What clouds the picture is that either crucial subordinate or corporate protégé may be initially spotted by his sponsor outside the corporation. They may be discovered in law firms, as did Roy Little in finding Bill Miller; or in banks, as did Leonard McCollum of Conoco in spotting Andrew W. Tarkington; or in consulting firms, as did David Sarnoff of RCA in locating John L. Burns; or in other industrial corporations, as did Robert S. Ingersoll of Borg-Warner in finding James F. Bere (from U.S. Industries). Other protégés or crucial subordinates may be discovered as colleagues on government committees. In the latter case, Peter G. Peterson, chairman of Bell & Howell, discovered a personal and business compatibility with Robert A. Charpie, head of Union Carbide Electronics Division, and made him his president at Bell & Howell. (He left a year later.)

They may have been friends at one time in school or college, as was William E. Zisch, forty-five, president of Aero-Jet Corporation who was secretary in 1939 to the founder, Theodore Von Karman, at Caltech's Aeronautical Laboratory before the latter left to found the Aero-Jet company in 1942. They may have been discovered in the military services. Vincent C. Ziegler met his sponsor, Boone

Gross, in the Army Ordnance Corps during World War II. He and Gross, one of his senior officers and a 1926 West Point graduate, had much in common. Both had been at Hiram Walker & Sons before the war. Ziegler made quite a reputation at Hiram by setting up a new marketing division. In 1945, after Gross had left the Army to become general sales manager of Gillette Company, Ziegler was asked by Gross to join him and became his executive assistant. As Gross moved up in rank, Ziegler usually was named his successor. The two made a great impression upon Carl G. Gilbert, the chairman. His added sponsorship, notably with Ziegler, brought mobility to both of them. Gross elected to accept early retirement at age sixty, and a year later Ziegler was named president. Shortly after that Ziegler became chairman and chief executive officer.

Inside the corporation crucial subordinates and corporate protégés may be discovered at any level high or low and even at such lofty heights as the board room. Walter W. Finke spent eleven highly productive years building Honeywell's electronic data processing operations up from scratch to an almost $300-million business. While emerging as executive vice-president of Honeywell, he had become a member of the board of directors of Dictaphone and a close friend of chairman Lloyd Powell. Finke had so impressed the board members and his long-standing friend Powell that he was invited to become president. In similar manner Henry H. Henley, who was president of McKesson & Robbins and director since 1963 of Cluett, Peabody & Co., left McKesson, with which he had spent his entire career, to become president of Cluett, Peabody in 1967. The point is that the place of discovery is not a significant factor in differentiating between the crucial subordinate and the corporate protégé.

But something that *is* a vital indicator concerns the extent to which the subordinate is crucially vital to his superior's own level of effectiveness. The exchange relationship between crucial subordinates and their superiors is greater and they treat each other more as peers or equals. The mentor does more for the protégé than the protégé can possibly repay, whereas the superior may need the crucial subordinate as much as the subordinate needs his superior. There is more grooming involved in the one relationship and more joint task effort in the other. Further, there is an implicit understanding that the intention of the mentor is to make the protégé his successor if the relationship works out. There is no such contract between the crucial subordinate and his superior. This difference may be illustrated by reference again to Roy Little and his protégé, Bill Miller, and his crucial subordinate, Rupe Thompson. As Textron's banker, Thompson had become intensely involved in Textron during the untidy activity centering around the American Woolen acquisition. Earlier he had been on Textron's board. Little needed a man who was financially more tidy than he was and who understood the intricacies of acquisitions and mergers. In addition, he needed someone whom he could trust to take over when he left, but who meanwhile could build a sound management team. By potentially complementing Roy Little's skills and personality, Thompson was brought back to the board in 1955 and made vice-chairman in charge of all the nontextile divisions, and in 1957 he was made president. Little's protégé, Bill Miller, was assigned at first to Little himself and gradually to Thompson. While Thompson proved crucial to Little's administrative format, Miller was learning from the master and from Thompson. Miller was never in a crucial managerial relationship to Little, his mentor, but became such to Thompson. Thompson made Miller chief executive officer in 1968, much to the pleasure of Roy Little, who by then had become aloof from corporate affairs as a consultant in waiting.

In the oil industry, the differences between crucial subordinate and corporate protégé are magnified as in no other industry because of the tradition that believes "no one but an oil man can run an oil company," and seldom do the top men not traverse the whole hierarchy, starting in the fields as laborers or engineers or geologists. Leonard McCollum was a happy possum at Standard Oil Company (New Jersey) with a good chance of becoming president. Having started at the bottom as a geologist roaming the fields of Texas for Humble Oil, his fast rise to the near top of Standard Oil made him a good prospect to take over the running of the ailing Continental Oil Company. After assuming the top job in 1947, his reorganization program for Conoco called for bringing in fresh blood, including non-oil men Ira H. Cram and Andrew W. Tarkington. The latter he found in 1948 tucked away in a Houston bank. As was the custom, Conoco had been run by a strong autocrat who had not developed anybody either by crucial subordination or by grooming, and McCollum had to have talent available both for running the corporation and building an in-depth managerial team. Under these circumstances, crucial subordination at a high level was what Tarkington quickly fitted. He came in as treasurer and helped make sense of Conoco's financial mess. After a year as assistant to the president, Tarkington served as vice-president and general manager in two domestic operating regions. Here there was an almost instant blending of his skills and McCollum's. In 1956 he became senior vice-president for marketing, supply, distribution, and transportation. In 1961, McCollum needed him to run financial and international business. By 1963 he had been all over the corporation and his global view proved the necessary factor to put him in the executive vice-presidency and, a year later, the presidency.

As in Tarkington's case, the crucial subordinate can stand on his own when discovered. From then on it is a matter of using him as he develops in areas that need his talents. Tarkington was one of the first among a few who made a route to the top without starting at the bottom. In an industry that does little grooming and believes that men should get there on their own, crucial subordination is the best explanation for a non-oil man taking over the top job. In short, you must stand on your own; this is precisely what the crucial subordinate does do whenever he is discovered and what the protégé seldom can do. This is why the latter needs grooming. At whatever level the crucial subordinate and his superior meet, their skills fit or interlock almost instantly, while the corporate protégé must be carefully prepared for subordination. Upon analysis of their backgrounds, it was found that of some twenty men who started their careers and became presidents of oil companies during the last two decades, eleven were clearly distinguishable as crucial subordinates and only two as corporate protégés. The others were traditional insiders without intimate sponsorship.

The ability to make an instantaneous contribution was a factor in Paul Wishart's becoming the successor to Harold W. Sweatt of Honeywell, Inc. Wishart went to work for Packard Motor Car Co. in 1932 and went up the ranks in manufacturing and sales. He became head of the field sales force before he bought a Packard agency in 1932. Shortly after Pearl Harbor, when he was found to be too old for active duty, he was approached by Sweatt to manage the factory operations. In 1946, he was made vice-president in charge of manufacturing and was well on his way to becoming crucial to Sweatt. He looked capable of taking the job of raising money for expansion off his boss's shoulders and Sweatt, tired of doing that sort of thing, told Wishart simply, "You do it." Knowing nothing about finance, Wishart groomed himself and came up with a figure of $16 million, which was what Sweatt quietly had figured out himself. Next came the job of getting the necessary capital, and, after learning his way around Wall Street, he proved capable of executing the capital expansion program. In 1952 he was elevated to the post of general manager to assume more of Sweatt's responsibilities, and a year later he became president. In 1962, Wishart was made chairman and chief executive officer. The relationship between Wishart and Sweatt gradually evolved the element of cruciality. It was not coerced or promulgated. In each new assignment Wishart had to find the skills within himself. His superior did not tell him how or where he could get the necessary means. Wishart could have lost his cruciality either by failing to learn and perform on his own or because no matter how excellent, his skills did not match those of his superior or were not what his superior most needed.

To become a protégé the executive must have tremendous amounts of exposure. A minimum amount of visibility is necessary because the superior discovers the protégé. With the crucial subordinate, the reverse is true. To become a crucial subordinate a minimum amount of exposure is required, but exposure of the kind which gains the attention of the immediate superior. This exposure to the superior must be intensive. The executive's visibility of the superior must be even more intensive. Visiposure allows both superior and subordinate to obtain the information necessary to fulfill the four conditions of trust. Without intensive visiposure, crucial subordination is not possible. Visiposure is the necessary condition for crucial subordination which, in turn, is the necessary condition for this kind of mobility. The condition that will guarantee mobility to a crucial subordinate is for the superior to be highly mobile himself. This means that the superior must in turn be a crucial subordinate to his superiors, etc.

Another difference between crucial subordinate and corporate protégé follows from their dispositions to legitimize the efforts of their superiors. The crucial subordinate has no authority over the mobile superior and, for that matter, neither does the corporate protégé over his mentor. But the crucial subordinate has vast amounts of power to influence his superior, while the protégé has much less. The crucial subordinate's power comes from his expertise and mental acuity. If the corporate protégé has power, it comes from his charismatic reaction to his sponsor, which produces the basis upon which the latter becomes fond of him as a person. He becomes favored. But because the protégé is basically an extended self of his mentor, his power to make independent claims upon him and to exert superior expertise is thereby limited. Then, too, the crucial subordinate achieves his power over his mobile superior within the broad framework of mutual trust with accessibility, availability, and predictability, the most common ingredients commonly shared by superior and subordinate alike. But the corporate protégé must show personal loyalty to his mentor, while his mentor need not return the same. Loyalty is the chief condition that evolves from the efforts of the protégé and is narrowly confined to personal loyalty. Thus, the protégé's modicum of power is precariously based upon deluging his mentor with huge showers of charismatic reaction of the type that make his superior appear wise and understanding.

If the reader desires to measure how far the industrial world has come from the days when traditional insiders emerged at the top after long years of simulating and internalizing the loyalty ethic, let him take note of the relative decline in number and importance of corporate protégés in executive suites and the great increase in value and number of crucial subordinates. In many corporations a whole new climate exists at the top as a consequence. There, trust is a managerial function that contributes both to corporate and individual effectiveness. Accessible, available, and predictable behavior allows for change, innovation, and risk. The crucial subordinate must make a managerial difference or he will not remain a crucial subordinate, no matter how personally loyal he is to his superior. Furthermore, the trust involved has only to do with the job in front of the crucial subordinate and his mobile superior and the position ahead of them. It is not a result of projecting what the subordinate will do someday, when he displaces his superior, as is the case in the sponsor–protégé couplet.

The corporate protégé has mobility in companies where the loyalty ethic is still in vogue. It is practically the sole consideration that allows insiders safely to anticipate that the protégé will put his company ahead of himself when he becomes chief executive officer. To trust him means that he will behave appropriately when he assumes the position of ultimate authority. Appropriate behavior means that the protégé will not do anything that will reflect on the achievements of his sponsor. The chief executive officer upon retirement often stays on the board not only because he is an insider who fears the outside but also to exert the effect of an elder statesman. His presence contributes to tying the hands of his protégé, especially if the latter feels true personal loyalty to this omnipresent shadow in the corporate wings.

Occasionally the protégé will prove to be rebellious. Perhaps he had been acting all along the route to the top, during which time he found it easier to simulate loyalty than to show the imagination, competency, and technical expertise of the crucial subordinate. Also, he found it less difficult to excel in interpersonal relations than to influence the decisions of his mentor. Whatever capacity the protégé now has to be different and to successfully defy the wishes of his mentor will depend upon the latter's willingness and ability to reassert his power and influence with the board to recapture his authority or at least put down, short of expulsion, the rebellious efforts of his once trusted successor. In not a few cases will the groom have to be expelled and replaced because he does not know how to placate, seduce, and allay the powerful corporate conscience of his mentor. In the shouting match that occasions confrontations between the corporate parent and the rebellious protégé, the numerous allusions to and accusations of disloyalty fill the offices of the executive suite with the resounding effects of an echo chamber. For years after the face-off, executives who witness the conflagration will remain uptight, as though the final blow had been struck against their freedom to defy convention and custom. As one executive remarked, "All you have to do to forever give up the idea that you should think for yourself is to watch one of these blowouts, especially when the old man wins and resumes where he left off." To repeat, the protégé must always be loyal to his mentor, but the mentor may be loyal to the protégé only when the latter fulfills his implicit contract of total fealty.

It would be misleading to leave the impression that protégés never go on to make major contributions to the corporation. Many who succeed to the presidency become effective agents of change. However, the protégé's cycle time between succeeding the mentor and becoming an agent of change in his own right is drastically longer. The study of corporate protégés shows that generally, after five years in the presidency or when the mentor dies or becomes incapacitated, the president discovers his spontaneous self. Thereafter he commences to flower into the colorful personality that moves his corporation. Crucial subordinates show much shorter cycle time between acting on their own premises and reacting as they had been trained. They are better developed to be centers of spontaneity and imagination. Because of this shorter cycle time, they fit the merging trend of the corporation to set short-run strategic goals and select presidents whose qualities carefully match them. Today, presidents stay in office less time, about five years on the average, rather than ten years or more as was the custom when traditional executives dominated the executive suite. In other words, the corporation's cycle time is much shorter, and its strategies cannot wait five years for a president to undergo the metamorphosis of a subordinate become superior. The recent tendency to encourage former chief executives to leave the firm altogether will greatly contribute to shortening the cycle time for their successors to get into the drivers' seats by themselves.

For these many reasons, the crucial subordinate represents the executive of the future. It is in his momentum—rather than the insider's inertia—that the greater resources of the firm reside, enabling it to master a rapidly growing and changing environment. He breeds highly flexible, imaginative replacements. To master change, the corporation must change. A former president of General Motors was fond of saying, "Change or you will be changed." His admonition has application to corporations and executives alike who aspire to be winners.

CHAPTER EIGHT

The Quitter

THE KEEPING TRACK of men in motion reveals a wide assortment of moves and movements. One cannot help but be impressed by the infinite number of strategies and tactics available to the mobile executive. The number and variety of his options depend upon what he considers to be his universe for achieving his career aims. The fewest options are provided by a single corporation. The insider has adopted the corporate universe as the only field in which he can pursue his career. However, the relatively few alternate routes to the top available in one company may suddenly be multiplied by merely redefining the scope of his career universe. The executive may decide that he will accept any route to the top irrespective of the kind of corporation. He may prepare to split the route into sections, with each part assigned to a particular corporation. When the executive runs out of challenges or momentum, whichever happens to be his definition of immobility at the time, he may transfer to another corporation in the hope of enhancing his probability of success. But to execute properly a career strategy that embraces a multicorporate universe, the executive must be able to enter the market for executive talent and wisely exchange his achievements for better opportunities.

Partly because of the influence of the mass media, the mobile executive is usually pictured at the point of arriving in a new, more responsible position. In every case of arriving, there is a prior act of leaving. And quitting, as we define it, precedes leaving. Knowing when, how, and why to quit is just as important as knowing what job to take next. Because many men in the executive suite quit first and find employment later, the aspiring executive can learn much about the strategies of moving by studying the many patterns or styles of quitting.

In mobile executives we can see that success is respecting the act of quitting. To them, winning requires more than willingness to quit; it requires thinking positively about quitting, as though it were as natural as staying. This quitting is not a freakish occurrence, not something of which to be ashamed, not a response to failure. It is a step in building a successful career, to be used objectively when the situation warrants.

In other words, if one does not manage his career, his company must assume the whole responsibility. Of course, a career cannot be controlled in the way the word "manage" suggests. The future is simply not that visible and predictable. Mistakes will be made in judgment, in tactics, and in performance. Because of this risk, the question of whether to quit or not to quit tends to turn a man into an executive Hamlet, endlessly weighing alternatives, too often making no decision at all until events are beyond his managerial powers. What is pinning him to his corporate executive suite is an engraved prohibition that dictates waiting patiently, biding his time for breaks, luck, and circumstance to do his work for him. He has failed at the number-one job, managing his own career. To do this he must treat as legitimate the option of quitting, even though he may not need to use it.

The quitter may be a fallen idol, an heir apparent, a well-groomed protégé, a passed-over vice-president, or a loser of a protracted battle for the presidency. He may blow the lid off a top-management dispute, or he may create a leadership void that threatens the continuity of the firm. The quitter may take talented people with him, he may slide into personal oblivion, or he may sue to gain in court what he lost in the executive suite. The quitter has been around a long time. Many of the most successful businessmen were quitters. Looking back into the careers of such historical figures as Carnegie, Rockefeller, and Chrysler, one can observe the same sort of restlessness that has come to mark the emerging generation of mobile executives. If the rate of quitting is any index of the degree of independence in the executive suite, contemporary executives are by far the most fearless generation since the early days of frontier America.

Quitters come in many varieties, but most may be categorized into either of two groups. The first quitter "fires" his corporation because of misuse or abuse, and the second leaves because he intended all along to work in several organizations and serve multiple careers or roles. The first mobility pattern relates to the characteristics of an immediate situation. It represents a mismatch between the executive and his corporation. The second takes its quality from a definition of life and is only incidentally related to the executive's present situation. For example, Allied Chemical Corporation for the first time in its forty-seven-year history selected an outsider for president. John T. Connor, fifty-two, was made chief executive in 1967. This outsider enjoyed the life of an outsider, for he was committed to a career of going where the challenges were greatest. After a wartime tour that included the Office of Scientific Research and Development and the Marine Corps, he joined Merck & Co. in 1947 as general counsel. Eight years later, at age forty, he became president of this Rahway, New Jersey, drug producer. He doubled sales and increased profit margins, laid the foundation for an aggressive acquisition program, and then moved on to a two-year hitch under Lyndon Johnson with the United States Department of Commerce—the youngest to have been given the portfolio in twenty-five years. When he joined Allied Chemical, this fifth-largest chemical company that thirty years before had been the largest, it was a sick company. Earnings had plummeted from a high of $2.62 a share to 64 cents, despite a slight increase in sales to $1.28 billion. Chester M. Brown, Connor's predecessor, had largely been responsible for developing the company into a major producer of bulk plastic and chemicals. However, Allied was hard hit by eroding profit margins in bulk chemicals. It had not moved aggressively enough into synthetic fibers and consumer products. It was overcommitted in agricultural fertilizers and had taken an especially heavy beating in ammonia. Critics complained that the corporation needed new leadership with more experience in marketing strategy and methods.

But Connor found a company with no real management, one that had abdicated control to division management and the technicians. He discovered his challenge in five areas that needed drastic attention: modernization of management that included position clarification, salary, and other programs; emphasis on planning at corporate and division levels; greater involvement of the board in policy decisions; greater involvement of corporate management in divisional operations; and the integration of the acquired companies into an integrated organizational format. The troubleshooter went to work, and his surgery included a personnel reorganization that made Brown's of some five years before look minor by comparison.

Of the three executive vice-presidents that survived Brown's reorganization, only one survived Connor's, Irb H. Fooshee. All other officials who reported directly to Connor were outsiders or relatively so, and being biased for the adversary process, many had been originally trained as lawyers. Many were quitters who had been in at least two companies before they joined Connor's team. Frederick L. Bissinger came to Allied in 1965 as vice-president. Trained as a lawyer and engineer, he started with Industrial Rayon Corp. in 1942 and in 1960 became president. In 1962 he quit to become president of Stauffer Chemical Co. After three years he quit, in late 1965, to become vice-president of Allied, and in 1966 he was made executive vice-president. He became chief operations officer in 1968, when Connor became chairman and chief executive officer. His vice-president for corporate relations, Herbert F. Walker, had been with General Foods and RCA. Brian D. Forrow, the new general counsel, came from a law firm. Naturally, some senior men quit when such youthful group vice-presidents as G. John Coli, forty-eight, and John H. Barnard, forty-six, occupied the inside route to the presidency. Whether or not Connor at fifty-five makes the turnaround at Allied, he will move to other challenges because this is the lifestyle of a true quitter.

Stanley de Jongh Osborne was no company man either. In his thirty-six-year corporate career he held high posts in several different large companies. He started in investment banking with Old Colony Corp. While there, his attention was called to profitless Atlantic Coast Fisheries. As he helped the turnaround, he rose to become the vice-president. After serving during the war as director of the United States Office of Rubber, he moved in 1944 to Eastern Airlines as vice-president for traffic control. During the six years at Eastern he proved his ability to manage during one of the most turbulent periods in the company's history. In 1950 he joined Olin Mathieson Chemical Corp. as treasurer and later became financial vice-president. Seven years later he became Olin's president and four years later chief executive officer. As project president he was assigned the difficult task of liquidating unprofitable operations and reorganizing. With his task completed, he quit in early 1964 to go back to his first love, finance, by joining the international investment firm of Lazard Freres & Co. as a general partner. His fourth major business career was to join the boards of troubled companies, sometimes as adviser to old managements and sometimes helping to select new, capable replacements.

Some corporations thrive on quitters of the Osborne and Connor type. Olin Mathieson's Gordon Grand, who succeeded to the executive vice-presidency when Osborne left, was also a trained lawyer who left his job of chief counsel of the House Ways and Means Committee to start his climb to the presidency of Olin Mathieson in 1965. In 1967 G. Keith Funston, a former college president, left the presidency of the New York Stock Exchange after sixteen years to become chairman of the board of Olin Mathieson.

Osborne, Connor, and Funston represent a breed of professional careerists who view life as consuming several diverse roles in a wide-ranging career universe. They are emotionally unprepared to put their fate in the hands of a single company. For them, life is continually quitting and joining, with healthy doses of challenge in between. They practice what the growing discipleship of this lifestyle calls "repotting." John W. Gardner, former Secretary of Health, Education and Welfare and himself a frequent repotter, used the argument to persuade Ernest C. Arbuckle to come to Stanford University as dean of the business school. "A man needs repotting every ten years," Gardner said. He pitched the right argument to the right person. Gardner was one of several trustees of Stanford's School of Business assigned to search for a new dean. At the time, Arbuckle was an executive vice-president of W. R. Grace & Co. After building the business school into one of the finest in the nation, Arbuckle repotted again to become chairman of Wells Fargo Bank, whose assets in 1967 were $4.7 billion.

When Arbuckle left the deanship he was replaced by another repotter who received from Arbuckle the same argument that enticed him to Stanford. Arjay Miller had started his career as a teacher of economics at the University of California at Berkeley while working for his Ph.D. degree. He planned to become a teacher rather than a businessman. But his war years were spent in the Air Force where he met Charles B. Thornton, and he joined him and the eight other whiz kids assembled by Henry Ford II at Ford Motor Company in 1946. He rose swiftly to the presidency of Ford and got caught in the supermove of Semon Knudsen. Having been at Ford almost twenty years, Miller accepted the argument of repotting to become dean at Stanford Graduate School of Business. Coincidentally, two other presidents of Ford were disciples of the repotting style of life. Ernest R. Breech has been at the top of three major corporations, including Bendix, Ford, and TWA, and Robert S. McNamara has been a professor at Harvard, president of Ford, Secretary of Defense, and head of the World Bank.

Arbuckle and Miller are illustrations of a trend toward repotting that has been growing since the late 1950s when Ralph Cordiner, former chairman of General Electric, wanted everyone around him to retire at the age of sixty so that they could do something else. He suggested teaching or government service. To become repotted, Cordiner believed that the retiring executive should leave the corporation altogether. Cordiner declined to serve on the board or as a consultant when he retired from the chairmanship. In this regard General Electric is representative of the trend. During the last ten years, over 30 percent of the retiring officers have been repotted. James H. Goss retired from General Electric at sixty to become president and chief operating officer of Automatic Sprinkler Corp. of America. Automatic had acquired a bad case of indigestion from too rapid expansion. Goss's case is similar to Knudsen's in that neither had a chance to be operating officer in his career firm. Although Goss was president of Canadian General Electric in 1955, he merely had his appetite whetted before he moved in 1957 to the parent company to head General Electric's consumer products. In 1959 he was moved to group executive for General Electric's operations in Europe, the Far East, and Latin America. The year before he left for Automatic he was consultant on international operations to General Electric's president. With his hands on the operating reins of Automatic, Goss found a challenge every bit as big as any he had in his career at General Electric.

Perhaps we have illustrated the point well enough. Suffice it to say that in the repotters one can see a form of quitting that is not an immediate reaction to a situation but rather a case of individuals who come prepared to quit whether or not they are misused or abused or challenged. The wide scope of their career interests makes quitting natural.

In this chapter we shall be more concerned about the second type of quitter who leaves because of disturbances associated with the immediate situation. We shall give the label "quitter" to this type to differentiate him from his more philosophical cousin, the repotter. Before C. Lester Hogan quit Motorola after building it up to one of the largest semiconductor businesses, he wondered what he could do for a second act. Robert W. Galvin, the proprietor of Motorola, had at least twenty years to go before retirement and showed little sign of making room at the top for Hogan. Hogan "threw in the sponge," so to speak.

Whether the quitter is strongly encouraged to stay or pressed into leaving, by definition he has irrevocably decided before that this is not the place for him. He "fires" his company. This frame of mind, that views staying as a strictly temporary condition, identifies the quitter. No enticement from another corporation has presented itself to goad him into this frame of mind. In contrast to the quitter is the leverager (see Chapter 9), who leaves only after he has found a better environment or job. In this respect, G. W. Woerner, who left IBM to join James Ling at LTV, was a leverager. He had not really intended to leave IBM because he had advanced rapidly to vice-president of the Data Processing Division and he was in charge of about one-third of the domestic computer business. The men above him were mobile, and he had every reason to expect continued upward mobility. When he was first approached with the offer to join LTV, he was not particularly interested; but upon persuasion he left. He did not quit, because the quitter quits mentally before he has a place to go and the leverager leaves only because he has a better job in his hand. In the latter case, an attractive offer triggers the act of egression and a career block precipitates the act of quitting.

The quitter has his freedom to express his career needs restricted and thus he is prepared to make an unambiguous break with his company. His blocks may appear in many forms, and they are sometimes more apparent than real. But real or not, they exist in his mind and are defined as real. When they are also defined as insurmountable, they sting his managerial ego into action. At the point of quitting, he may appear to be making an irrational decision. A flurry of personality-directed invective may be exchanged between him and his superior and colleagues before or after he quits. Or he may depart in a most amicable fashion, with going-away fanfare and parties in his honor. He may appear to be walking away from a golden opportunity, or he may be likened to the spoiled brat who quit because he could not have his way.

As irrational as his move to quit may appear to the public, he is at bottom following a stern, inner logic that consistently argues for maintaining and enhancing his sense of identity. He sees himself as more competent than his job and superiors allow him to be. Winners do not quit willy nilly. The point to be made is that the immediate situation facing the mobile executive, the situation that triggers him to quit, is not his sole cause for leaving. In fact, it is not meaningful in and of itself. His past achievements, present opportunities or blocks, and future goals come together to provide an overlay by which his immediate situation is intelligently evaluated.

His act of quitting only *appears* to be instinctive, impulsive, irrational.

Furthermore, we can see in the mind of the quitter the essence of mobility. His mind avoids blocks and seeks opportunity for expression. Momentum must be maintained because the slowing down of his rate of personal development produces stress and pain. The more mentally mobile the executive, the more likely he is to quit. And he may quit several times before he finds the situation that fits his pattern of personal development. At each point of quitting, he acquires an enriched view of himself. Mobility is his strategy of finding and carving out a niche for himself.

But he may appear to leave suddenly. What exasperates corporate officialdom is the sudden departure of executives. This peculiar quality of the quitter stems from his unmasking his own self-deceptions. Corporations need good men at all levels, particularly in the executive suite. Because many men want to become president but few can, the corporations must keep executives well-motivated. For example, to keep vice-presidents functioning, superiors often allow them to make assumptions about opportunities that do not exist. Many are promised promotion as a motivation to perform. Some of this spurious motivation seems inevitable, whether devious or not. But some of it is downright mismanagement.

The author discovered, in 1964, in a corporation with thirty vice-presidents, that among the ten youngest full-route and split-route mobile executives, six had been "promised" the presidency. By 1967, four of these vice-presidents had quit, and among their replacements two had been "promised" the presidency. Under such circumstances, a mobile executive has to be very skeptical of "promises." The moment underutilization of his abilities and experience sets in, he must read his maze very carefully for the real answers to his future opportunities.

His greatest enemy is not the bad promises made to him but his own capacity for self-deception. This last step to the summit is so enticing that he can manufacture hope that exceeds even the lies and carefully planted suggestions. A self-deceived executive can waste years of career time until he is too old to be attractive to other companies and useful to his own. Thus, while he may promise himself the presidency, someday, of some corporation, he dare not commit himself to his present circumstance. This would be painting himself into a corner.

Even a company that anoints an executive for future promotion to the presidency must be suspect, for it may have to renege due to changes in its future plans. Raymond H. Milford was told in 1959 that he would be the next president of Owens-Illinois in exactly one year, during which time he served as an assistant to the president. He was given an office and a few specific responsibilities, including traveling with the president and chairman. About the same time the glass container division got into trouble and, before he could begin his training for the presidency, he was thrust into the arena as vice-president of the troubled division. After making the turnaround, he succeeded to the presidency almost three years later. But suppose, under conditions of high visiposure and crucial subordination, Milford had failed? Needless to say, his future would have appeared considerably less bright if the powers that be had had to reconsider their promise

In a similar manner, Robert Galvin, chairman of Motorola, having learned from Lester Hogan's abrupt departure that maybe he should remove the cork from the bottle after all, set up a line of succession. William J. Weisz, vice-president and general manager of the communications division, was anointed in the winter of 1969 for the presidency in 1974. The laying on of hands this far in advance is generally regarded by industrial corporate officials as foolhardy. Now, what about the twenty-four vice-presidents, among whom is J. R. Welty, who partially took up the slack created by Hogan's departure? Over half of them were eligible in age for the presidency, and based upon the probabilities that usually obtain in this position, we may assume that over half of them probably felt frustrated by being passed over. No doubt Galvin wanted to create a line of succession to remove the uncertainty that attended Hogan's quitting, but he erected a barrier every bit as troublesome. As one mobile executive exclaimed upon hearing of this plan of succession, "It is very apparent to me that I've been entombed." Of course, some executives under similar conditions may hang on in the face of highly improbable odds. Unpredictable events may suddenly force aside succession plans. A project president with different skills may be required in five years and a hitherto unanointed executive may find himself thrust into the presidency, or key figures may suddenly expire or be forced to retire. Gamble, forty-four, at Pet Milk, suddenly died and forced overnight the careful contrivance of a new line of succession. While dreams and hopes may be validly built upon these arguments, still only a few from a bevy of vice-presidents can succeed to the top in the period of a decade. Aside from these probabilities, there are always more who think they can move up than the powers that be consider eligible. Obviously, some executives deceive themselves.

Because the executive is prone to commit self-deception with a minimum of encouragement from well-intentioned bosses, the quitter will not emerge in him until he breaks through his self-delusions. Few quitters do not psychologically "fire" their companies and rehire them several times before they actually acquire the resoluteness that guarantees eventual physical departure. This is the painful, tormenting process whereby the executive unmasks his own self-deceptions. But there is no force as formidable as that which takes over a mobile executive when he can delude himself no longer. When he announces that he is quitting, he has mentally gone already. There is very little a corporation can do to keep him. If he has promised himself the presidency, no amount of internal mobility short of the top job will be an adequate substitute. Nor will money suffice. Mobility and money or their equivalents will work only for the executive who is still deluded. When the true quitter utters "no" to these enticements to stay, he means "No, you had your chance," and out of pride he will leave because he cannot be had again. Always the public version of his quitting appears more sudden than the mental activity itself.

Much has been made of the reasons for quitting, and the digit "1" followed by a series of ciphers, preferably five, is presumed by many to have a magical hold on executives. The news media, pressed for space to account for the many quitters, may focus upon salary and other financial incentives. No doubt some increase in compensation is integral to the transaction. In August, 1968, when Woerner of IBM accepted the bid to head up Dallas-based Computer

Technology, he signed a five-year contract for $85,000 a year plus incentive pay of at least $10,000, options on 75,000 shares of Computer Technology stock, and a loan to buy 50,000 shares of stock immediately. By November, Computer Technology stock was selling at twelve times what Woerner had paid for it. Woerner became a millionaire before he could pack his bags and leave IBM.

As is so often the case, money was not the only reason for Woerner's departure. His friends at IBM reported that he saw in the offer an opportunity to turn the computer industry around by displacing in-house data processing staffs with his organization's staff. If Woerner can increase the profitable use of data processing equipment, he and his former company, IBM, the major manufacturer of computers, will greatly benefit. Also, knowing the inefficient use of data processing equipment by companies and governmental agencies, Woerner could hardly refuse the challenge.

The opportunity to be his own boss represents a dominant motive of successful winners. Late in April of 1968, Ken McAllister resigned his six-figure executive vice-presidency of Thomas J. Lipton, Inc., to become president of Mars, Inc., at about half his former salary. He showed the quitter's independence, self-confidence, and career loyalty when he explained that he was fully competent to hold the president's job and W. Gardner Barber, the president, was his same age and did not intend to give up the reins. He took about six months to get located with Mars. It is interesting to note that McAllister found his place finally after spending twenty years with General Electric, Columbia Records, Inc., and Benton & Bowles before he went to Lipton.

In a similar vein, Arthur W. Wishart left Corning Glass Works for Westinghouse to set up a large glass manufacturing division to produce for the company's own needs. Suddenly, Westinghouse reversed its tactics and continued buying its glass from Corning. A chance of a lifetime evaporated overnight. Wishart recalled that it was like retirement at full salary. With nothing to do, he quit. Later, he was given the chance to be boss at Knox Glass, a small, sick company on its last legs. He seized the opportunity to build something from scratch with his own hands.

A whole career may be spent to find challenge. Phillip W. Scott wandered in and out of companies before he found a job that would give full scope to his talent. He started his career with Dresser Industries in shipping, gradually moved up to secretary and treasurer of Bryan Heating Company, to vice-president of Affiliated Gas Equipment Company, to administrative vice-president of a division of Borg Warner, and then to Budd, where he became president and chief executive officer. Running a company in the rapid transit car industry was a tough assignment, but it proved challenging enough to keep his interest. Scott's advice, gained from his many arrivals and departures, is that a man should quit if he finds his job unworthy of his talents. This advice represents the true belief of a quitter.

The mobile executive is the big-business version of the small-business world's entrepreneur. It is normal for him to struggle for command rights. David J. Mahoney left the executive suite of Colgate Palmolive to become president and chief executive officer of Canada Dry, and later he became president of Norton Simon, Inc. Upon leaving he said, "I have the normal tendency to want to be boss, and here (Colgate Palmolive) they've got a good boss. I wouldn't leave though unless I thought I could make Canada Dry swing." Mahoney speaks instructively and authoritatively for the mobile executive. The entrepreneurial mentality considers it normal to want to be boss and to keep a steady eye out for the main chance. Walter Finke summed it up well when he left after eleven years with Honeywell to become president of ailing Dictaphone: "In general, someone in professional management is always attracted by the chance to be chief executive of a good company—to run it." [1]

To run it may not mean to own it or to build it from scratch. Yet it is a mistake to believe, as is common, that the mobile executive is entirely different from the entrepreneur who starts a business venture from scratch. They both want the feeling of initiating actions that flow from their individual talents and skills. This motive may be slow in capturing the full force of the personality. There are late bloomers among mobile executives as there are in entrepreneurial types of endeavor. But when the drive to be boss emerges in full

[1] *Fortune,* January, 1967, p. 42.

bloom, there is nothing more persistent. To be boss, to be account-able for the whole complex of men, money, and materials, is a so-phisticated version of the human need to be in control of circum-stances. This universal need is expressed in many forms and degrees of subtlety. In management it means to make things happen by will and design. The lure of a new, more challenging managerial job in another company beckons the mobile executive no matter how well-paid he may be.

James W. Wright was well-paid at Ford and had amassed a small fortune through his stock options. But he did not want to sit out a long wait for the presidency, never being sure he would get it. So he quit and was picked up by Federal Mogul Corporation as president and chief executive officer. He ran into a conservative board, domi-nated by several retired executives and a chairman who was not ready for Wright's flair for acquisitions and his strong management style. The struggle came to a head when the board overruled Wright and voted to sell Federal to Bendix Corp. Wright would have become a division head, a position he previously held in the much larger Ford Motor Company. Wright balked and issued an ultimatum, only to find that after he had isolated himself the board reversed itself because of hints from the United States Trust Depart-ment that the deal with Bendix might not be approved. Now Wright, fifty-five, had time to enjoy the money he made at Ford from his stock options. However, this usually proves small consola-tion to a man who has put his career on the line.

Opportunity and money are two of the most powerful lures, and while there may be others, these may represent the minimum. We may suggest that these two motives overlap. In a larger sense, money affords the opportunity to be in charge of life's opportuni-ties. In this sense, money may be more of an incentive to change for the financially unestablished executive than for men like Wright who have enough to live comfortably. For them, money is a kind of indicator of how much their efforts are appreciated. Many were mis-led when Semon E. Knudsen chalked up a $181,000 paper profit by using his options to buy 10,038 General Motors shares a few days before he quit to become Ford's president. His new contract called for stock options and bonuses that would surpass those offered Ernest Breech, who is credited with saving the ailing Ford Motor Company in the postwar years. A deeper purpose lies in this unprecedented job hop. Knudsen wanted to hold the reins and prove his mettle, and it was unlikely that he could ever be chief executive officer of General Motors. He had inherited millions of dollars from his father, who was once president of General Motors. At the time of his job hop, he held 42,507 General Motors shares worth more than $3.3 million. When it became apparent to him that his arch rival, Edward N. Cole, had been nominated to the presidency, "Bunkie" Knudsen could have sat back and managed his many financial interests. In part, General Motors's lavish bonus plan was intended to allow men passed over to live with dignity and in comfort. But not Knudsen. He and many financially established executives during the past decade chose to quit.

Keeping money and challenge in the background, we may note the function of momentum. The greatest threat to the mobile executive is the arrest of his upward mobility. Boredom represents the lack of challenge. Anxiety ensues from the inability to remove obstacles to his upward mobility. The mobile executive is not threatened by boredom but by an uncertain future. He is most prone to the effects of career anxiety in or near the executive suite. Here the demand for continuing momentum runs into a structural characteristic of the corporation. At the top he incurs the vulnerability of being blocked, sidetracked, or otherwise terminated at the vice-presidential level or its equivalent. Arrested upward mobility, one step away from the presidency, represents the ultimate risk. After all, the sloping sides of the corporate pyramid guarantee very little room at the top. General Electric, for example, in the decade of the sixties, had three presidents but fifty-four vice-presidents. General Motors plucked three presidents from a bevy of fifty vice-presidents. AT&T had forty-three vice-presidents, three presidents. IBM had nearly forty and three. Of course, not every vice-president wants to be president. As many as half are happy to remain in second rank. But scratch an executive and one will probably discover a future president. At least, he has promised himself the presidency, and this capacity to self-nominate greatly increases the probability that he will eventually become a chief executive.

The comparison between vice-presidents who broke out of their positions and those who stayed in them reveals a crucial dimension of winning that is not well-understood. We must first note that the presidents did not stay at the second level below or its equivalent much longer than seven years. The question that faces the vice-president who has put in his seven years concerns what to do next. Some may stay and take their chances, but others may leave to become presidents of other corporations. They move before they experience intolerable amounts of career anxiety. One of the executives most apt to leave had traversed the whole corporate hierarchy. In full-route types the itch to take the last step is directly proportionate to three variables, all of which represent mobility rates. They are the duration of his nonmanagerial career, the degree of incline in the managerial ranks, and the diversity of his experiences. Vice-presidents who start their careers at the bottom in nonmanagerial jobs and move swiftly to managerial responsibilities acquire huge amounts of confidence. Most full-route presidents worked three years or less as nonmanagers before they were given managerial responsibilities. The more time it takes to become spotted as managerial timber, the less will be the executive's confidence that he can go the full route. His urge to become president will be further increased by the steepness of his incline to the vice-presidency. In addition, if he has been in at least two functional areas in addition to his specialty and at least another division besides the one he started with, the expectation of becoming a president will be gradually transformed into the telltale promise that identifies the vice-president who will never allow himself to become blocked or sidetracked.

Among split-route executives who bypassed the nonmanagerial level and part of the lower supervisory routes, such as when the young man is brought in as an assistant to the president or some member or near-member of the executive suite, the capacity to self-nominate depends upon the speed of the ascent and the degree of cross-functional and divisional mobility. However, these split-route types with this unkickable habit of success usually came into their entrance positions in staff assignments. Hence, the less time an executive spent in staff before becoming a line manager, the more likely that he would not be able to adjust to a second-rank future.

The attempt to develop executives did not set out to breed presidents per se, but this was the indirect result. The shortening of the distance to the top, the acceleration of the rate of climb, and the increase in the diversity of experience produced executives with strong capacities of self-nomination. They promised themselves the presidency. Frustrated by the prospect of years of servitude in a vice-presidential job, these mobile men took off for opportunities in other corporations. Hence, the executive suite became a conduit to the outside. The more mobile the executive, the more prone he was to go outside. During the latter half of the sixties, the egress rate of full- and part-route vice-presidents shot up to the degree that keeping a talented second-string team became a principal challenge for many chief executives. One such first-stringer complained, "We brought them along rapidly and made them vice-presidents, often ahead of many men senior in experience, age, and tenure. But before they got themselves established as vice-president they left for presidencies of other corporations." We must reaffirm that if the executive thought that he had a good chance of becoming president, he would probably have stayed. But the uncertainty of this probability forced the executive to practice self-nomination. Hence, challenge, money, and the drive to reduce career anxiety represent a trilogy of needs that variously relate to the act of quitting.

It should be indicated at this time that not all quitting is done to improve one's managerial opportunities. The executive may egress because he wants more technical challenge or to maintain his momentum. No doubt this was the factor behind Baughn Beal's leaving North American Aviation after a decade as director of research to assume the same post at Cummins Engine in a brand new $23-million research center. Beal cashed in his many achievements at North American for the challenge of exploring the possibilities of producing a commercial turbine engine that would be as light and powerful as a diesel. The challenge was there for Beal if for no other reason than that J. Erwin Miller, chairman, had his own money on the outcome. To ensure the success of both the old and new ventures, Miller raised Beal to head of the domestic engine division. There he had a better chance to make sure that his division got the necessary resources and attention to bring off the successful development of the turbine engine.

If Beal relocated for the sake of greater technical challenges,

Theodore H. Maiman relocated to find a more permissive and comfortable environment. He, too, was not concerned about managerial mobility, although he discovered a latent desire to manage for the purpose of producing better technical results. While at Hughes Research Laboratory in 1960, Dr. Maiman acquired a luminous reputation for developing the laser—the word stands for "light amplification by stimulated emissions of radiation." While developing the project, he got little support, and one superior even tried to phase out his project because he thought Maiman was wasting his time. When the laser beam was working, he received sudden support from the most unexpected places, but not from the budget—the most likely place from which to expect support. When Maiman was ordered to get some research and development contracts from the government, he immediately became outward bound because he did not fancy himself a fund raiser. He relocated at Quanton, a small electronics laboratory where he could become a big fish in a small pond. Unfortunately, it turned out that the president wanted Maiman to put the company in the laser business, for which there was no available market. He relocated again to Union Carbide to work in the autonomous Korad Corporation. While fighting to keep it autonomous he managed to build a market for the laser, and Korad grossed over $3 million in sales in 1967.

The quitter must have a high degree of self-regard. He must be firmly convinced about who he is and what he wants to become. This self-insight permits him to relocate. The study of quitters reveals that they gain tremendous insight into themselves that cannot be gained any other way. Maiman discovered that Hughes Aircraft, like other big aerospace companies, was a poorly managed conglomeration of scientists and engineers with a tremendous turnover, lots of red tape, political bushwacking, and concern about status and position rather than job. He decided to go to a small company, Quanton, and found that they were poorly managed too. He then set out for a large corporation which allowed him to spin off a separate autonomous venture, only to discover that that environment was not to his liking either. He left and formed his own enterprise in Los Angeles, Maiman Associates, to help set up and advise on new high-technology enterprise. At this point he changed roles from a distinguished scientist to a fledgling businessman. He was deeply challenged by the opportunity to rationalize science, organization, and entrepreneurship. His introduction into this new role of businessman was not without pain and anxiety. For a scientist it seldom is. But he is at the top of a business now and leaves behind a string of lessons from which others can learn about how to manage men. And it may be said that the insight he will gain about himself as an entrepreneur and manager of his own business firm may cause him to move again to another role or environment.

Hence, self-insight backstopped by the trilogy of momentum, money, and motivation constitutes the makeup of the typical quitter. There are other factors that represent peripheral or precipitating conditions. These lie in the environment, while the basic causes inhere in the executive himself. The structural condition of the pyramid which we have previously identified may be considered a situational factor. Another situational factor concerns an executive team backstopped by young, aggressive talent. For example, Bell & Howell has always wanted its presidents young. Charles Percy, a director at twenty-three and president at twenty-nine, was succeeded by Peter G. Peterson, thirty-four. Seeing his path blocked, William E. Roberts, forty-four, executive vice-president, quit to become president of Ampex Corporation. We have previously noted how companies that vigorously recruit young managers and force feed them in a corporate training program are most apt to find that they have unintentionally created a log jam at the near top. This is especially likely if the corporation is not growing as fast as it is grooming men for command positions. It is paradoxically correct that growth corporations attract and develop talent better and, in turn, talent may be better developed by and attracted to growth firms. It is easier to move into new positions opened up by growth requirements than to climb over a set number of men in fixed positions. When growth is not fast enough to absorb talent, young executives and old may feel the squeeze. Seen in this light, it is not by accident that as the age level of top executives declined, the quit rate went up. A case in point was Lloyd M. Powell's effort at Dictaphone Corp. to lower the average age of managers to forty-four years from sixty. A few years later the corporation lost three of its most able young managers and the quit rate was far higher than before the youth drive. Apparently, Powell did not have faith in his young management team, because two years later he brought in Walter W. Finke as chief executive officer from Honeywell. Finke, fifty-nine, and Powell, sixty-seven, had to put people in charge to avoid reaching outside again for replacements.

Youth is not without its problems. Whether the top team is uniformly young as at Bell & Howell, or half young and half old as at Dictaphone, rivalry between generations represents another common basis for relocating. John Lawrence, forty-six, president of Joy Manufacturing, could not get along with L. F. Rains, sixty-four, head of the executive committee. William L. Wearly, forty-two, next assumed the presidency, and after four years of intergenerational conflict, resigned "for personal reasons" and was replaced by James A. Drain, fifty-eight. In Fairbanks Whitney Corporation, Alfons Landa, sixty-four, resumed the chair of the executive committee. He resigned when the board blocked his attempt to oust president Dave Darr, forty-three, Landa's one-time crony and proxy-day ally.

Similarly, forty-three-year-old Raymond Rich left Philco to become president of Avco and ran into chairman Victor Emanuel. Considerably younger than the top man was Marshall S. Lackner, forty-three, when he clashed with the chairman of the Pabst Brewing Co., Harriss Perlstein. Formerly a vice-president of Colgate Palmolive Co., Lachner threw in the towel and built a successful consulting firm.

The quitting of Lawrence, Wearly, Karr, Rich, and Lachner occurred during the middle to late 1950s. In this period intergenerational strife was widespread. Wide age discrepancy between superior and subordinate was a relatively new phenomenon, and the older generation was ambivalent about recruiting young men for positions immediately below it. The young men were more educated and were more mobile and susceptible to accepting an offer to move. In time, the idea became more acceptable, largely because the younger breed proved themselves. But it was a rough period for each generation.

In many cases, a wide discrepancy in ages will not be the precipitating factor. The situation will represent conflict over policies, objectives, or organizational format and, of course, a generational gap will tend to magnify differences and arguments. Under the leadership of William C. Stolk, American Can acquired Marathon Paper Company, and its president, Roy J. Sund, was made head of the parent company. Sund was plainly ticketed to become the chief executive officer when Stolk reached the mandatory retirement age of sixty-five. Now, Sund believed in a highly decentralized structure in opposition to the highly centralized organization that Stolk was building. Roy Sund resigned because he did not want to take over a company that did not have his style. Sund went over to Champion Paper and took George Walker with him. It was up to William F. May, fifty-one, to transform American Can from a fragmented federation of almost autonomous divisions into a highly centralized operating structure. His president was Elmer T. Klassen, who was in the running with May for the chief executive job when Stolk stepped down. He had come from manufacturing and May had come from planning. At the annual meeting in 1968, the shareholders were told of the sudden resignation of president E. T. Klassen. His decision was due to a difference of opinion regarding policies of the company. The exact nature of this conflict was never revealed by Klassen or May. It was ironical that Klassen's sudden departure forced the division heads to once again act like presidents. Until May filled the void made by Klassen's departure, Canco was a tightly centralized organization without strong operating direction.

Roy Sund went to work for U.S. Plywood–Champion Papers, Inc. Karl Bendestsen had been the head of U.S. Plywood and proposed to Gene C. Brewer, the head of Champion Paper, that their two corporations merge. Bendestsen was to be chairman of the merged company, U.S. Plywood–Champion Papers, and Brewer the president, but they were to share the chief executive's authority in a kind of office-of-the-president arrangement. They would have made a complementary team in that Bendestsen was a hard-driving, brusque executive and Brewer a soft-spoken, warm type. But Bendestsen wanted to reorganize the executive staff to make division executive vice-presidents and won approval from the board. He was appointed chief executive officer. Brewer would be supervising several presidents of relatively autonomous divisions. He felt sand-wiched in between Bendestsen and these division vice-presidents and quit. Sund, who left Canco because he wanted the divisions strong, fell heir to the presidency of one of the divisions. It was an ironical twist of fate made no less probable by his capacity to quit.

In most instances a resignation without explanation of "for per-sonal reasons" is a code message for deep personal conflict of a de-gree that cannot be rationally expressed. The suddenness of the de-parture leaves the arch rival in a very bad situation that cannot help but reflect adversely upon him. Power struggles may break into the open because the central figure acquires a reputation for being difficult to work with. Charles F. Adams, Jr., formerly a part-ner in an investment banking firm, was given the reins of Ray-theon. Adams proved to be a poor administrator and, under the strain of a massive number of military contracts, he brought in Har-old S. Geneen for relief. The new executive vice-president clamped on tight cost controls and made deliveries on time. Up went the price of stock from $15 in 1956 to $70 in 1959. Differences with Adams over authority caused Geneen to move to International Tel-ephone & Telegraph and Adams picked up as his next president Richard E. Krafve, who had headed up the ill-starred Edsel project at Ford. Krafve, a vice-president, took up where Geneen left off and built the management team. Thomas L. Phillips, forty, vice-presi-dent of the Missile and Space Division, was passed over Krafve for executive vice-president. Krafve immediately resigned without com-ment and Phillips took over. The dispute in both cases centered around the boundaries of authority of president and chairman. In-tegral to the dispute was the fact that Adams was fifty-one, Krafve fifty-four, and Geneen forty-nine. Adams was too young to begin thinking of retirement and the other two were too young to stand in the wings. While Krafve might have been mollified by adequate amounts of authority, Geneen wanted Adams's job. In any case, Raytheon underwent four major management shifts in eight years.

The shakeout at American Airlines after years of management turmoil produced many quitters. G. Marion Saddler, fifty-three, stepped in between two rough veterans of the skyways: C. P. Smith, president since 1934, and William J. Hogan, sixty-one, executive vice-president. Saddler was made president in January of 1964 and Hogan chief financial officer. George A. Spater, fifty-four, was made vice-chairman. In October, Saddler resigned for personal reasons. A week later Smith had succeeded in persuading Saddler to change his mind and return to the presidency. The conflict stemmed from circumscription of Saddler's authority. Hogan, Spater, and Saddler reported to Smith. Hogan was responsible for long-range planning in addition to his financial duties. Saddler felt that he could not responsibly determine the competitive strength of the firm if he could not influence the financial and capital programs. Apparently Smith had intended to train Saddler for the job by not giving him all the responsibilities normally accorded the president. The power struggle caused many vice-presidents to leave and neither Hogan nor Saddler became chief executive officer. In 1968, Spater became chief executive officer. Saddler, after undergoing two operations, resigned, as did Hogan after suspecting that Spater had the inside track. The winner picked up all the pieces of authority that Smith divided up among the triumvirate.

But such was not the case of Curtis Publishing. The power struggle at Curtis started over the issue of corporate objectives and policies and ended in a great palace revolt against top authority in which no winners emerged. The word of the revolt eventually became widespread in the trade and raised public attention. This great corporate disaster focused initially around a junta composed of editor-in-chief Clay Blair, Jr., thirty-nine, and Marvin D. Kanter, thirty-seven, chairman of the Curtis magazine division. The man they were out to topple was president and board chairman Mathew J. Culligan, forty-six, brought in two years earlier to restore to health the ailing company. In addition to these chiefs, the junta included thirteen top-ranking editors and advertising executives. The head of what was once the greatest magazine publishing empire in the world was under attack by a youthful congeries whose principal charge was mismanagement. With strong indirect support from representatives of leading bankers, Blair and Kanter took their case to the board, composed of fifteen members, including six who were holdovers from the family group that controls one-third of the stock. The stodgy, conservative board refused to heed their advice in spite of the fact that corporate losses continued to add up: $4 million in 1961, $19 million in 1962, $3.5 million in 1963, and $2 million in the first half of 1964. The situation, having gone from bad to worse while the board sold off assets to keep operating, required drastic action. The junta, led by Blair, convened a secret meeting in a restaurant near Greenwich, Connecticut, and framed a bill of particulars which they sent to the board. The fifteen rebels served notice that they intended to resign en masse unless Culligan was relieved of command. After being suspended by the board, Blair and Kanter quit, as did eventually a half-dozen other junta members. Later, the revolving door caught Culligan, who was asked to step down. But the power struggle was not over and the junta had achieved very little. The two chairmen who succeeded Culligan failed to stem the tide of huge, uncontrollable losses. Finally, Martin S. Ackerman, thirty-six, a securities lawyer from Rochester, New York, who put together Perfect Film and Chemical, invested $5 million to cut down Curtis to profitable size. In 1967 he dissolved the company that published the venerable *Saturday Evening Post*.

It is easy to miss the right step and quit the wrong job or quit the right job for the wrong reasons. The consequence may prove disastrous in either case. To quit or not to quit—that is, of course, a career question; but the answer will first depend upon the way one handles the blocks to his authority, and each executive has a style of removing blocks. In less than seven years, John L. Burns quit three jobs, never having satisfactorily resolved the problem of control and authority. Burns graduated from college (B.S., Northwestern University; Ph.D., Harvard) in 1934 and after a short stint of teaching at Lehigh University, he went to work for Republic Steel in Chicago as a common laborer. He was quickly identified as talented and was placed in charge of the research laboratory. A year later he was promoted to plant manager of the wire mill and, despite a strike, he put the mill on a profitable basis. He next accepted a job as management consultant for Booz, Allen, and Hamilton and in one year was made a general partner. In his position as partner in charge of the RCA account, he attracted General David Sarnoff's attention. General Sarnoff *was* RCA and asked Burns to study RCA for purposes of reorganization. For ten years he was in and out of RCA, but never as an employee. He started his public career in 1957 as chief operations officer of RCA at the age of forty-seven. Whereas color TV became a moneymaker under his leadership, his ambitious plans for data processing and control products affected the profit picture adversely. Burns resigned for "personal reasons." He vowed never to accept a position without full powers of control.

In 1961 he set up a group of businessmen to buy Rawlings Sporting Goods Company, but, wanting the helm again, he accepted the offer of the board of directors of Cities Service to become chief executive officer. In 1965, at the age of fifty-seven and a lot wiser, Burns completely reorganized the dilapidated organization and management. Sales and profits increased spectacularly and he turned his agile mind to find in conglomerates the key to still further increases in sales and profits. The board, in a series of highly controversial and intense discussions, resisted. When he saw his power checked by important stockholders working through the board, Burns, fifty-nine, quit again and joined the board of Studebaker-Worthington and the executive committee. The question is: What did he achieve by quitting? He did not have to quit RCA or Cities Service. He could have tempered his ambitious data processing plans by taking the sage advice of several elder statesmen and well-intentioned colleagues. He did not have to push quite as hard, all at once, in Cities Service for his conglomerate plans. As a matter of principle, Burns left when he found his power checked. A cue to his style of quitting is found in his inability to use tact and diplomacy and salesmanship to remove the power block.

Leaving when the going gets rough is characteristic of the quitting style of Pasquale J. Casella. Starting his career as a store manager for Montgomery Ward, he moved to RCA and acquired during Burn's regime a reputation as a hard-driving, relentless executive. After becoming president of Canadian operations and director of a wholly owned subsidiary, he was made vice-president of the parent company in charge of the messy consumer products division. With costs out of hand, he cut them sharply and inadvertently reduced quality control. His high-handed "Napoleonic" style produced a harsh reaction and many enemies. He was removed and found a job in the international division. After six months he quit, and after six months of unemployment he became senior vice-president in 1961 of Endicott Johnson and returned to his home town, Endicott, New York. Pat Casella, forty-eight, was made president when it became apparent that his troubleshooting, cost-reducing skills needed the backstop of the president's office. Endicott Johnson was struggling for its life and they at first accepted his harsh measures; but by 1963 he had succeeded in alienating the family members. A $700,000 net loss only abetted his enemies. He abruptly quit. He next joined the Elgin National Watch Company as president and chief executive officer. But not all the board members supported his nomination. The president of Zale Jewelry, who annually placed orders amounting to 5 percent of Elgin's gross sales and was guarantor of some of its debts, viewed him as a bull in a china closet and brought in his own man, Irving Stein, to be chief executive officer. Casella as president barely survived the power struggle, but he was denied a seat on the board. Stein became chairman. The inevitable happened—Casella left. A very common quitting style is to "leave before one has to."

Louis T. Rader represents an interesting quitting style. This Illinois Institute of Technology professor who had worked for General Electric returned to GE and, after a rapid set of promotions tapered off, was left in the wings much too long to suit him. Harold S. Geneen of International Telephone & Telegraph picked him up at age forty-nine and made him vice-president. Geneen, who believes that if you cannot change your environment you should get out, gave Rader his head, and he promptly made the division over in his own image. A year and a half later he received a call from Dause L. Bilby, a dropout from IBM and now head of the Remington Rand Division of Sperry Rand. Bilby saw in Rader the ideal match for his troublesome Univac Division. Plagued with frequent changes of top management, personality clashes, stubborn middle managers, and obsolete facilities, Rader accepted the challenge, as it looked similar to the situation he had successfully dealt with at ITT. In 1963 Rader headed the division when it was set apart from Remington Rand, but he unfortunately made a prediction that Univac would end up in the black in 1963. It did not by a long shot, and Vickers,

the head of Sperry Rand, wanted to know why. He put Frank Forster in charge of a task force to investigate Univac. Rader saw the
true meaning of this move. Vickers was the president, chief executive officer, and largest single stockholder in Sperry Rand. He
thought a lot of Frank Forster. They were close friends and compatible at work. Forster had successfully headed Vickers' hydraulic division and ran it so efficiently that he became widely suspected as
heir apparent. Bilby's job was dissolved and the Rand units were
split up. When he quit, he left his protégé, Rader, exposed. Having
stood in the wings too long at General Electric, he was not about to
make the same mistake again. He quit to head up the industrial
electronics division at General Electric. His decision was correct. J.
Frank Forster became president of Sperry Rand in 1965 and chairman and chief executive officer in 1967. Forster had for some time
been groomed for the top job. He had the inside track over all others. Rader was without sponsorship.

Unwise, careless quitting can produce the worst of all blocks,
causing the executive to pull the ejection string. Robert O. Fickes
went to work for General Electric in 1932 and, after completing his
business training program, he started a slow, plodding rise, as was
customary in those times, up the ladder to manager of the electric
blanket and fan department. After thirty years in General Electric,
nine of them as department manager, he quit. He did not want to
spend the rest of his life as a department manager. Fickes had been
too long in one department, a nonpriority department at that, to be
eligible for broad corporate assignments. During his last ten years at
GE he had been bypassed by many younger men. But age is one
block that cannot be removed simply by quitting. So much depends
upon where the executive goes and the peculiar characteristics of
his new managerial environment. The older the executive, the more
cautious he should be in choosing his options. He must be careful
to find the precise environment that matches the energies and style
belonging to his age. Fickes moved to Elgin National Watch, a politically upset organization in which various forces were contending
for power. Fickes never knew what hit him, so accustomed was he
to doing his job with the implied consent and support of his superiors. Because of a disagreement with the owners and board members,

Fickes left after thirteen months. He had no immediate job open to him. Several months later he moved to head up Borg-Warner's Norge appliance division. While back into elements akin to his General Electric experience, he was far afield from his abilities. He quit to become vice-president of Ford and president of Ford's Philco subsidiary. If there ever was a politically, financially, and managerially explosive environment, this was it. An apparent policy dispute with Semon Knudsen got the best of him and he quit the job in 1968. Fickes, a late bloomer, never knew when to quit quitting, but he also never knew how to pick his next spot.

The quitter must be flexible enough to change his mind if events change to cause improvement in his situation. Patience pays off quite often. Charles S. Mitchell rose steadily to the executive vice-presidency of Cities Service Co. after joining the firm in 1930. In late 1965, both the presidency and chairmanship were open due to retirements. Just as he thought he had one of the jobs in hand, John L. Burns moved in from RCA as chairman and chief executive officer. Mitchell got the consolation prize of the presidency but was not particularly happy. Burns, fifty-seven, was only a year older than Mitchell, who could see himself retiring in step with the chief officer. Mitchell saw Burns develop difficulties with the board and decided to bide his time. He stayed clear of the fracas that developed over Burns's aggressive acquisition program and inherited the top job when Burns quit two years later.

Leaving now the several reasons for and styles of quitting, we may next explore the problems that besiege corporations. One problem arises because an outbreak of quitting may reverberate through the executive echelons and strip a corporation of its most promising talent. Shortly after Virgil Boyd was brought to Chrysler by Lynn Townsend, the president, from American Motors where he had made a spectacular record, he succeeded to the presidency after Townsend became chairman. Boyd's subordinate, John Riccardo, was moved into the job Boyd vacated to become president. Two years later, Boyd was sidelined to vice-chairmanship and Riccardo made president. However, Robert Anderson had once supervised Riccardo and found himself now working for his former subordinate. This proved unworkable and Anderson was moved out of the line of succession into the vice-presidency for planning and development. He quit to become president of the Commercial Products Division of North American Rockwell Corp. and later became executive vice-president of the corporation. In 1970 he became president. Meanwhile, back at American Motors, Boyd's leaving helped Victor G. Raviola, former Ford executive, to become number-three man after William Luneburg, president, and Roy Chapin, chairman. But he, too, got caught up in a log jam at the top. Chapin was fifty-two years old and Luneburg fifty-five, which meant that Raviola, fifty-four, would retire one year later than Luneburg and two years before Chapin, the chief executive officer. Rather than wait around for a truck to run over either one, Raviola quit.

This chain reaction that went through Chrysler and American Motors was more noticeable in "Bunky" Knudsen's job hop from executive vice-president of General Motors to president of Ford. Almost overlooked in the excitement of this supermove was the fact that, to make room for Knudsen, Arjay Miller was bumped from the president's chair of Ford and out of the line of succession to the chief executive job. Henry Ford II created the job of vice-chairman of the board and Miller was given long-range problems to solve. Shortly after Knudsen arrived at Ford, Miller decided to drain the gasoline from his veins and become dean of Stanford's Graduate School of Business. The vice-chairmanship was dissolved when Miller left in 1969. Caught in this squeeze at the top was Lee (Mr. I) Iacocca, who at forty-three was in direct line for succession to the presidency. That was before "Bunky" showed up. Still, Mr. I of Mustang fame could afford to sit around and absorb the attitudes of his new mentor while he headed up the billion-dollar Ford car operations and later the Lincoln-Mercury division. But age was working against his vice-president for product development, Donald N. Frey, forty-five. After seventeen years with Ford and unwilling to wait behind a superior younger than he was, Donald Frey quit. With twenty years of career time ahead of him, Frey took his small fortune and considerable management savvy to General Cable Corporation. As president, Frey succeeded A. Leon Fergenson, fifty-six, who became chairman and continued as chief executive officer. Both Knudsen and Frey had decided to quit before they had other jobs.

Meanwhile, back at General Motors, things were never to be the same. When Edward N. Cole won by a narrow margin the board's vote for presidency, the organization chart was redrawn to provide a division of labor at the top unlike any in GM history. It was drawn to make use of the talents of the men available to manage. James M. Roche, sixty, was chairman and chief executive officer. George Russell was vice-chairman of the board and chairman of the finance committee. Knudsen, executive vice-president, was responsible for the 20 percent of the business that belonged to nonautomotive United States operations and GM overseas business. Cole, of course, was president and was responsible for 80 percent of the business— domestic autos and trucks.

Knudsen did not report to arch rival Cole but to chairman Roche. It was clear that both Cole and Roche were extending themselves to take account of Knudsen. When Knudsen left for Ford, Edward Bollert was named to Knudsen's post, but not to head the GM Canadian division as Knudsen had. He was responsible to Cole rather than Roche. Harold G. Warner was elected to the board and promoted to Bollert's post. Then Donald L. Boyes was appointed to succeed Warner; Richard L. Terrell to succeed Boyes; and Harold W. Campbell elected to vice-president and general manager of the Frigidaire division. Although the final toll of moves is not known, the author was able to chart, with the help of several aides, some thirty-five moves in GM and Ford that occurred as a consequence of Knudsen's move. A man who quits sets in motion a swirl of forces that can lead to unpredictable consequences. Some of these consequences represent chain reactions that cut across corporate boundaries to create simultaneous chain reactions in several firms. When men quit and join other corporations, they cause others to quit in numbers that exceed their arithmetic proportions. Even the men who stay may have their careers greatly affected. In a mobile world there is no such thing as immobility, even for those who want it.

Another problem with quitting is that it builds a momentum of its own. Soon a whole industry may be infested with quitters. This spiraling effect ensues directly from the quitter's intelligent understanding of career blocks. He removed *his* barricades by quitting and now realizes as a chief executive that he must be careful to not block others or *he* will lose good men, too. Thus, a quitter is most apt to give men challenge and opportunity. But at some time the sloping apex will produce more men eligible for the top than there is room for. Thus they too will quit, and thus quitters will unintentionally produce quitters. Two examples may serve to illustrate this spiraling effect.

Under the guiding genius of Charles B. (Tex) Thornton, the cofounder, Litton Industries has unintentionally become a major breeder of quitters (and leveragers). Litton graduates have flooded the executive suites of major corporations. They refer to themselves as "LIdos," an acronym for Litton Industries dropouts. These executives were turned on by Thornton's philosophy of maximum autonomy and mobility. After climbing to the executive suite, they move on to occupy, usually, one of the three top spots in other companies or to start their own companies.

Many who moved into the top job immediately upon dropping out of Litton were quitters and others were leveragers. They included William E. McKenna, president of Hunt Foods & Industries; Russell W. McFall, chairman of Western Union Telegraph; George T. Scharffenberger, president of City Investing Co.; Frank R. Moothart, vice-president and treasurer, Republic Corporation; Seymour M. Rosenberg, executive vice-president of Mattel, Inc.; Frederick J. Mayo, senior vice-president, American Export Industries, Inc.; and Fred R. Sullivan, chairman of Walter Kidde & Co. Henry Singleton started his own company, Teledyne, Inc., as did Crosby Kelly of Crosby Kelly Associates.

The moment each of these left, another executive received a promotion. The departure of McKenna allowed Litton to move up five promising executives, and their application of fresh skills and minds more than offset the loss of any one key executive. With the loss of these many talented executives, most companies whose sales grossed nearly a billion dollars or more would collapse, but not Litton. It was disgustingly healthy with reserve strength. To Thornton, a certain number of quitters is healthy in that it revitalizes the organization by the replacements that come forth to fill the voids.

The key to understanding the capacity to breed quitters at Litton is found in the background of Tex Thornton, who is himself a dropout from Ford and Hughes Aircraft. After World War II Henry Ford II, twenty-eight, eager to revitalize the ailing Ford Motor Car Company, made a deal with ten young officers who were itching to try out in private business the statistical financial controls that were developed in the Air Force. His group included Colonel Charles B. Thornton, the leader, Robert S. McNamara, James O. Wright, Ben D. Mills, Arjay Miller, J. Edward Lundy, Charles E. Bosworth, W. R. Anderson, George Moore, and F. C. Reith. Ernest R. Breech had been brought in earlier to be president. He brought with him Lewis D. Crusoe and promoted from within Delmar S. Harder. The Breech-Crusoe-Harder team in turn moved in a dozen or so men above the Thornton group, so that Thornton decided that the management environment was not conducive to his objectives. Thornton quit in the spring of 1968. Eventually most of the "whiz kids," as they had become known, left. Reith became president of the Crosley Division of Avco Manufacturing Co.; Moore became an automobile dealer; Anderson went to California to manage Bekins Van and Storage Company; Wright moved over to head Federal Mogul Corporation; McNamara became Secretary of Defense; and Miller, as we noted, became dean of Stanford a year after being relieved of the presidency of Ford.

Thornton moved on to Hughes Aircraft as vice-president and assistant manager and in five years helped to increase sales from $82 million to $200 million. He came into conflict with Howard Hughes, as he had earlier at Ford with Harder, and struck out for himself, taking with him Roy Ash, assistant controller, Hugh Jamieson, research scientist, and Henry Singleton. With the help of Lehman Brothers, he invested $1,500,000 in a small, highly profitable producer of microwave tubes, Litton Industries in San Carlos, California. Thornton and Ash practiced assiduously their formula of giving youth unlimited autonomy and authority, routine mobility, and careful coaching and guidance. The result was a free-forming organization and informal managerial style that kept them in rapid motion and, of course, spun off a goodly number of quitters (and leveragers).

A second major breeder of quitters (and leveragers) is International Telephone & Telegraph. Under chairman Harold Geneen, ITT has been growing so fast that it has not had time to develop enough of its own executives. This is in spite of the fact that Harold Geneen is believed to be a wizard at spotting and developing executive talent. The alumni of ITT include the following presidents and chairmen of major corporations: George A. Strickman, chairman of Colt Industries; Richard H. Griebel, president of P. Ballantine & Sons; Neil Firestone, president of Turner Corporation; William M. Duke, president of Whittaker Corporation; C. J. Witting, president of Crouse-Hinds Co.; M. H. Dubihier, chairman of Esterline; Glenn W. Bailey, chairman of Keene Corporation; J. C. Lobb, president of Crucible Steel Co.; Henry E. Bowes, president of McCall Corporation; D. J. Margolas, president of Colt Industries; J. A. Unker, president of Astrodata, Inc.; Cortes W. Randell, president of National Student Marketing Corporation; Gerhard R. Andlinger, chairman of Esterline; John Morse, president of Gerber Life Insurance Co.; Robert Kenmore, chairman of Family Bargain Centers; Earl H. Tiffany, president of Bartell Media Corp.; David C. Scott, president of Allis-Chalmers; and John W. Thompson, chairman of Advance Ross Corp.

In addition, ex-ITT men, often referred to as "exITTs," are presidents of over twenty other companies or other subsidiaries. Such exITTs hold high executive positions in Litton Industries, Colt Industries, Electronic Association, Celanese, Teletronic Systems, Singer, General Dynamics, and General Electric. Some twenty-nine entrepreneurs, including Randell and Morse, were once with Geneen and split off to found their own companies.

The chief product of Geneen's president machine is Geneen himself. As a dropout, he practiced firmly the quitter's belief that if he cannot change his environment to please himself, he should get out of it. After studying accounting at night school and working during the day as a Wall Street page boy, Geneen in 1934 went to work for the accounting firm of Lybrand, Ross Bros. & Montgomery. With his C.P.A., he moved to the accounting department of American Can, to the controllership of Bell & Howell, and then, in 1950, he became assistant to the president of Jones & Laughlin Steel. During the early fifties, Geneen was interviewed for the controllership of Chrysler by Tex Colbert, who suspected that Geneen was so ambitious that he would have tried to take Colbert's job away from him. Unhappy with a dominating, suffocating boss at Jones & Laughlin, Geneen next left for Raytheon, where he made a great name for himself. After World War II, Raytheon found itself saddled with shallow management and sagging earnings. The founder, L. K. Manball, went outside to snatch Charles F. Adams from an investment banking firm in Boston to assist him in rebuilding the organization. Before he could rebuild Raytheon, it became deluged with military contracts in the mid-1950s. Adams called in Harold Geneen as executive vice-president and gave him the simple mandate, "make some money." Geneen installed controls, moved out the deadwood, made deliveries on time, and started to build a management team. Earnings went from $2 million in 1956 to $11 million in 1959, and Raytheon stock jumped to $70 from $15. However, Adams wanted to keep his hand on the wheel while Geneen was trying to drive. So Geneen left in 1959 to join ITT. He built ITT from a company of $700 million sales in 1950 to nearly $3 billion in 1969, all the while increasing earnings every quarter for thirty-four consecutive quarters.

To build and sustain this earning growth, Geneen had to excel in identifying and developing competent, aggressive executives. He got them wherever he could find them, mostly from outside the corporation. Men who could not adapt to his acquisitive-minded, control-dominated, and detail-oriented managerial style quit or were fired. From the United States government he got Harry Perry, from investment banking he got John C. Lobb, and from General Electric he picked up Louis J. Rader. From RCA he selected John Graham, Glen Bailey came from Chrysler, and John Ireland, Jr., left Alleghany Corporation for ITT. Within one month he hired three men away from McKinsey Company, including Martin Dubihier. Four men had been presidents of companies before they joined Geneen at ITT.

Geneen's formula is only slightly different from Tex Thornton's. He presses much harder on details and holds his men to a back-breaking schedule, but he believes in giving young men with solid performance backgrounds inordinate opportunities and salaries. As a catalyst of talent, he has made a reputation for making men who otherwise might have died an early career death. Bailey was dying a slow death in Chrysler because he was too young for line responsibility and because he had the wrong background for his superior's likes. Geneen took a chance on him and in two years he was running a major division. Geneen found another source of talent in the executives of the firms ITT absorbed under Geneen's aggressive acquisition program. He offers management of firms he is about to acquire five-year contracts and huge salary increases to both make his merger proposal attractive and to attract and keep executive talent. In short, the bait Geneen uses to attract and keep talent is opportunity, and opportunity comes in many forms at ITT. In so doing he unintentionally produces egressors, of whom not a few are quitters.

Litton Industries and International Telephone & Telegraph are the newer, more spectacular producers of quitters. A few older, more established corporations have produced a fantastic number of presidents and senior executives. In the period of 1961 to 1965 some forty presidents of the largest industrial corporations had served stints of five years or more as vice-presidents in a dozen corporations, including General Electric, where dropouts called "GEdos" are so numerous that we dare not attempt to list them. IBM has been effective in reaching down and bringing young men along at rapid speeds. In so doing, it has incurred the same liability as did other companies who failed to keep them adequately challenged. Such mobile men as Mike Kama left for Xerox, Dause Bilby for Sperry Rand, John Haanstra for General Electric, and Fred M. Farwell for Underwood and later ITT.

The surprise of the sixties was the number of young executives that Ford Company lost after it has so strongly emphasized the attracting and keeping of youthful executives. If there was one company that needed youth, went out to get youth, developed youth, but could not keep the products of one of the most aggressive youth-oriented talent hunts in business and industry, it was Ford.

Ford could not afford to lose her exceptional talent as she fought a dueling battle with General Motors. Chase Morsey and R. I. Eggert left for RCA, for the positions of executive vice-president and vice-president of economic marketing research respectively. James P. O'Neill also went to Xerox as vice-president and manager of operations in the business products and systems division. Victor G. Raviola, William V. Luneburg, and John C. Secrest went to American Motors. James J. Kelley left for LTV and later TWA, Charles Beck for American Bosch Arma Corporation, John Frey for General Cable, and Robert Rowen for Great Western Sugar. Phillip Buckminster and W. Stewart Venn joined Chrysler, Richard Krafve went to Raytheon after Geneen left, and Lowell E. Drug went to Olin Mathieson and then to the presidency of Standard Packaging Corp. Although Ford is not generally revered for the ability to breed large numbers of highly talented, youthful executives, her quitters made as good names for themselves after they left Ford as did the dropouts of other, more prestigious corporations. Chrysler, American Motors, General Cable, Bendix, TWA, and Xerox would be hard-pressed without the services of their many former Ford executives (FOdos).

The Ford case illustrates the fact that even companies short of talent experienced high quit rates during this era of rapid growth and change. Probably the airline industry best represents the tendency of corporations to pirate from each other's quitters when none could afford to lose whatever talent they had developed or acquired. In the sixties, executives were joining and leaving American, TWA, Pan Am, United, Northeast, Northwest, Delta, and Eastern in such numbers that if an executive had not been in at least two of these airlines he was not really established. Bud Wiser left American for the presidency of Northeast and then became president of TWA. James O. Leet took Wiser's place at Northeast and had been at Pan Am and Irish Airlines. From executive vice-president of Continental, Lawrence Harding left to become president of Braniff. Floyd Hall left TWA to become president of Eastern, replacing Malcolm MacIntyre who had been counsel to American. At American, Ralph Damon and four other executives left to become presidents of other airlines. Over twelve executives left to become vice-presidents eventually, and over a hundred became executives at lower levels in other airline companies. Only a few who occupied the executive suites in the major airlines came from outside the industry. Among these executives was Richard M. Bressler, who quit General Electric to become vice-president of American. Many outsiders had backgrounds in industries akin to aviation. Ernest Breech and Charles Tillinghaust of TWA had strong aviation backgrounds obtained from North American Aviation and Bendix. For the most part, airline suites were occupied by airline people. Further, few left for companies outside of the airline industry, and when they did, they kept close to some phase of the aviation industry. For example, A. V. Leslie, TWA's able finance chief, went to Douglas in 1962 and became senior vice-president of finance. Carter Burgess left the presidency of TWA and became president of AMF.

The quitters have several things in common. Once they leave, they usually make another move before they settle down. Furthermore, the longer they have been with the parent company the more likely it is that they will move twice more before finding a niche. For example, Cortes W. Randall quit GE and ITT before he built his own company. Louis T. Rader quit GE, ITT, and Sperry Rand before returning to home base—GE. Simon Ramo quit General Electric for Hughes Aircraft before he helped found Ramo-Wooldridge Company, and Bob Wooley quit General Electric and Omnetic Corporation before he got established at Discom Corporation. One reason for this job hopping is that the parent company and the one to which the executive goes first are too contrasting. The letdown may cause him to leave again, and this time he will be more careful in picking his next slot.

The second quality that quitters have in common is that they largely hold to their industry backgrounds. In this sense the airline industry represents an extreme version of the tendency for executives to stay in the industry that relates to their functional and technical backgrounds. There are, of course, notable exceptions to this principle. John Carter left Corning Glass to become president of Fairchild Camera. John Burns left RCA to go to Cities Service Co. via Elgin National Watch; P. J. Casella left RCA for Endicott Johnson; Paul Stickt left Campbell Soup for the vice-chairmanship of Federated Stores; Henry H. Henley left the presidency of McKesson & Robbins to become president of Cluett Peabody Co.; Robert Morris left Monsanto to become president of Wheeling Steel; and David C. Scott left Colt Industries to head up Allis-Chalmers.

The relatively small number of executives who truly parted from their established functions or technical backgrounds suggests that few executives feel that they can manage anything that is manageable, regardless of background. The mobility patterns of dropouts strongly suggest that they mostly hold to their backgrounds in selecting their moves. The pure generalist is not as common as the industry specialist with strong general management skills. Apparently, mobility is a marriage between one's feeling of security and confidence and opportunity to leave. Or, to put it differently, an opportunity is one that attracts the confidence of the executive that he will perform effectively. This confidence is based upon familiarity with a given industry. Putting the factor of self-confidence aside, the executive has fewer opportunities to leave the less he has established himself as an industry type.

The rovers are not without representation, however. George Bunker had been a jack-of-all-trades before he settled down to successfully nurse ailing Martin-Marietta back to health. He had been at Campbell Soups; Wilson & Co., the meat packer; and a consultant with McKinsey, Kearney & Co., Kroger Co., and Trailmobile Co. Donald Burnham was chief engineer at Oldsmobile before he left to become an executive at Westinghouse. He helped reorganize Westinghouse, and as president did a fantastic job of developing a strong earnings base. The rovers were as apt to be successful in running their companies as the industry types. Or, to put it differently, it would be difficult to prove that the industry type was more capable than the rover type. The failures in both categories can appear quite conspicuous. General Electric claimed that the professional executive could manage almost anything regardless of his technical background. But the disastrous computer division at the Phoenix and General Electric Bull operation in France forced General Electric to recognize the need for executives who had mastered computer technology. General Electric brought in Richard M. Block from Honeywell and John W. Haanstra from IBM after first enticing Louis Rader back from Sperry Rand. But the successes in both categories can be offsetting.

Corporations have gone outside their firms for top executives more than ever before. The majority of these executives have strong relevant technical or functional backgrounds. However, the trend to acquiring executives without relevant technical skills is increasing and is a function of the scarcity of capable executives in general. Louis F. Polk was brought to General Mills by General Rawlings in 1960 shortly after Polk's graduation from Harvard Graduate School of Business. Polk knew Rawlings as a boy in Dayton, Ohio, and placed him in finance, where he sparked much of the company's growth. When he was passed over by James A. Summer for the chief operating officership, Polk quit at the age of thirty-eight and became president of MGM after having been discovered by an executive placement company that was commissioned by Edgar Bronfman, the largest single stockholder of MGM. Polk was completely out of his industry element, but the movie industry is accustomed to outsiders. In the past twenty-five years, there were only a few industry career men who became chief company executives. They included Jack Warner, Harry Cohn, and Darryl F. Zanuck. Polk had as good a chance to succeed as had many of his predecessors. Unfortunately he was released after less than a year in the MGM slot by Kirk Kerkorian, who gained control away from Bronfman and put Jim Aubrey in the presidency because he wanted someone who was technically qualified. However, in more cases than not, it is not the lack of technical or functional competency that causes career failure. The lack of managerial capability proves far more telling.

In conclusion, if you cannot quit, you are not really mentally mobile. This powerful theme has embraced masses of executives whose career strategies will not allow them to waste away on corporate shelves. Some quitters will leave prematurely, not knowing that they could win by staying. Many will escape imminent failure. Still others will avoid the slow death of executive obsolescence. The latter condition has plagued many corporations and executives during the sixties. But few executives are truly obsolete. Rather, many are merely misplaced and belong in a different environment and job. The aroused itch to move and the increased "pirating" of executives are combining to cause a better utilization of executive abilities and skills in the economy. What the quitter has and the executive with the insider's mentality does not have is the courage to quit before he has a specific opportunity to go elsewhere. This act requires a high degree of self-confidence. Hence, some of the most self-confident executives are quitters, a fact that flies in the face of the traditional notion that quitters do not know who they are or what they want to become. Men who are most capable of standing on their own two feet are the most capable of running. Miller and Knudsen were two of thousands of executives who, during the decade of the sixties, responded to the inner logic of self-affirmation. However, not a few executives lacked the substance within to fall back upon. Having allowed their sense of identity to become eroded by too many years of stony identification with their corporations, they could not pull themselves out of their depressions and self-deceptions. Their failure to adjust to sudden, unexpected change illustrates the fact that a winning strategy is dependent on placing a high value upon past achievements and acquired reputation. Many executives, old and young alike, particularly insiders, never realize the value of their skills in the marketplace. Having been defined by their corporation to be of low strategic value, they do not believe that they could be of critical value to other organizations, including nonindustrial types. In a society growing beyond its talent resources, a failure in one sector may become a success in another, and almost everyone may lead a useful life. It all depends upon what men define themselves to be. Time and again the author watched insiders allow their corporations to define for them their limits of usefulness. They accepted as final their corporation's judgments. Thus, while some executives took to quitting, others sat and ate their hearts out. It was a weird decade in which overly alert executives worked alongside others who were barely alive to their opportunities. New opportunities emerged too swiftly for men too long entrenched in old habits.

The appearance of mobile executives in large numbers did more than any single event to break the incestuous ties of inbred executives and relieve their suites of the stale, suffocating air expelled and inhaled by men who lived most of their careers together. The quitter has found a dignified way out of the corporation mired in mindless conformity or preoccupied with games of hard work and corporate loyalty. He represents the emerging triumph of the individual over the corporation. He can also mean a triumph for the corporations that have the foresight and capability to build their fortunes on his style and competency. The insider's attitude—"Mirror, mirror, on the wall, who is the fairest of them all?"—is rapidly giving way to the attitude that men who egress out of philosophical commitments (repotters) or situational circumstances (quitters) may acquire more competency than if they had stayed. The quitter may be the fairest of them all.

CHAPTER NINE

The Leverager

THE CHIEF CHARACTERISTIC of the mobile executive is his antiorganizational posture. He does not view himself as an organization man. While the quitter will not allow a corporation to set a brass collar around his neck and throw away the key, the leverager is skeptical about the usefulness of a ladder to climb the corporate slopes. Rather, he believes that few executive positions require for their performance the lengthy preparation of a subaltern employee. The potential talent exceeds the number of men formally prepared and aggressively seeking promotion to high-level assignments. Success requires the courage and craft to nominate oneself for these higher positions and to leave if his request produces an outright rejection.

Immobility comes from a fixation on the immediate job and on getting to the next job above it. If an aspiring executive can do his present job, he may, with more effort and attention, perform effectively at several levels above. The possibility of performing ineffectively at several levels above a given station is not substantially greater than the possibility of failure to perform an entirely different job at any point in the corporate hierarchy. A president accustomed to managing executives may have as much difficulty learning to manage engineers and scientists at lower levels as a scientist may have learning to manage senior executives.

The leverager has spotted the fact that there are discontinuities in the structure of the corporate hierarchy. A job three levels above is not necessarily three times more difficult. It is likely that the preparation and background required to be an effective member of the executive team is not related to the experiences that may be derived from middle-management positions. The leverager is not intimidated by a corporate pecking order. He spends little time worrying about who and where he is and attends almost exclusively to the question of where he can go and how to get there. In short, the leverager prizes opportunity over company, he gives ambition priority over loyalty; he prefers self-nomination to nomination by others.

This polarized version of the leverager has a degree of mental mobility that relatively few men possess. However, few men who move to the top rapidly do not subscribe intuitively to many of the leverager's values. Early arrivals have achieved a high degree of acceleration or upward mobility. So have the late bloomers who have suddenly shot straight to the top after serving long periods in lower management positions. In the mobility pattern of early arrivals and late bloomers, ample evidence may be found for the efficacy of the leverager's belief that careers can be greatly accelerated by aggressively pursuing opportunities.

The Depression years, during which there were more men available than jobs, were not conducive to leveraging. But during the decade of the sixties there were more jobs than available men. This situation brought about an unprecedented shortage of executive talent. The large industrial corporations became huge human magnets that attracted men of all types to fill the executive offices. Even the breeder companies, consuming talent in unprecedented quantity, developed voracious appetites that could not be adequately fed by men mobilized from the lower managerial ranks within these companies. Outsiders of industrial and nonindustrial backgrounds and specialties found abundant opportunity to pursue careers in corporations that formerly were suspicious and disdainful of men not of their own stamp. These strangers came from government, banks, investment houses, law partnerships, public accounting firms, educational faculties, advertising agencies, and consulting firms. Some were hired for their broad general backgrounds and others because of their precise technical skills. Of the many brought in to perform technical, nonadministrative roles, a surprising number became full-fledged line officers of their corporations.

As industrial corporations became favorably impressed by these outsiders, they stepped up their recruitment from these institutions. Some executives came in relatively young, others in advanced stages of their careers. It was not possible through mobility patterns to find any evidence that these outsiders proved any less capable of managing their executive assignments than their counterparts with pure industrial backgrounds. What goes into making a topflight executive remains a mystery. The fact that many mobile executives today hold an M.B.A. degree cannot be used to argue that training in business management is a requirement for becoming an executive. In fact, graduates of the military academies are well represented at the top. When James A. Summer, a West Pointer who headed the British subsidiary of General Mills, was nominated for the executive vice-presidency of General Mills, he beat out Louis F. Polk, a graduate of the Harvard Business School. Although military academy [1] graduates in 1961 to 1966 were far less numerous than graduates of collegiate schools of business, academy graduates occupied almost twice their expected per capita share of offices in suites of industrial corporations. Although the number of men in executives suites with M.B.A. degrees exceeded twice their per capita share, this figure is not very impressive. After all, they are business school graduates. Also, corporations aggressively recruited M.B.A. graduates and executive placement firms were strongly biased toward them, which was not the case for military academy graduates. It is widely suspected that graduates of business schools are better trained for middle and lower management. It is questionable whether graduate business schools produce talented executives or

[1] West Point and Annapolis graduates who entered industry as full-route or part-route types.

whether talented men go to graduate schools of business. There are still a goodly number of lawyers at the top, as well as engineers and liberal arts graduates.

All of which suggests that the mobile executive's faith possesses considerable validity. Managing is something that can be learned and practiced by diverse types of personalities with equally diverse kinds of backgrounds. Some of the most successful presidents did not come through the ranks. Others bypassed whole sections of middle management. Still others made unspectacular records at lower levels. What accounts for their successes has less to do with background and where they come from than their opportunities and motivations. An aspiring executive must be mobility-bright, which means that he must efficiently crank out of each move the competency that inheres in any position.

However, experiences, while not completely interchangeable, are not necessarily sequential or summative either. That is to say, an aspirant need not start his ascent at the bottom. He may start it at any point, including the top. What is more important than where he starts his career is his capacity to learn. A few of the basic rules of success may be learned at any level, and they are most efficiently learned at the level that matches the aspirant's learning capacity.

Further, he may learn the basic elements of the game in an outside environment. An aspirant may learn better by first working in banks and then, at midcareer, he may transfer to the industrial corporation. He may thus be more effective and may contribute more than if he spent his whole career in the same organization. Not everyone can learn to manage a corporation by the opportunities provided solely within it. The reason that some men may better start their learning at higher levels or in outside environments is because the corporate hierarchy of positions is not an efficient learning device. The concept of organizational structure was originally contrived to efficiently produce goods and services, and it was later adopted as a vehicle to transport men to the top. The organization itself came to be utilized to train men for higher positions. While all of this was happening, aspirants took to using the hierarchy as a ladder, and the pyramid became a teaching and learning instrument. We know now that few men learn according to the traditional rules that guide climbing. While set up to get work done, the organizational structure was expected to do something that it was not intended to do and to produce something it could not efficiently produce—learning experience. It took the demands of growth and innovation and the widespread scarcity of capable executives to make the pyramid an obvious anachronism. The rapid upward mobility rates showed that many could perform executive roles without climbing the ladder one step at a time. Many of the new generation of executives started their careers at the near top. Oftentimes, what others who took the traditional route learned below constituted negative learning that misprepared them for life in the executive suite.

Now, in addition to being a place to work, the corporate universe is rapidly becoming a learning environment. The shortage in available manpower is due largely to the inability of corporations to simultaneously get work done and prepare men for other responsibilities. The deficiency is in learning power, not in manpower. Because many men can assimilate experiences faster than they are allowed by their corporations to climb the ladder, a premium is placed upon the capacity to self-nominate. But this skill must be backstopped by a rapid and efficient learning capacity or the executive's mobility will be ahead of his ability to assimilate experiences. This condition almost guarantees a loser. In addition to being mobility-bright, he must be mobility-directed,[2] and here the critical quality is the courage and self-confidence that is basic to creating, finding, and exploiting opportunities. The act of career acceleration requires the willingness to cash in one's gains and achievements and invest them in inordinately bigger and better jobs. This is the basis of leveraging and has become one of the most popular techniques for making big jumps up the corporate ladder, for getting ahead in another company when the executive has immovable blocks in his home company, or for getting to the top before retirement ends the whole game of trying. Leveraging takes a dim view of the ladder itself.

Archimedes of Syracuse, the most famous of ancient mathemati-

[2] See Chapter 3 for explanations of the terms "mobility-directed" and "mobility-bright."

cians and natural philosophers, exclaimed, "Give me a place on which to stand and I will move the world." He used this allegory to illustrate the principle of the lever, but unfortunately he did not apply the social equivalent of his principle to spare his own life. The besieging armies of Claudius Marcellus that were held at bay for three years finally took Syracuse and, against the express wishes of the victorious commander, Archimedes was killed. He failed to find his fulcrum.

In a world where talent is scarce, every aspiring or established executive has a potential fulcrum. He has something of value to his present corporation or to another—something that is not being utilized or recognized to the extent that it might be if he were to aggressively expose and push himself. Leveraging is indigenous to an affluent, growing society possessing a strong faith, bordering on neurotic fixation, in the success ethic. Children are admonished to go farther than their parents. In the middle-class family wherein parents sacrifice for rather than with their children, the parents' achievements, resources, and gains serve as a huge fulcrum by which the child advances ahead of his parents and others. For true believers in the success ethic, college education is less a preparation for manhood than a fulcrum for launching successful careers. Teachers, parents, and businessmen encourage students to major in a particular curriculum because of its utility in the world of commerce and industry.

Young people often choose colleges and universities that will look good on their résumés. Not a few educational institutions counsel graduating seniors about how to sit for an interview, organize a biographical data sheet, and take employment exams. For parents and their children alike who are among the most ardent worshipers of the success ethic, preadult life is one grand fulcrum for assuring instant success. The fact of fast mobility to the top by unprecedented numbers of young men afforded tangible, visible evidence that there were shortcuts, right turns, and efficient moves to be emulated and copied. To the leveragers, the American dream is more a demand than a hope. Their plans to go into business include the many fulcrums that are available to them in an opportunistic society. If, in preadult life, they learned anything from their elders, it was that leveraging is the *modus operandi* for managing careers intelligently. This they believe will enhance and accelerate career success as much or more than classroom exercises in engineering or accounting.

During the decade of the fifties, the pall of the Depression continued to constrain the efforts of many insiders to aggressively advance their career interests. Long accustomed to underestimating their value to other corporations, most insiders were asleep to the possibilities of moving rapidly to the top. They labored under the delusion that success was achieved by taking one step at a time up the corporate slope. They were admonished that if they rose too fast they could fall too hard to recover. Men stayed in their jobs long after they had learned them, and eligibility for the next job was more often achieved by patient waiting than aggressive seeking. By the late fifties, a few saw that implicit in a growth economy were opportunities that led to better opportunities, and that some jobs could be exploited to gain inordinately bigger and better jobs. Silently hidden within the exploding economy were fast tracks to the top waiting to be traveled by those courageous enough to defy the conventions of the insider. These implicit chains of discontinuous positions that transcended corporate boundaries attracted mostly the prematurely wise, college educated, former GIs of World War II. Their success was more conspicuous than their technique.

At first, leveraging was adopted for compressing the time period that elapsed between starting at the bottom and arriving at the top. The leverager still had to be unobtrusive because he had the stigma of a job hopper, a bum of sorts who failed in every previous job and would probably fail in the next. He was a poor risk. But the arrival at the top of increasing numbers of executives who used leveraging to some degree and in some manner showed that the climb could be greatly accelerated. More importantly, since he spent less time waiting around for some insider to retire, die, or be fired, the leverager made more efficient use of his career time. Because he left soon after he had learned his job, he was able to compress experience. He proved younger and more competent for his age than the company executive who overlearned and overstayed on each rung of the corporate ladder.

The value of leveraging was augmented by several conditions

that fit in with the advent of the growth economy. First, corporations failed to breed enough of their own men. They had to go to the market and found it more advisable and ethical to go to the alumni of prestigious corporations than to their employees. Although this procedure was entirely logical given the ethics of breeders at the time, it contributed to leveraging. Because the egressors were selectively recruited to avoid the stigma of pirating, quitting became reinforced, as did parlaying of one's achievements into better jobs.

Secondly, within their corporations men were moved about to accommodate the growth cycle. In many growth corporations, men were so scarce that they were often moved out of the functional specialties to do a critical job. As they moved laterally, the best also moved vertically. By the early sixties, a few growth corporations began to see in these mobile types the benefits of both time and experience compression. The exigencies of a changing market and economy called for the flexibility of the younger, more mobile types who were accustomed to change and movement. Corporations turned more energetically to the few executive placement firms to find executives, and more often than not the most movable executive was one who had quit or was about to and who was not above looking seriously at a tender. As corporations used executive placement firms, executives used them too, and the mushrooming of recruiting firms attested to the growing respect for men who could make the most of their achievements and opportunities.

In not a few corporations, administrative slugging matches evolved between the new breed and the old generation, with youthful competency more often than not winning the field over noisy desperation. Eventually corporations had to go to currently employed executives, who often would not leave without ensuring the safety of their loyal subordinates. Some executives were allowed to bring their protégés and crucial subordinates with them. Parallelism gradually set in as corporations discovered that one way to get executives was to pick up a man with a team. As outsiders brought in outsiders, insiders were often encouraged or forced to leave. Being intelligently self-concerned, these insiders adopted modest versions of the leveraging technique. (Notice we did not say they quit; an insider cannot quit easily.) By the late sixties, the largest manhunt in history was furiously trying to catch up with the highest rate of executive turnover.

The most dramatic form of leveraging is to jump over and past several rungs and thereby accelerate upward mobility. The conservative version is to jump to a sequential level such as a level above the present position. Whether the jump is big or small, the technique may be one of two types. Tactical leveraging occurs at a specific point in the executive's career when he decides to quit and turns to the outside to make the most of his reputation and achievements to land a better job. Strategic leveraging is a master plan for managing a total career. It is a strategy of life and involves a long-range, overall battle plan for going to the top. Here leveraging is not simply a tool of advancement, it is a philosophy. Quitters may practice tactical leveraging, but by definition they cannot practice strategic leveraging.

Tactical leveraging was most common in the late fifties and early sixties, but strategic leveraging became increasingly evident in the makeup of mobile executives at the close of the sixties.

Seldom is leveraging of either type not involved to some degree in a career move. It is impossible to present oneself to a prospective employer as a cipher. Not even the graduate fresh out of college can do this. Intelligent behavior dictates that the aspirant use his college experience in and out of the classroom to favorably impress his prospective employer. In a different vein, George Kozmetsky, who assembled Litton Industries' digital computer group, dropped out with Harry Singleton to help him form Teledyne. They each put up 225,000 shares to start the company. Kozmetsky was executive vice-president but was hopelessly blocked behind Singleton when he left in 1966 to become dean of the graduate business school at the University of Texas. His initial investment had grown to be worth $44 million. It would, of course, be ridiculous to assume that Kozmetsky did not apply leverage to gain his job at Texas. Of course, Kozmetsky may not have helped build Teledyne with the idea of someday becoming dean of a business school in Texas or anywhere. In a rapidly changing society, future opportunities cannot be easily predicted. But Kozmetsky, an M.B.A. graduate from Harvard, had previously taught at Carnegie Institute of Technology, where he picked up an appetite for education. He had thought of someday returning to pick up this career line. While he was at Teledyne, the events that made his career change possible fell neatly into place. Not the least of these events was his success at the practical side of running a business. He leveraged, as do most executives who attempt to make the best move that past achievements will allow.

In making career decisions, the executive may not have the opportunity to be completely thorough and methodical in planning the moves that may be required to maximize his past achievements. But whenever strategic leveraging is used, the executive will take the necessary time, because he believes that nothing counts as much as maintaining momentum. He does not believe in losing irretrievable amounts of career time by staying too long or by departing without careful inspection of his options. When this quality of strategic thinking dominates the executive's mind, he is the pure leverager and dramatizes in bold form the craft by which some aspiring executives will attempt to move swiftly to the top. No contender who hopes to use tactical leveraging can fail to learn about the power of leveraging from a close inspection of the winners who used strategic leveraging. The gaining of inordinate amounts of exposure and visibility and parlaying the results into a major career advance is what leveraging is all about. For example, young, aspiring executives may go to work for wholesalers to get the exposure and visibility and experience they need to land a good job in a retail company and become established. Graduating lawyers may go to work for high-ranking law firms with important clients in order to gain business exposure and visibility. Miller at Textron did not invent this technique.

Many an executive started his climb to the top of business by going to work in a bank. Because few young men went to work for banks during the Depression years, banks have a critical shortage of officers at the vice-president level. Men can climb rapidly to that level and, if it is a big, prestigious bank, they may be elected to the board of directors of a corporation. With this exposure and visibility, the next step is not difficult. Young, aspiring executives have used investment firms, brokerage houses, stock exchanges, public accounting firms, advertising agencies, and management consulting firms. Space agencies, Pentagon departments, and military programs have proved to be effective sources of exposure and mobility. In addition, going to work for individuals well-known for their capacity to spot and develop young, talented executives is a well-used, intelligent move. Men such as Harold Geneen at ITT, James Ling at LTV, or Tex Thornton at Litton Industries are a few of those to whom young men have turned in order to accelerate their careers.

The strategic leverager has learned from the experience of failure that making the right moves at the right time is not easy. Leveraging is a tricky game, and the more numerous the players, the more sophisticated their skills. It is the tactical leverager who is most apt to jump into a nonadvantageous situation. He leverages more out of desperation than policy and is not apt to be methodical and thorough about knowing all his options and executing the principle of the lever. All too often he must make another move to correct his bad move, and this next position may be little better than his prior job. Precious amounts of career time can be lost because the leverager is not aware of the elements that make for high risk.

A careful scrutiny of successful leveragers shows that they may use but are not preoccupied with the institutions and instruments that help them to execute their moves, including executive placement firms, executive counselors, professional and trade associations, biographical data sheets and résumés, news releases, publicity agents, speaking engagements, published articles and books, community and civic organizations, social engagements, and family ties. The failure-prone leverager is too concerned with résumés, executive placement agencies, publicity, and advertisements. These concerns may be properly called "the tactics of leveraging" because they most commonly identify the limited resourcefulness of a tactical leverager. The successful leverager is more oriented toward the strategic or basic factors that precede the tactical. His more professional mind includes subtleties that escape the notice of the tactician. These strategic factors—which combine to make the fulcrum—include the executive's reputation, the image or reputation of the corporation from which he egresses, the opportunities available to him in the ingressing corporation, and the general shifts in the patterns of executive turnover and recruiting in the economy.

The members of the fulcrum must be delicately interrelated or the result will be something less than leveraging. For example, if two executives who have everything equal but the size and reputation of their corporations are randomly selected, the results will be spectacularly different. Ben is a manager in a large, well-managed company (firm X) whose reputation is so outstanding that many corporations would snap up one of its managers at a moment's notice. Competitive and noncompetitive firms instruct their members to be on the lookout for managers and executives in firm X who might want to leave or could be tempted away. Bill is a manager with a reputation equal to that of Ben, but his fulcrum is a smaller company (firm Y) with a bad reputation for managing. Bill would have decidedly more difficulty in landing a higher and more responsible job than Ben. The career advantage inherent in leveraging is gained by using the corporation's image to parlay the competency, skills, and reputation of the leverager. Tapping the power inherent in leveraging will be effortless for Ben and may only entail discreetly dropping a hint to a few selected businessmen in the industry and in the associations to which firm X belongs. The men at the top of the industrial establishment are a tightly knit group who communicate frequently through the media of business dealings, trade association meetings, conferences, and social events. It would be difficult for Ben's intentions to remain secret after a few initial contacts.

In examining the image of the corporation from which egress is contemplated, generally the larger the corporation, the greater the advantage to leverage into other companies, large or small. The managerial skills related to scale and the trend toward bigness make executives in large corporations highly marketable. Somewhat related to size is the rate of growth, with the advantage favoring the sustained-growth corporations. It is easier to leverage from a corporation with the good growth rate of Sears Roebuck than from a corporation with the poor growth rate of Montgomery Ward. Next is the factor commonly referred to as "managerial quality" and, of course, the higher the caliber of management, the greater the leverage advantage. Part of this factor concerns the ability of the men at the top to identify and develop top talent. If one or several are known for having this rare talent, the advantage will be extremely favorable. Ernest Breech, while at Bendix, Ford, and TWA, was widely regarded for having a green thumb, and the men he identified and developed for top positions were always in high demand.

Few executives are in greater demand than mobile insiders of corporations that are known for their superior breeding capacity. Of course, most if not all corporations attempt to breed their own talent, but many have to go to the market occasionally or often to fill their voids. The best market for talent comprises a few corporations that are known for the quality of their quitters. Hence, each represents an important and viable route to the top and a fulcrum of immense power.

These breeders are known as academies because of the large number of corporate presidents and top executives that they unintentionally produced in the course of breeding their own kind. The academy is rushed by aspiring executives, many of whom may be leveragers wanting to get its name on their résumés. The advantages to the academy are apparent. It gets a broader base from which to select candidates than a nonacademy corporation. The academy can afford to be more selective and, with its superior breeding capacity, it will have available a higher-quality graduate for itself. However, the academy products are highly in demand by less efficient breeders. The academy, vulnerable to being pirated even in a relatively slow economy, comes under extreme duress from pressures within and without in a rapidly expanding economy. It must develop more talent to supply its own growth needs while at the same time it acquires more vulnerability to the executive raider. A vicious circle may start up in which the academy steps up its breeding efforts to make up for increasing losses. It may even have to go to the market to recruit talent. Because of its reputation as an academy, it can import quite easily. But the academy must be careful not to undo its own breeding efforts. By the recruiting of outsiders, it could cause more insiders to leave than normal. Thus, the academy must rely largely upon its own breeding capacity. In this way, the academy ends up overbreeding executives.

In the fifties the established academies included such companies as General Motors, General Foods, IBM, Sears, Standard Oil Co. (New Jersey), American Telephone & Telegraph, Procter and Gamble, Du Pont, Firestone, and General Electric. In the sixties, these old-line academies were joined by fast-growing companies such as International Telephone & Telegraph, Litton Industries, Textron, Bell & Howell, Xerox, Kodak, General Mills, and Texas Instruments. These corporations became reluctant academies by producing large numbers of leveragers that identified their more established academic peers.

Leveragers from academies utilize the value that other corporations ascribe to their experience and competency. From such eminent academies as IBM and General Electric, many men have leveraged into entrepreneurial roles. GEdos (General Electric dropouts) abound in the peripheral computer industry that services computers with soft goods. In 1956, General Electric moved its computer division to Phoenix, Arizona. After a great initial success in selling electronic data processing systems to the Bank of America, the manufacture and sale of computers took a nose dive. General Electric periodically injected huge doses of fresh management into the division, and after each time, more men left. The technical personnel alone have had to educate five generations of top-level management since 1956. Many of the more capable technical and managerial personnel left the company and went around the corner to set up shop. According to Robert Colten, executive vice-president of the Computer Research Bureau of Los Angeles, there are nine peripheral computer companies that were started by GEdos in the Phoenix area alone. Colten himself is a General Electric dropout. According to one of the presidents, there are more than two hundred GEdos working in computer firms in Phoenix. Donald E. Oglesby, a GEdo and president of Data Computing, observes that most of the GEdos who built own companies left after Bob Wooley quit as head of the peripheral equipment engineering department to become general manager first of a department in Omnetic Corporation and then of Discom Corporation.

In one area of the company, advertising, the dropouts were so numerous that they formed the GE Old-Boy Club. GEdos who have in common the fact that they are graduates of General Electric adver-tising training courses number over three hundred and get together once a year over cocktails and dinner to glance back upon their experiences at the starting gate of their careers. Dropouts from other areas of General Electric could form a similar alumni club and almost as many would be eligible for membership. No company has had as steady a stream of dropouts as General Electric. In spite of this turnover and except for its computer division, General Electric has enjoyed a great reputation for its management depth.

IBM has bred and lost many talented executives to competitors. In one area, computer software technology and services, IBM has had a large number of successful dropouts. Among the six hundred largest independent computer software companies, over two hundred of their founders had been at IBM. H. Ross Perot was a supersalesman with IBM in 1962 until he became unhappy because he was told he was at the top of the salary level of his position. He left to build a computer software business which six years later was worth, on paper, over $300 million. George S. Collet took six with him from IBM when he left to build his company. Harvey Goodman did to IBM's training program in computer programming what many men have done with General Electric's advertising training program. He used it to get the training in skills and concepts he needed to go into business for himself.

Keeping uppermost in mind the parent and the other company, we may describe several common patterns of leveraging. The first is leveraging down, a maneuver which John Logan executed when he left the executive vice-presidency of Olin Mathieson to become president of Universal Oil, a substantially smaller corporation. Of course, by so doing he went up a notch on the career ladder, and the word "leveraging" implies this intention. But the concept of leveraging "down" means he used the fulcrum of a large corporation to catapult into a small firm. By going down he goes up. The leveraging down pattern has been increasingly used by executives since the early sixties. Before this time, the executive of a large, well-established corporation was reluctant to join a smaller corporation with a reputation tainted by the lack of success or growth. There was great pride in belonging to a large, successful corporation. The public was overawed by the power and position of executives in such corporations as General Motors, General Electric, American Telephone & Telegraph, and New Jersey Standard Oil. Not a few of the executives in these companies felt that they were members of the ruling class. Large corporations did things in a big way, including producing larger-than-life executives. But the eternal log jamming at the top and the growing desire to reach out for challenge rather than enhance status produced the high rate of leveraging down that identified the late sixties. It became respectable to go up by going down. A challenge was a challenge, regardless of the size or reputation of either company. Once again, we see the concept of opportunity at work. What kept many executives inside their corporations at lower than desired levels were the trappings of status, reputation, and glamour. As one insider remarked, "I never thought I would leave General Electric. I knew that I would never be president, but I had been told all of my twenty years in the company that we were the best. There was nothing comparable to GE. Anything else would be a step down. I got the idea, as did all of the men around me, that it is better to be on the second rung of a strong ladder than on the first rung of a weak ladder. I stayed and stayed, and then one day I said to my wife, 'It's better to have fun on the first rung than eat your heart out on the second.' I got the heck out when a president became needed in a manufacturing firm one-twentieth the size of my company. Man, have I had a ball!"

Challenge can be found in leveraging up. This may be done by going from a small to a larger company. The new position may or may not be higher than his old job, but it offers a greater opportunity to go up eventually. Or he may actually go up the ladder in terms of his evaluation of challenge and responsibility. Once again we see the large corporation, when shorn of its pride and eager to get talent from any quarter where it may be found, reaching down into the numerically smaller firms. The latter have always had difficulty keeping talented executives, partly because of the glamour associated with being a team member of a large, prestigious corporation. In both breeding and importing men, the corporation appealed to the superior advantages of being on a first-rate team. Some leveraged up for this reason. But others leveraged up for the purpose of taking advantage of the opportunities created by the extreme shortage of executive talent.

In executing either the leveraging down or up patterns, the executive must be careful not to walk away from a golden opportunity. The question of who has an inside track to the top can never be easily answered. Many a mobile insider left a better opportunity because he did not really know his stature in the eyes of his ultimate superior. Corporate protégés and crucial subordinates were known to make this mistake frequently. A young man was being groomed for the presidency of a large corporation without being fully aware of it. At thirty-four years of age and after a rather rapid rise to the level of assistant vice-president of marketing, he became a party to an intergenerational struggle with his immediate superior, who had three years to go to retirement. This struggle went on for almost nine months before it broke out enough to become evident to the president. Feeling great warmth and sympathy for the sixty-two-year-old senior vice-president of marketing and not wishing him to retire in the middle of a dogfight, he pulled the young protégé out of the department and parked him under the vice-president for public relations with instructions to the latter to keep the young protégé busy until the old man (the marketing vice-president) retired or he (the president) could line up a better job. The protégé interpreted this transfer to the nonpriority function of public relations to be a consequence of his attack upon a corporate deity and decided to leave. A short time later he became vice-president of a corporation one-eighth the size of his former company. But when the president initially heard of his resignation he fell into consternation. The protégé was scheduled to become his replacement in five years or less. There is nothing comparable to the shock that erupts when the leverager is apprised of the golden opportunity that he unwittingly left behind.

The leverager should be equally concerned about the color of the opportunity on the other side of the street. It may turn out to be somewhat less than green and definitely not gold-plated. All successful moves are based upon having the kind of information that comes from exposure and visibility. The outsider typically lacks the insider's view of opportunities. The duties and responsibilities of a position may be difficult to assess. But the value placed by the corporate authorities upon performance in that position is even more difficult to determine. This information may be difficult to acquire even after a considerable period of time in the corporation. Then, too, the strategy of the corporation—which partly determines the value of a position—is always subject to change. The executive may not know for some time that he has leveraged himself out of the line of succession. To avoid misassessing the opportunity factor of a given position, one must have a creditable source of information within the firm. Contacts made through various media—including social, political, community, professional, and trade association activities—are helpful. Leveragers are avid joiners and use the elaborate networks of organizational membership to keep in touch with unfolding opportunities and to find the man who knows about a specific situation in a particular organization. It is true but perhaps tragic that the nine-to-five executive who is home every night with his family does not have a chance in the opportunity game. There is more leveraging initiated and negotiated outside the company than inside.

It should be noted that a propitious condition of leveraging has developed from the immense rate and speed of long-distance traveling by businessmen. When the executive traveled less frequently and less rapidly, his opportunities were limited to his regional base. Today, the well-traveled businessman has as his potential opportunity base the whole country and a substantial part of the world. Because he travels extensively, through contacts with associates, colleagues, and friends, he has the potential ability to become eligible for positions that were unknown in premobility days.

Of course, having a sponsor in the other corporation represents a distinct advantage. One such sponsor may be a former superior who has been in the company long enough to know the ropes and his way around. It is almost as common for an executive to reach back to his former employer for a man or two as it is to take the subordinate along with him when he moves. Both the delayed type of parallelism and the immediate type may involve leveraging. Getting wind of the fact that the boss is thinking about leaving allows the subordinate to indicate subtly that he is ready to go too. Or, after the boss has gone, the leverager must not be averse to contriving a situation to properly renew his contact with him.

The problem is that the superior may not level with the subordinate about his own opportunities, and the subordinate *could* hitch himself to a falling star. This lack of candor could be present in the case of immediate parallelism. In leveraging, one must carefully observe the principle that if one cannot trust the sponsor completely, one should not move with him. Because trust is a common problem in both types of parallelism, the delayed type emerges superior because at least one of the parties to the move has had exposure and visibility, which is not the case in immediate parallelism. Of course, if the superior enters the corporation at a command level where he can actively control the future opportunities of his subordinate, the problem boils down mainly to knowing what value the boss places upon the leverager. In other words, is the leverager being hired to clean up a mess, to be a troubleshooter and hatchet man, after which he will be of little functional value? Or will the leverager assume a critical position in the superior's overall view of his mandate?

The lack of exposure and visibility in the other corporation is less serious if the leverager is hired for a project assignment in addition to filling an established position. What the leverager really wants requires exposure and visibility after he gets in the firm. He wants to be discovered as being more capable than his achievements of the past indicate or his new position requires. A project can be better assessed than a position. This is because projects are more specific in nature and more subject to objective evaluation. A corporation cannot hide a weak financial position from a competent finance man nor deny the success of the finance executive in improving the financial condition. But corporate officers may exaggerate the value of a position in their scheme of things to an executive in order to attract him to the corporation.

In short, having sponsors and being assigned to projects are two ways in which a leverager can overcome the deficiency of inside information about the other company. An intelligent leverager does not move to another company without being aware of what he is joining as compared to what he is leaving. Still, the risk is great and leveraging is no game for the faint-hearted. Even among the best leveragers, one move is often followed shortly after by another move, but the leverager does not stop when he draws a dud. He moves again and perhaps a third time before he finally obtains the catapult effect inherent in the lever principle. Many a resourceful leverager has made three moves in ten years. Contrary to the conventional wisdom of the insider, it is the rapidity with which he makes his moves, not the number of moves, that could injure the reputation of the executive. Generally speaking, the executive should allow at least two years to elapse between one move and the next. He must stay long enough to perform, to be evaluated, and to give the corporation an honest try. Then, if he moves, he is merely being intelligent and realistic. Every mobile executive is aware that opportunities can turn into blocks with no discredit to the executive himself. There is one exception to this two-year waiting period. Mobile executives report that they are allowed one move in a career that comes within ninety days after joining a corporation. But whether the time elapsed between moves is three months or three years, an opportunity is evaluated regardless of when it comes to the executive. And while he seeks the next opportunity, he is diligently making the best of what he has. He continues to build his reputation. In fact, because his performance may help him to leverage, he may outproduce the company executive who works patiently in the insiders's track or sits serenely on a corporate shelf.

The opportunity factors that may exist in the old and new corporations do not represent the fulcrum by which the executive successfully catapults. The fulcrum is composed of his reputation and that of his corporation as viewed by members of the other corporation. A distinction exists between achievements and reputation. What an executive has actually done and the credit he is given may be disparate. An executive's reputation travels better than his achievements. In his home company he may be given only partial credit for an accomplishment because others were also acknowledged to be partly responsible for the success of the project. In another company he may be given total credit. The news media partly account for the difference between achievements and reputation. In reporting the promotion of an executive who was the nominal head of a major automobile division in General Motors, a leading business analyst noted that he was the mastermind behind the spectacular improvement in the market position of the Cadillac during the late sixties. Many factors coalesced to make this feat possible, not the least of which was a rising standard of living, inflation, a trend toward buying the larger, luxury cars, and a poor marketing, designing, and advertising job by the Lincoln men at Ford. More specifically, the Cadillac division had several extremely talented men aiding the marketing, sales, and design functions at the time, and these men almost carried this division head on their backs in order to produce the Cadillac phenomenon. But the leading business analyst's story was repeated and repeated by a host of reporters so that not only did most of the business world believe the story but not a few men in General Motors believed it as well. This leads to the recognition of an important tool of the leverager. He knows that becoming exposed to the business community partly depends upon becoming known to members of the news media. This, in turn, means making speeches before civic, professional, and trade groups. If such a meeting is not well-covered by the press, the leverager will have the corporate public relations officer prepare a release to the press about the speech. A reporter, needing background information, may report that the executive is head of a division whose chief product is making a spectacular show in the market. Before technically oriented groups, the executive himself may refer to several of the problems that had to be solved in the attempt to achieve a certain marketing or production objective. There are any number of techniques that he may use to achieve high exposure to the business community via the press short of hiring a public relations firm. And the latter has frequently been done by mobile executives.

Parlaying reputation is what leveraging is all about. What helps is the tendency for the executive's strengths to travel better than his weaknesses. The old cliché that an expert is a man 50 miles or more away from his hometown is certainly appropriate here. The executive who has remained in the same firm most of his career has become a known entity. He is known by both his strengths and weaknesses. At the top, however, the subordinate's weaknesses are more carefully examined than his strengths. They are weighed more heav-

ily because the assignments are more critical and involve closer tolerances of success and failure. When the tolerances between a successful program and a failure are close, weaknesses are subject to
critical analysis. Superiors must know precisely what the executive
can and cannot do. The author has often observed that one executive may be promoted over another because he had fewer weaknesses than the other executive. As one president remarked to the
author, "When the selection committee gets down to the lint-pick-
ing stage, I usually observe that they will accept a man whose
strengths and weaknesses are fewer. We will trade off a few less
strengths for a few less weaknesses." In the other company, his
weaknesses are less known than his strengths. Or, to put it differently, it is harder to check out his weaknesses. Besides, the corporation often brings in an outsider for the sake of qualities they could
not get by promoting an insider. The executive is recruited because they want fresh blood, which means that they expect to get
different strengths and weaknesses than the chief inside candidate
has. As long as the outsider's weaknesses are not identical to the insider's, the outsider has his strengths undiluted. And since it is seldom that the outsider's weaknesses will be as well known and,
hence, equally valued as the insider's, the outsider has the margin
of victory.

The intelligent leverager is aware of these subtleties and knows
how to maximize his reputation and his strengths and minimize his
weaknesses. He may appear to the company executive to be playing
games, but his reply is that strengths and weaknesses are relative to
the corporation and there is no universal arbiter. Who, then, can
say that he is trying to give a false impression? Besides, the leverager contends that what you are is not important. Who knows the
answer to this question? A man can contemplate his navel while a
whole horde of opportunities pass him by. A publicity-minded society and a public-oriented generation of businessmen have helped
to create many executives whose reputations go far beyond their actual achievements. A president who has observed this process at
work remarks, "If men at the top were suddenly stripped of their
reputations down to their actual achievements, many of us would
look puny by comparison."

The executive's corporation has a reputation of some kind that is derived from the quality of its products, the efficiency with which management utilizes stockholder equity to produce a profit, the individual reputations of its top executives, and the respect accorded it by members of the capital lending institutions and brokerage houses. Corporate reputations that become established acquire an inertia of their own. As stereotypes, they endure many short-run cycles of the economy. At any given time they cast a halo over corporation members. The executive's reputation and that of his corporation reinforce each other to produce more than their arithmetic sum. Although the insider has not the instinct for quitting, he stands to gain a greater advantage from leveraging than an executive who has been with the corporation for a short time. We are assuming that his corporation has an excellent reputation.

Men who are relatively unknown to the business community but who are products of well-reputed corporations have a better chance to leverage than well-known men with reputations tainted by the dim halos of their corporations. However, corporations tend to become known for their styles of managing. The other corporation may not be interested in the executive whose style of managing represents a radical departure from its own. The executive may want to leave because his style of managing is somewhat idiosyncratic within his present corporation. General Mills had a reputation for conservative, tight managerial style. Louis Polk rode to the vice-presidency on a free-forming organizational emphasis. This was useful, if not desirable, at levels below the command level and in several sectors of the corporation, given their problems at the time. But at the chief-executive level and as an overall pattern of managing, it may be deemed undesirable by the powers that be. What was idiosyncratic at General Mills became functionally desirable at MGM's board of directors, where Polk leveraged to the command post. The other corporation may wish to depart radically from its established management style. If an executive with an idiosyncratic style in a well-reputed corporation fits the needs of the other corporation, he may become a prime candidate for a crucial position. The advantage of leveraging diminishes considerably if the executive with an idiosyncratic style has a close identification with an unreputed corporation. He must stand or fall on a weak fulcrum.

Part of the leverager's fulcrum comprises the rules by which executives join and leave the corporation. When the ingress and egress rates are both low, a favorable advantage accrues to the leverager. If, over the years, a corporation sustains a high earnings reputation, a low ingress rate shows that the corporation knows how to identify and develop talented executives from within. The corporation is well-managed or it would have a higher ingress rate. A low egress rate has become recognized as indicating that such a corporation also knows how to maintain and enhance talented people.

A less favorable advantage exists for the executive when his corporation has a high ingress rate and a low egress rate. Such could be a growth corporation that has had to go outside to augment its capacity to find and develop executive talent. A prospective employer would think twice before he hired an executive from a corporation in which many joined and few departed. A leverager from this company would stand out like a sore thumb and the prospective employer would probably want to investigate to see if he had one of those that not even a growth company would want to keep. It is obviously true that high ingress and egress rates would not produce a high leverage advantage.

The exceptions, more conspicuous than numerous, largely concern the amount of average relative time that executives stay between arriving and departing. If the average relative tenure is ten years, the advantage would be to stay five years or less among the leveragers. A man may acquire the bad habits of a corporation's incompetent executive staff if he stays longer. Besides, it should not take him more than five years to realize that he has joined a poorly managed corporation, one that offers few opportunities for personal growth. It must be noted that in corporations inferior to other members of an industry, many have executive talent that another corporation considers more than adequate for its purposes. In short, the leverager's reputation emerges as the foreground and his corporation's reputation as the background.

A brief note should be added on the opportunity to leverage that arises with cyclical shifts in demand for executives. The demand for executives does not increase uniformly for all levels and for all kinds of executives. For example, in 1965 there was such a shortage of division presidents and general managers that an executive at one level and oftentimes two levels below could easily leverage. Anyone in sight of the division level has the whole world of industry as his oyster. Likewise, staff men in corporate planning became a scarcity at about the same period. Managers of technically oriented managers and nonmanagers were in high demand throughout the decade of the sixties. These variable changes in demand for executives were recorded by several executive placement firms, of which one of the foremost was the Chicago-based Heidrick & Struggles. The smart leverager keeps an eye on these cyclical demands as they will help him plan and time his moves. They also indicate the probability of receiving a bid if the leverager is in one of several markets or industries being heavily raided.

The probability of receiving a bid increases with the ability of the executive to bring talent with him to the other company. Men who successfully jumped company lines moved together in twos, threes, and even in sets of eight and ten. This act of several executives leaving a firm for a common destination is called "parallelism." The practice may serve various purposes and those who become involved in it may be quitters or leveragers. For example, James A. Yunker quit ITT to take over financially troubled Astrodata, Inc. He took with him Robert Baker, thirty-eight, as vice-president of finance and James Somers, thirty-five, as vice-president for administration. In this act of parallelism, Yunker was behaving as a good disciple of his mentor, Harold Geneen. When Geneen left Raytheon he took several executives with him to ITT, including Richard H. Griebel, George Strickman, and David Margolis. In 1963, Strickman took Margolis with him to Colt Industries. When Roy Sund left American Can for Champion Paper, he took George Walker with him. Rarely does the pirated firm get a chance to reverse the flow of men, but such was the luck of Bell & Howell. William Roberts left in 1961 to become president of Ampex Corporation, taking several colleagues with him. In 1968, Bell & Howell had to go to the market for vice-presidents, and it hired back two of its former men from Ampex. This is reverse leveraging at its best.

Probably the most bizarre case of parallel leveraging occurred when C. Lester Hogan left Motorola for the chairmanship of Fairchild Camera. To explain this we must note that departments or divisions may become known by the quality of the men that staff them. A corporation as a whole may not be known for the quality of its people, but a part of it may have that status because its executives are in high demand. Thus, engineering managers at Boeing, finance executives at Ford, technically creative executives at Shell, research executives at Raytheon and Westinghouse, manufacturing executives at McDonnell Aircraft, and marketing executives at Douglas have generally high marketability. Other corporations have members in functional or technical areas that are of interest to the job market because of cyclical needs of industry. The semiconductor operation at Motorola was known for its staff of competent personnel. Hogan always had trouble keeping his highly respected team together. Then, suddenly, Hogan himself quit when the semiconductor industry as a whole was showing low profit margins and good technical and managerial personnel fell into very short supply.

The events leading up to one of the most controversial cases of executive leveraging and pirating started when John Carter left a vice-presidency of Corning Glass Works to become, at age thirty-seven, the president of Fairchild Camera. Lured by the promises of a free hand from the founder, Sherman M. Fairchild, Carter tripled sales, an achievement for which he was assured the chief executive officer's job in 1962. In 1967, five divisions suffered a combined operating loss of $4,800,000 on $19,800,000 sales. Since most of these divisions were started by Carter, he felt the need to attempt to make them profitable, but Sherman Fairchild had different thoughts. Carter resigned and Richard Hodgson, imported in 1958 from Chromatic Television Labs, was named chief executive officer. He lasted seven months before he was kindly boosted up to the vice-chairmanship. In June, 1968, Robert N. Noyce, vice-president and director, quit because he was not offered the presidency, and three months later Hodgson joined ITT as senior executive officer of the president for operations. In addition, several other big executives quit because of the unexpected importing of Lester Hogan, a near-legendary figure who built Motorola's semiconductor business from scratch to the point where it was second only to Texas Instruments in the billion-dollar semiconductor field. At Fairchild, two-thirds of the company's business is in semiconductors, which is Hogan's forte and that of the seven key managers whom he took along with him.

Robert W. Galvin, forty-five, chairman and son of the founder of Motorola, had transformed the company from an ordinary maker of radio and TV sets in 1956 into a broadly based electronics complex. He was not about to see his firm robbed of its talent resources and financial gains. On the day of the announcement of Hogan's shift to Fairchild, Motorola's stock dropped to 129 for a loss of eight points. Galvin and his family own over 1 million of the 6.1 million shares, and they incurred a paper loss close to $100 million. While Motorola's stock fell 10 percent within a week, Fairchild's stock spurted ahead 19 percent. Within three weeks of Dr. Hogan's resignation, Galvin filed a complaint in the Federal District Court in Phoenix, Arizona, against the ex-Motorola men and asked an injunction prohibiting its former employee from working for Fairchild and from disclosing trade secrets. It also asked that any financial gain by these dropouts resulting from their move be held in trust. Meanwhile, to boost his company's sagging image, Galvin boosted Stephen Levy, forty-six-year-old former assistant to Hogan, to command of the semiconductor division and lured back John Welty, also forty-six, who had left earlier in the year to head Philco-Ford's Microelectronics Division. Ironically, while Galvin was crusading in and out of universities arguing that big business is exciting and challenging, Hogan was allegedly consulting with and interviewing other employees about the fun of going with him to Fairchild. Hogan denied he recruited at Motorola. Dozens of people wanted to go with him, but he could not use that many. The day before he left, one employee was reported to have been at his home crying and pleading to go with him. Ironic also is the fact that by quitting Carter made more money than if he had stayed. Hogan drove the price of Fairchild up considerably.

The growing trend of parallel leveraging is producing another problem. If one executive leaves, one unoccupied position results. But if several leave, as was the case with Lester Hogan at Motorola, a whole department or division may have to be rebuilt. Parallel leveraging is becoming popular because the executive can bring his own team and ensure the success of his new venture. The other corporation can use the executive to obtain talent in addition to that of the executive himself. Raiding other corporations, particularly academies, is a cheap way to get high-caliber talent. But it could be costly to the academy and disastrous to a corporation with a less productive breeding capacity. To defend itself, it must then raid another corporation. The question, succinctly put, is: How much is one man worth? The answer may be that he is worth all the men that may leave with him.

The Hogan case of parallel leveraging and the suit that followed put a slight crimp in the quitting and leveraging trends. Actually, the Motorola case was just one among many. Similar suits against former employees have been filed by United Aircraft; Texaco, Inc.; Defense Electronics, Inc.; and Air Inc., a subsidiary of Control Data Corporation. What is at stake in the outcome of these legal cases is the right of the executive to better himself and the right of a corporation to exclusive use of trade secrets. In the years between 1965 and 1968, key industrial states such as New York, California, Illinois, and New Jersey have strengthened existing statutes making the theft of a trade secret a criminal offense. But legal precedents are still lacking. The facts vary in every case. What is stealing in one case might be carrying away personal experiences in another. In any case, these lawsuits have cramped the freedom of mobility in only a small segment of the mobile executive population. This is in the highly technical areas where men are extremely close to the research and development activity and where parallel leveraging is involved. Most of the suits involve two or more people leaving one firm and joining another. The majority of imports are singles and are not in sensitive, technical areas where trade secrets are likely to be involved. As it now stands, managerial quitting and leveraging bulks too large to be reversed substantially by legal rulings.

If the factors of corporate size and growth rate, management quality, ingress-egress rates, executive reputation, and cyclical demands coalesce in favorable amounts, the advantage accruable to the leverager could be substantial. General Motors is one of the very largest corporations with an excellent reputation for producing profits and earnings, with a well-established market position, and with a well-accepted line of products. It is generally regarded as having one of the finest in-depth management teams, and the in-gress-egress rate at division levels and higher is one of the lowest in the country. Using General Motors as a fulcrum would in itself produce an advantage to the leverager that could not be gotten by any other means. Because post-Depression General Motors had not lost many of its top executives, when it finally did begin to lose them each made unprecedented amounts of news copy. Witness for example, the leaving of Semon E. Knudsen, executive vice-president of General Motors, for the presidency of Ford. His advantage in le-veraging is not accruable to a Ford executive of equal station and reputation.

The leverager must be diligent in his regard for the power of the fulcrum. He must know his company well, and he must know how it is regarded by other companies. Too often the leverager makes the mistake of attempting to make contact with a corporation that does not regard his employer highly. Or he fails to use his compa-ny's reputation to the fullest extent possible. The act of leveraging must not be undertaken with haste and lack of forethought. Time and patience are required to reap the advantage inherent in the ex-ecutive's particular kind of fulcrum. The executive who is tempted to accept a tender too early without checking other prospective sources or who does not know his corporation's standing may not spring into the highest or most challenging job that is potentially within his fulcrum's capacity.

A major impetus to tactical and strategical leveraging has come from a communications gap between corporations and executives looking for jobs. Corporations do not know how to say the right things to executives who have quit or are movable, and the latter do not know where the good jobs are. Temporary gluts and voids of executive talent occur in companies and industries. To fill the gap, executive recruitment firms have sprung up in spectacular numbers. These middlemen, known as "headhunters" for middle and top management, acquired a stigma in their early years because the insiders viewed with disdain any effort to pirate executives. In

1959, a dozen of the more established firms attempted to spruce up their bad image by forming the Association of Professional Recruiting Consultants. They had time and a growing executive shortage on their side. By the late 1960s, the placement function had achieved widespread acceptance among industrial corporations. In 1968, electronic data processing equipment kept track of the thousands of executives in the headhunters' files and it also served to record the deluge of requests for executive talent from business and industry. A clear trend toward specialization was evident. Some headhunters recruited for banks and investment houses, others for aerospace firms, and some recruited for regionally based firms. Lendman Associates specialized in lining up, for corporations, all types of young men fresh out of the military service. In 1968, Lendman Associates placed almost three hundred junior officers aged twenty-two to twenty-nine who were draftproof and eager to start their careers.

Executive placement firms are not to be confused with executive counseling firms. Often called "handholders," executive counseling firms advise executives about their prospects and offer guidance, but they do not arrange placements. Placement firms are contacted by the company, which expects them to find the executive and arrange for his transfer to his new employer. Counseling firms specialize in offering self-insight and teaching their clients the manners, graces, and techniques of being interviewed and of successfully landing a job. The executive pays the fee of the counseling firm and the corporation pays the fee of the placement firm. By 1968, executive counseling firms had developed such a stigma that hardly anyone had anything kind to say about them. The many complaints from clients of executive counseling firms provoked a rash of investigations by various groups including the Federal Trade Commission, the Licensing Bureau of New York City, and the New York State attorney general's office. The allegations charged that handholders wrote attractive résumés for people and told them, for a high fee, that they had career possibilities. The résumé game became so widespread, largely because of the aggressive activity of executive counseling firms, that résumés themselves came into question. Be that as it may, in 1968 the executive placement firms placed more than thirty thousand executives and counseling firms did more than $25 million of business.

The widespread use of the services of executive counseling and placement firms attests to the need of executives for help in making intelligent career moves. It is easy to fault these firms, particularly the counseling type, but they are largely sustained by tactical and strategical leveragers. They facilitate the planning of career moves in advance or at the point of quitting and tactical leveraging, and they help executives who are least likely to leave without a better place to go. They have increased noticeably the egress rate among insiders.

In addition, the services of headhunters and handholders are absolutely needed by the victims of a mobile society. The high turnover rate shatters the self-identities and egos of many executives whose personalities forbid them to advance their own interests aggressively. Little is known about the trauma inflicted upon men in the middle and older age groups who suddenly discover that they are not wanted or needed by their employers. The headhunter may be useful in placing them in another job, but the improvement and defense of shattered careers often requires more than help at leveraging. The executive may be so emotionally disturbed that he cannot intelligently use the services of a placement firm. A tender via an executive placement firm may, to an emotionally strained executive, appear to be better than it really is. In his confused state of mind he may jump from the proverbial frying pan into the fire. Actually, his self-confidence is shaken because he is not certain about who he is and what he wants to become. He needs self-insight to help restore his self-confidence before he can intelligently make any career moves. The problem is that his symptoms are below the level of easy identification. He is not disturbed enough to be diagnosed as such and to receive the special attention and skill of a psychiatrist or psychologist. He needs the services of a sensitive adviser or counselor. While in this disturbed state of mind he may gravitate to an executive counseling firm, and he is often a sucker for the gladhander who tells him anything that makes him feel good. While it may be valid to indict some handholders for taking advantage of him, he is quick to read into their advice and suggestions what he wants to hear to restore his feelings of worthiness. Whether the counselor is associated with an executive placement or counseling firm or is a private practitioner of psychology or psychiatry, the executive needs help in order to be certain that his next move will be to his best advantage. The advantages inherent in leveraging will accrue if he has been helped to resolve his problems of identity. Unfortunately, a mobile society accustomed to hearing many success stories is largely incapable of understanding the crucial value of small but timely doses of self-insight. Oftentimes, the difference between a winner and a loser is the addition, at the right time, of the self-understanding required to start a new career or to rebuild an old one. The ethical headhunter and handholder can be bridges that move men from one organization to another, helping them to avoid or resolve career disturbances or to accelerate their rates of career success. The executive and the corporation and society in general stand to gain from the mature use of leveraging.

CHAPTER TEN

The Shelf-sitter

WITHOUT WARNING, the executive's whole world—the career of his choice, his successful reputation—may be demolished by the frenzied movement of an unexpected flush of executives from unexpected quarters of the company or from the outside. Too experienced to go to pieces over the broken promises of the corporation, the executive yet fears that his upward ascent has been permanently arrested and that he may not even be able to stay at his present level. With these terrifying thoughts the executive commences the torturous life of a shelf-sitter.

Suppose you were one of some thirty executive vice-presidents, corporate vice-presidents, and subsidiary presidents who were suddenly confronted with an executive who came in over your head as the number-two man in the corporation. Suppose you were one of several executives who were eight years or more older than the top two men. These circumstances or similar ones often emerged in corporations during the sixties. At Bell & Howell, Robert A. Charpie, forty-two, came in from Union Carbide to be president of Bell &

Howell under Peter G. Peterson, chairman, age forty-two. Fortunately for many vice-presidents, less than a year later he leveraged to Cabot Corporation, where he could manage with full responsibility.

Or suppose you were an executive in Cudahy Packing Co. who believed in experience and frowned upon education. This was your formula and background too, and out from nowhere came eleven new officers who were college graduates and new to the meat industry. How would you feel if you were one step away from the executive suite and, at age forty-eight, you were eight years older than the new outsider who now occupied the suite where your formula says you should be sitting? One reason for this high incidence of arrested mobility is the increased competition for mobility at all levels in the corporation but particularly at the middle-management levels. Increased competition is generally attributed to the rising expectations of the members of our society to be able to improve in education, position, and status. The mobile executive came from World War II better equipped to garner career success. He proved to be a better college student, more skillful in handling people, more confident in managing tough assignments, and more ready to pay whatever costs would be incurred in total success. The managerial ranks were freshened by a steady flow, in and out, of highly motivated, educated, and technically skilled men.

Due to the GI Bill, the ranks of the educated were inordinately enlarged. By the time of the Korean War, the explosive growth of technology and the near exponential rise in the economy had begun to generate a huge demand for managers and professional men with the latest education and up-to-date skills. The better-educated managers had higher estimates of their own abilities and expectation of opportunities and rewards that seemed brash to the insiders of the older generation of executives. When the new breed of future executives confronted old-time middle-level insiders, who had learned their profession the hard way through master–apprentice type relationships and had been reared on the sacred virtues of patience and corporate loyalty, the intergenerational strife and clashes could be heard all around the private sector. Older men left in a huff when they saw better-educated and less experienced youngsters making faster progress, and young men took off when they encountered a slow-moving superior whom they could neither bypass, dislodge, or respect. Competition for mobility broke all bounds and many got hurt, bruised, and permanently injured, with their careers shattered by their inability to work and compete at the same time.

Always the many have been left behind and only the few promoted ahead. But relatively more have been left behind since the middle fifties. The girth-apex shape of the corporation necessitates this fact. The number of managerial employees has increased faster than the number of nonmanagerial employees and executives at the top. In terms of relative growth rates, the corporation cannot be represented by the usual pyramid. The relative increase in the number of managers—men between the worker and the executive suite —requires that we describe the corporation by the profile of a light bulb in which the widest part (the girth) represents middle management. Here competition has been greatly intensified. There have always been more managers than executives, but the relative proportion of managers to executives has nearly doubled (only in the years 1965 to 1969 did the executive ranks at the top begin to swell greatly, and during this period headquarters staff grew proportionately as fast).

The swelling of the managerial ranks may be accounted for by a number of factors. One is the increased use of automation that has reduced the relative size of the work force and has made economically possible an increase in the number of managers and in their salaries. In addition, the number of managers of managers has increased because the numbers of managers that are managed by any one superior has decreased. Project assignments and special task forces of all kinds have reduced the effective span of control. The result has been that at the manager of managers (MOM) level, more men have failed to maintain their upward mobility. Another way to say this is that relatively more men have made it to middle management and relatively fewer have reached the executive suite above it.

The passed-over generation is found preponderantly in the second, third, and fourth levels of management. While the public sees the larger number of men who carry the prestigious titles of corporate executives, it does not see the vast number of middle managers, nor does it see the large number who have had their upward mobility arrested and now sit precariously or recline gracefully on their corporate shelves. This is not to say that the executive suite has no shelf-sitters. This would be a gross misrepresentation of the facts. Among any ten men who sit in the executive suite who are not president or chairman, at least three and as many as five are not eligible, for a variety of reasons, for the top job. In a study of three thousand executives by C. Wilson Randle (in connection with Booz, Allen & Hamilton, a large management consulting firm) to identify promotable executives, only slightly more than one-third qualified for advancement. If we study the number of men who sit around the corporate chieftain and never get his job, this figure is extremely conservative. During 1961 to 1966, about 35 percent of the men at the top were in the age bracket from fifty-five to sixty-five—making retirement necessary within ten years or less. The rates of death, disability, and turnover added another 10 percent. Roughly one of every two were prime candidates for the presidency. The average time in the presidency during this period was approximately five years. This means that during the time it takes two men to occupy the presidency, three of ten men have been cooling their heels and three or four have reached retirement, have died, have become disabled, have taken early retirement, or have left for another company.

Indeed, the executive suite has its share of shelf-sitters, and experience shows that they are the most difficult to manage. Being so very near the top, they are prepared to make persistent claims as few at lower levels can. The question is: How do corporations and individuals tolerate each other when neither appreciates the other to the extent desirable for a smoothly running executive team? The vice-president one step removed from the top may become a thorn in the side that hinders the efficiency of management. Life on the corporate shelf usually provokes a long, continuous confrontation between the executive's essential self and his corporate superiors. Of course, the psychological consequences that generate deep managerial disturbances may extend to all levels. Because this is true, we may examine closely what the men who recline on shelves in the executive suite do every day other than work.

Success in business depends more often than not on what a man thinks of himself. Every businessman has a self-image—a mental picture of himself as an executive. Much of what is called "executive behavior" has to do with the need to feel important as a person. Decisions are made, organizations are changed, personnel are moved because of the executive's need to act like the kind of man he is or wishes he were.

The executive is not alone in this struggle to live up to his self-image. The improvement and defense of one's self-image is probably the most potent of all human needs. Life is filled with events that challenge each man to act as he thinks he ought to act. The compulsion to do so comes not only from within him but also from the men about him who insist on dropping each other into slots. Each executive becomes known for the kind of person he is, his speed of ascent, his special capabilities, his personal idiosyncracies, his spectacular achievements. The executive has, therefore, his own private picture of himself shaped in part by members of his corporate environment and in part by what he thinks he is and what he wishes he were. This self-image serves him well when his corporate universe gives him wide freedom of action. Unfortunately, a happy marriage between the executive and his corporate world is a delicate contrivance. Contrary to popular myth, executives are not cut from the same cloth, especially mobile types, and they do not have identical opinions, attitudes, and prejudices. Contrary, also, to a widely shared public stereotype, many will not do *anything* to succeed. On their climb to the top they grow in self-awareness, self-respect, and powers of self-expression. This is in part a function of motivation, rate of mobility, and variety of experiences and achievements. As the executive evolves a strong sense of self, he becomes better prepared to register a complex of beliefs and values, often formulated as a style, which make for individuality. The self-image produces his mandate to act and, because it is backstopped by reputation and character, he must support in the presence of his colleagues, excluding superiors, the image for which he stands. To do otherwise is to feel guilt and shame and appear to others to be cowardly or capricious—a sort of chameleon.

It is because of self-respect that the talents of men at the top can-

not be easily meshed. Yet an executive organization must be con-
structed to some extent with each change of chief executive. The
greater the mobility in the executive suite, the more free-forming
must be the executive organization and the greater the flexibility required among the members. But flexible men have their limits too.
An executive cannot manage another man's show if his mandate
precludes believing in it. His self-respect and that of his colleagues
is at stake. Yet the chief executive must set the corporate strategy
and assemble his cast, including his crucial subordinates. He knows
that some executives will be unable to fit into his format, and it is
his as well as their responsibility to discuss the conflicts openly. If,
as a result of the attempt to rationally find areas of mutuality, the
dissenter cannot be integrated into the team, he will either have to
accept a secondary spot on the team or quit. Being honorable men,
neither superior nor subordinate expects the other to give his full
measure of effort and devotion to what is essentially a conflict of
principle and policy. To some executives, to stay under these conditions would not only be wrong but unproductive. A shotgun wed-
ding sustained and coerced by rewards extrinsic to job satisfaction
(such as status, salary, pension rights, and stock options) is eminently less productive to all concerned than a happy marriage freely
entered into by the challenge of individual expression. Hence, the
struggle between two men of conflicting mandates often leads one
to retire psychologically or physically from the field altogether. The
quitter makes his position available to another more mentally prepared to work the other man's show.

We have previously noted that quitters do not limit themselves to
the professional or career universe of a single corporation but
choose instead that offered by the economy or society in general.
Wherever they serve as subordinates they prove to be difficult to
manage for they, too, have private mandates that determine their degree of flexibility. As superiors they have to set strategy and reorganize their staffs. They, too, expect to be able to bow out honorably
if they are forced to do so after expressing their honest disagreement. If they do not choose to leave and are not forced out of the
corporation, they have to accept minor positions on the new team.
In this way a high ingress and egress rate will augment the rate of

quitting and leveraging. Because of rapid mobility within and among corporations, a pattern of rising individuality has developed that infuses a militant self-respect and a highly audible self-expression. Suffice it to say, executives are tough to push around—and they are getting tougher.

But a high ingress and egress rate has also augmented the number of shelf-sitters. During the scarcity conditions of the Depression, coercing oneself to fit into a limited slot that truncated individual expression was indeed necessary. Then career management meant getting and keeping a job—any job. But values have changed. The economy has grown out of the circumstances that caused men to waste away doing only what they had to in order to make a living. Still, many will accept a tertiary responsibility when they could leave for greater opportunity to fulfill their mandates. Of course, some are too old to easily relocate or take up new careers. Our society affords them the luxury of withholding aggressive expression of their mandates if they choose to. But unless he is approaching retirement or is maimed or disabled, an executive cannot comfortably sit on his shelf. Unless, of course, he has no mandate to begin with and has always worked and done what he was told and never developed strong managerial beliefs and values. This form of flexibility may make for a good second man, but never a strong first man.

However, lately it has become questionable whether such a man makes a good member of the team. The executive organization must be a finely integrated complex of skills and interests, and chief executives increasingly take a dim view of men who lack initiative and aggressiveness. Executives without mandates do anything or nothing to succeed. As chameleons, they bring to the team everything except diligence in the improvement of competency and in defense of their beliefs and judgments, the two most essential ingredients of a topflight executive team. Still, the mechanics of a shortage of men with initiative prescribes that a certain number of reactors who will do what is expected of them be utilized. Few corporations excel in the tricky art of breeding such superior talent that all members of the executive organization are first-rate performers. The corporation must manage shelf-sitters. Men who do not have strong mandates may easily adjust to whatever the corporation offers them. But then they may not be wanted either.

What gives corporations headaches are shelf-sitters who cannot adjust to their immobility yet will not quit. Their reasons for staying are numerous. Some continue to live with their self-deceptions. If just a flicker of hope remains, they will continue their daily treks to the office. Others will have exceeded their fondest dreams of success and will work only to conserve their gains. Then, too, many shelf-sitters believe that they have rights because of tenure and experience. They show the pattern of the past, when there were always a few executive positions that were often sinecures which held men until retirement. But the biggest headache of them all is one who works for the extrinsic rewards of money, status, prestige, and power. These values that represent kudos to the mobile executive have displaced the intrinsic satisfaction of professional managing. Perhaps such an executive came into his career this way or developed this attitude through years of monotonous effort. But his mandate can just as severely press him into action as can that of the executive who stands up for his professional skills, beliefs, and principles of managing.

His mandate, his mental picture of himself at his future best—shared in part by his colleagues and friends—is what is at stake as the shelf-sitter attempts to adjust to his special niche. Some never make friends with their shelves and live wretched lives, and others salve their egos, find compensations outside the company, redefine their purposes in life, and gradually enjoy the quiet existence of a man who is going nowhere and is under no pressure to prove himself. He no longer lives on the ready, he is prepared for but not alert to opportunities, and he is unwilling to enter the race again—to put his identity on the line. He is now a confirmed, established shelf-sitter.

This problem of shelf-sitting is complicated because shelving has not occurred through systematic or planned effort. As one president said, "It is not a rational, well-conceived device, but rather one that grew up surreptitiously to meet needs." Sound shelf administration was slow in coming because breeder firms were unwilling to acknowledge that not all men had a chance of going to the top. They wanted to keep alive the myth that the route to the top was open to everyone. They were afraid to recognize that to some, if not many, the top was closed. To do so would have been to shrink the carrot before the very eyes of men who most needed it to maintain their faith in hard work and corporate fealty. The result was that those who were left behind were not given the dignity that comes from a frank acknowledgement that all cannot go to the top and that good men are needed at all levels. Breeder firms increasingly recognize that policies are needed to respect those who stay beind and reward those who move ahead, and that careful coordination of the movement and arrestment of men is necessary to make the best use of a firm's manpower talent. The first step in such a program is to identify the several kinds of corporate shelves and the characteristics of the men who occupy them. Shelf-sitters may be men who are illustrated below:

	PA*	AE+	
Man A	A+	P+	Unsatisfied but capable
Man B	A+	P−	Unsatisfied but at ceiling or incapable
Man C	A−	P+	Satisfied but capable
Man D	A−	P−	Satisfied but incapable or at ceiling

* Aspiration + Potential

The column headings PA and AE refer respectively to private aspirations and authorities' evaluation. Private aspirations are the desires of the individual—what he would actually like to do. Authorities' evaluation is a composite of a superior's impression as to whether an individual has promotable talent. For example, let us refer to executive A. Under PA the A+ indicates that he has great expectations of continuing his present rate of mobility or of increasing it. In short, he wants to go higher. Under column AE, the P− rating for this same executive indicates that his superiors believe that he has talent, that they expect him to achieve higher levels of performance and are willing to advance him as fast as the opportunity allows. Similarly, the rating of A− under PA indicates that the executive in the case, C or D, is satisfied to remain at the same place or level and wishes to conserve his gains. A letter P− under

column AE means that the authorities have judged this executive
to be at the peak of his ability and do not expect any sudden change
in his pattern of performance.

Let us now consider executive A. This executive has a temporary
block to his continued upward mobility. He may be temporarily
shelved for several reasons, of which the foremost is that movement
to the top is never an unbroken series of promotions but rather an
uneven series of fast moves spliced unpredictably with slow ones.
During the slow moves he may appear to be more arrested than he
really is. The corporation cannot always program people in keeping
with their developmental and mobility needs at any given time.
There are always some executives and managers who are performing below their mobility and developmental levels. For example, at
least one out of every three executives in the top levels is carrying
responsibilities that are routine to him. He is doing the job "out of
his back pocket," so to speak. He is positioned to be ready for the
call, but he must wait for someone to retire, to transfer, or to be
promoted.

Temporary shelving may occur because business today requires
multiple offensives to meet unexpected needs. Every firm needs
what the sports world calls "a strong bench." Stockpiling of executive talent sometimes two and three layers deep is necessary to assure adequate succession during sudden deaths of key men and
crises of growth and acquisition.

Breeder corporations attempt to maintain a kind of managerial
bank, with many executives waiting to be cashed and drawn into
action and others destined to be deposited. Rich is the corporation
that has large talent deposits, although these will nevertheless de-
preciate if they are left uninvested. The men in the talent pool are
the most valuable to other corporations and are most vulnerable to
leaving if they are sidetracked too long. No amount of challenge
through changing his assignments will overcome an executive's feeling of arrestment if he is not promoted sometime soon after he feels
personally ready. As one corporate vice-president put it, "I was on
the ready line for two years before I got executive vice-president.
Meanwhile, they had me going to Europe every other month on
troubleshooting missions. I did not exactly mind except trouble-

shooting makes lots of enemies and I was wondering if I would get shot down before promoted up. My promotion came one year too late and I almost quit."

Executive A is easily misread because of the growing practice of "outspanning." This term is derived from the practice of unyoking work animals before they fall of their own fatigue. In corporations there are positions in which the stresses are so great that executives cannot be left in them longer than two years before they need the "outspan" or rest. Normally, the higher-placed executives stay in their positions longer than mobile middle managers. One exception to this is the executive in the stress position. For him, two years is the average time which compares favorably with that of mobile middle managers.

Before the sixties, the concept of outspanning was not widely known. What gave it widespread recognition was the fact of rapid corporate growth. During the period, priorities were assigned to functions or divisions and limited objectives were established to be met in a relatively short period of time. Executives arrived and departed, and each of these attempted to execute different limited objectives. Those who did well under the pressure were often moved to another job of equal or more stress. In the second or third job of this kind, good men were often ruined. It became apparent that a sequence of stressful positions had to be spliced by positions that were relatively routine by comparison. At first the executive completing a stress assignment was moved laterally to an outspan position for the purposes of giving him a rest and of saving him for another critical job in the near future. Executives soon discovered that the relatively easy and slow work in the outspan assignments afforded them an opportunity to gain perspective about what they had learned in the stress job. They soon grew impatient in the outspan assignment and their desire to get back into the stream of stress again was renewed. The outspan positions, however, gave them the vital resources of insight and added drive, which were lost from severe amounts of unbroken stress.

Executives who stayed in the stream of stress too long showed a pattern which we may identify as stress reaction. It is most commonly found among men who have executed several sets of objectives in the same stress positions without relief. An early symptom is an inability to tolerate anything that is relatively routine and slow. One day of vacation and the manager is ready to go back to work. He may be unwilling even to consider a vacation. He has a strong tendency to withdraw from any problem that requires careful, meticulous thought and inquiry, a preoccupation with minor aspects of that part of the job that is crucial, and a tendency to freeze his perception of the nature of problems at the point where they are first identified. As one executive undergoing stress reaction said to a staff member, "For god's sake, don't find any more problems than we have now. We've got our hands full as it is."

A later symptom of stress reaction is an inability to react at all to stressful events. Conditioned to handle stress, the executive is unable to get his adrenalin moving at all. He appears almost apathetic. Actually, he becomes careless about critical objectives, treating them as routine and common. When he should spring into total and personal involvement, he relies upon second-hand evidence. His actions become partial and ill-timed. He may sense that he is not reacting as he should and tell himself that tomorrow or the next day he will really sail into the job as he has done many times before. But the zip is gone, and in some cases it may never be retrieved again. The author has seen executives burned out as early as their middle forties because they were not relieved at strategic times. Corporations are much wiser today about the relationship between mobility and stress.

It is hard to control the levels of stress. If a mobile executive is put into a position that has become widely recognized as a stress type, he knows that he has to accomplish limited objectives in two years and he will then be relieved. This knowledge and the desire to maintain his reputation as a high performer will not reduce the amount of stress. A man who knows that he must give his all for a short period of time will attempt to give more than he has in him. On the other hand, if he knows he will be in the job four or five years, he will pace himself as though he were in a cross-country track event. Too often he approaches his stress position much as though he were running a 100-yard dash. This factor of self-induced stress may become as great as the stress inherent in the job itself.

The problem is that an executive's superiors have little control over the amount of stress that he may self-induce. They may warn him not to overreact, but he knows that if he fails in the job, he alone will be held responsible. What his superiors can control is his next job assignment, and if they are wise, they will move him out of the stress stream. He knows, however, that they will do this whether he succeeds in the job or fails. The only thing he can do is to throw his whole self into the job, and the fear that even this is not enough may force him to exceed the limits of his ability and energy. This may solve his short-range problem but create a long-range one. If he cannot apply good judgment in a stress job, what evidence is there that he will make the best use of the outspan—his opportunity to rest and refresh himself?

The advantage of a stress assignment followed by an outspan is found in their geometrical relationship; the one helps the executive discover his potential; the other helps to keep it available to the corporation. The corporation is always in need of identifying the executive who can perform in critical positions, and the executive's potential to do so cannot be fully assessed unless he tries his hand at a high-stress position. The yields are so great, aside from those gained by achieving the objective of the job itself, that one cannot imagine a corporation that does not make instrumental use of stress outspan positions.

The executive in an outspan position has not failed in his previous position, although the rumor mill in the firm will suggest it. What is important is that he know the kind of shelf he is occupying. The pun "shelf insight" is not to be taken as lightly as it sounds. For example, one president put a promising executive on an open assignment merely to keep him busy for a while. This man made the assignment a permanent job simply because he did not understand what was happening. He is still assistant vice-president, but he could by now have become a vice-president in his own right. Another temporarily shelved subordinate, who took the pause too literally, quit because he thought there was no longer any future for him. All of which makes good shelfmanship a prerequisite. Almost everyone who has gone to the top has at one time or another found himself a reservist. The strategy that seems to be most successful for the individual is to move along with the assignment without too much change in his style or thrust. He should not lose his drive or his head. Any change out of the ordinary may suggest immaturity and anxiety.

Turning to executive B, he sits on one of the most densely populated corporate shelves that holds the men whose superiors have judged them unable to advance. The men believe otherwise. Consequently, they rest on their haunches, ready at any moment to spring into action. While this shelf-sitter is the most difficult to handle, he also represents a group that is most diverse in its characteristics. Some members of this group are young, but many are past their prime. Some have been in the organization all their working lives. Some are eminent retired military men, public servants, or educators who contribute counsel or improve the public image of the company but are expected to carry only nominal administrative weight. Many of these "trophies," as they are sometimes called, used to being in the thick of things in previous employment, are unhappy on the shelf and work hard to get off. Sometimes they do so by showing ability previously considered lacking. But in many cases they violate the conditions of their entrance into the firm and are ejected or else moved to what appears to be a more responsible shelf. As one executive puts it, "This shelf-sitter is given a quiet place to think about an important problem that will never be solved." Also among the shelf-sitters are company heroes who carry the scars of great past victories. One may have been the president who once saved the company; another, the engineer whose patents have given the company its secure economic position. Whatever the case, the company has passed them up, but they still hope for a miracle that will restore them to power. Meanwhile, they are treated with dignity and respect.

Next to them is the administrator emeritus who once was a high executive. Because the company wants to maintain the high prestige and honor of all top positions, his status is not tampered with although his authority is withdrawn. However, he still strives to influence and persuade. The real problem is to help him be influential in ways not critical to the program. This is easier said than done, and no amount of added prestige and money will quiet his inner urge to regain power.

All these are less tragic than those who have been inadvertently

dropped down one of the many personnel crevasses of the organization. They may be lost at any level, including near the top, due to
faulty communication, personnel assessment, and training programs.
They may be on a shelf due to rigid adherence to traditional patterns of succession. For example, in many companies the executive
in charge of personnel can never become the company president. A
staff man may never become a line executive. Or, after a certain
age, executives are often not promoted to higher positions because
their tenure is about to expire.

These shelf-sitters have one thing in common. Because they feel
dissatisfied with their superiors' judgment, they are prone to be
overly aggressive to get off the shelf. This, of course, is expected.
After all, if they completely adapted to shelf life, there would be few
competing for top positions. Furthermore, management could be
wrong in its judgments, and this error would not be corrected. The
problem is that they may become active in negative, unconstructive
ways. For this reason, many shelf-sitters who have been incorrectly
judged are lost to the future because they are not able to control
their growing antagonism. Their destructive behavior serves to confirm their superiors' judgment. Some never really give up, and all
find it hard. Managers who have been conditioned by visibility
never give up entirely their hope of going higher. Some will refuse
to read the intended and unintended messages that indicate their
loss of mobility, namely the decreasing amount of exposure, visibility, challenging assignments, and opportunities to evaluate and
nominate. Finally, there is the tendency for superiors to overesti-
mate their mistakes and underestimate their successes.

Executive B's difficulty is that he may not know who the superiors are who hold negative evaluations of him. Only a few, if any,
actually inform him of their true opinion of him. Nor does he always know why he is valued negatively. What causes him to sustain
hope is the ambiguity of the messages that flow from the evaluators.
The more desperate he is for visibility, the more he reads into these
messages. He can easily be misinformed by the literal, benign message. It is odd, but the more the corporation gives respect to a person, the more difficult he finds it to assess the information of his
evaluators. A smile that comes from a superior's desire to make him

feel comfortable may be interpreted as a cue that he is not arrested after all. The same smile may be interpreted the next time as an attempt to patronize him.

Another reason that he keeps alive the hope for mobility is the tendency for superiors to be very mobile and to come and go frequently. The shelf-sitter knows that in a mobile organization an executive can be on a shelf one day and in the stream of action the next. He may want to impress the next superior, and the next, and so on. A third reason for the shelf-sitter not to accept his fate is that managers who are effective only at the present level may be transferred to a different position on the same level. A corporation may move a shelf-sitter laterally and geographically. With each move, he has a chance to gain exposure and visibility. There is always a chance that he may pick up support or even sponsorship.

Some shelf-sitters acquire a sour-grapes attitude. They rationalize that they are better off where they are, life above them is excruciatingly stressful, and that the advantages do not offset the risks. In actual fact, the men who move to the top have been given gradual increases in stress, and with each round of stress they achieve mastery that enables them to undertake a greater amount. Of course, some mobile executives move up too fast and fail to absorb the stress or handle it predictably, but most do not make the big leaps that exceed their stress tolerances.

A classical shelf-sitter in the B group is the "retro-fit." Momentum will carry executives beyond their abilities. A shortage of executives will cause corporations to promote men above their ability. The retro-fit actually is fitted to perform better the position or positions below him or to the side. While his aspirations lie ahead, his abilities lie behind. A retro-fit creates difficult human relations problems when his condition is known. What does a sensitive superior do to him? Does he demote him or let him keep his title and change his job content? If the latter course is adopted, the corporate ladder is distorted because his position is no longer what it appears to be and aspiring to it is fraught with the distinct possibility that it is bigger than it really is or less than it appears. In one case, the division manager of the office products division of a moderately large computer company was discovered to be a retro-fit within two years after assuming the job. The company merely took office copiers from his division, leaving his division with typewriters and dictating equipment. Two men below him quit because they did not want a job that was shorn of one-third of its sales and appeared to them to have lost its priority with the councils of power. Rather than demote the retro-fit, they reduced his job to the point where it matched his span of ability. There are many retro-fits; men who are ahead of their abilities and should revert to levels of matched ability. The problem with kicking the retro-fit upstairs rather than down is that he will distort the picture of the company organization as a ladder which insiders may climb rung by rung. Some rungs do not lead to higher rungs because they are blocked by shelf-sitters who will occupy them longer than they would if they were mobile. Or the positions have been created for the shelf-sitters. For example, the sluggish consumer electronics market in 1967 caused an executive to revise his whole line management in a large semiconductor corporation in the southwest shortly after he succeeded to the presidency. A vice-president of the semiconductor division had a manager reporting to him, but when the new president eased the division head upstairs to vice-president for corporate resources and services, he replaced him with the subordinate. By the fall of 1968 there had been other changes and a rash of departures during which the subordinate was made corporate vice-president. His boss's position was created for him and evaporated when he quit. As a staff position it made sense, but as a position on the corporate ladder it was without significance. Few intelligent executives would aim at his job, and yet the manner in which the executive conducted his job affected the opportunities of people at division level to move up. If middle managers had midmountain blurring, they would not be able easily to decipher the staff executive's degree of influence. Actually, he was a shelf-sitter, but one man in particular did not know it and therefore gave the shelf-sitter inordinate amounts of influence over him. This was called to the attention of the new president, who stepped into the act by reassigning the staff executive, at which point he quit.

The executive in the C group is still another problem. We shall assume that executive C has not rationalized his immobility. He literally feels useful and honorable at his level and does not want to improve his lot; but his private aspirations, or the lack thereof, are not legitimate in many organizations. Mobile superiors do not really understand the manager who is happy where he is. The corporation puts considerable capital resources into the development of men at any level and does not usually feel that the man has the privilege of turning down a promotion. To do so is to say that the company has no right to gain a profit from its investment. Besides, the man who is contented is more difficult to get to jump. Mobile executives maintain that men hungry for promotion are more controllable. For several reasons, then, superiors want the sole prerogative of positive or negative promotion decisions.

The surprise of the past decade was the growing number of shelf-sitters who had unused ability. Often they have decided against future advancement because of the risk and additional responsibilities involved. If they already fitted comfortably on a shelf, it was difficult to move them. Management devised tricks and levers to cope with this problem. "We sometimes send these shelf-sitters to university executive programs to have their sights raised or self-confidence developed," comments one business executive. "We may increase their salaries unusually to stir the pecuniary instinct," says another. A third observes, "We may cut their salaries sufficiently to spur them on."

Some companies have been known to manipulate the executive into such a crisislike position that he either quits or decides to move up. Typically, they find he does the latter, but the decision will not come unless superiors force the issue. Then the big problem often is to get the executive to enjoy his forced promotion. This satisfaction is seldom achieved. "One can force a promotion but one cannot force happiness," said a disappointed president.

What complicates this problem is that this shelf-sitter may attempt to overshoot his actual shelf to allow for a demotion. In such cases, threat of demotion only plays into his hands. He arrives then at the level which he set out to reach in the first place. This shelf-sitter may seem to be easily identifiable because of his abundance of both skill and satisfaction. However, this is not always the case. Many executives entertain a secret desire to sit comfortably on a shelf. They will work diligently to get there. Having arrived, they are not disposed to show too much satisfaction for protective reasons. Not only will they hold their display of satisfaction in mild reserve, but they will also hold back their ability. Shelfmanship here becomes a trick of appearing to be fully capable of holding down the present job but not quite capable of moving higher. Equally dangerous is the art of strategic incompetency, which is displaying a lack of higher executive skills at a few critical times.

The only executive who is free from the anxiety of mobility is the executive in the D group of shelf-sitters. He does not want to go higher and he cannot. He is viewed as performing effectively at his present level and he enjoys the thought of staying at his present level or in his present position. There are not enough of this kind to go around. They represent a happy agreement about their future. They often show all the productiveness of those who are satisfied but able. In fact, they are known occasionally to outproduce them because there is little unused ability to be wasted. However, they can be made to feel insecure, and management must take care to assure them that they are needed. Because they are not expected to assume greater responsibilities, management must not allow them to become sloppy and complacent. Ideally, they enjoy both freedom and security. In a way, these shelf-sitters are less vulnerable than the satisfied but able type because they seldom are forced to take a promotion or to extend themselves.

The satisfied but unable, however, does fear destruction of his shelf through reorganization or changed policies. He will react aggressively when faced with this danger. At such times he may become oversensitive to his and others' mistakes. To get the most out of him, he must be allowed to enjoy his shelf, and this is the crux of the problem. This shelf-sitter can, through the years, become a marginal effective who does just enough to hold his present position and conserve his gains. Corporations are riddled with marginal effectives who resign themselves to their fates and gradually decrease their investment of energy but hope to increase their benefit and rewards. The superior must encourage such a man to do a good job, but he could easily rekindle in him a false hope of going higher. The motivation to do a good job is related to the motivation to go higher. It is difficult to increase the one without increasing the other. Many superiors, therefore, take little action in regard to executive D and instead concentrate their efforts on the more developmental executives A and C.

Of course, the evaluations of superiors are subject to error. There are many shelf-sitters who are developmental but who have been mistakenly shoved aside. The longer they stay in positions with little visiposure, the more difficult it is for them to show developmental talent. Shelf-sitters may have more competency and talent than their reputations suggest. The corporation that becomes hard-pressed for managerial talent has learned to search for it within the corporation. Some breeders keep track of shelf-sitters, and after a number of years at a given level, some are promoted on the principle of testing their evaluations, which in many cases have become stereotypes. The result is sometimes pleasantly surprising. It is less costly to promote some shelf-sitters now and then than to bring along young men to levels above them. Even if the success rate is one or two out of ten, the fallout advantage will justify the effort.

Executives in the D category can easily move from the status of a marginal effective to a noneffective. Such a man is often called a "loser" or an "it" or a "nonperson." In a way, the hazard of the executive life is being pushed by the flux from being "in" (an inside insider), to becoming an outside insider, and finally to the level of an "it." Many executives fail to consider the feelings of a person who once held the reins of authority and power and who now has no presence or weight at all. These "nonpersons" are seen but not listened to, patronized but not evaluated. The "it" can make mistakes with immunity. He poses little danger for the superior or the corporation because he is performing the most perfunctory of responsibilities. The shelf-sitter's mistakes are underestimated, as are the errors of the crucial subordinate, but for different reasons.

There is a kind of executive who is not going anywhere. He may or may not be happy, and in this sense he does not fit squarely into these slots of shelf-sitters. His value lies in his ability to make an individual, functional contribution. A few breeders call him an F.I.C., for functional individual contributor. He is more competent than his label sounds. In fact, the F.I.C. is indispensable to modern corporate management. He may be a lonely scientist working steadfastly in his small lab, a psychologist, a medical doctor who is used whenever his specialty is required, or an executive with a special ability or skill. He may have been a line executive when his rare contribution was first discovered. In most cases, he is extremely happy and his salary level may be comparable to that of his superior or to the best of the executives in group A. He is respected in greater degree than his title and salary merit. And some shelf-sitters attempt to cast themselves in his form. They attempt to show a unique skill that is irrelevant to their job description or position or level. There is an F.I.C. in every executive. Each would like to be known for his individual contribution and as being different from all others. The F.I.C. is this without the need to claim this distinction.

Several times the author has seen a well-loved executive bypassed by a more capable man and gently shunted off to the side, only to reappear with great stature because he cultivated a timely, functional skill. A finance man with great statistical know-how was asked to give way to a young, better-trained accountant type of executive with a strong background in investments and banking. The company wanted to make better use of its cash flow and reserves. The passed-over finance executive went to college evenings and became extremely competent in computer technology and systems theory. In the quiet of his back office, away from the stream of line activity, he drew up a plan for computerizing the control function and was asked to supervise the installation and perfecting of it. Before it was completely perfected, he asked to get more training in information theory, and several years later he popped up in the councils of authority as the expert on decision making theory and communication program design. For ten years he made functional individual contributions that have stamped the corporation as one of the most efficient and progressive in the business world. No one had more access to the board and the president's office. His staff consisted of a secretary, two assistants, and anyone in the corporation he could excite into action. All shelf-sitters who despair of their lowly status and ineffectual positions can take a chapter from this F.I.C.'s book. Opportunity abounds for men to make individual contributions. A shelf is just the right environment for men who want, quietly, to reorder their careers. This is one form of self-nomination.

One of the ways in which a mobile executive may have his upward route arrested is by becoming a subordinate to a shelf-sitter. He often refers to this kind of superior as a "blocker." If the blocker knows that he personally is not going anywhere, he may attempt to hold down the mobile subordinate. He is more apt to do this if there is a wide discrepancy in age between him and his subordinate. Superiors, by the very fact of their presence, tend to block both the exposure and visibility of their subordinates. Some do this more than others. The mobile superior will tend to inform his superior of the excellent work and results of his crucial subordinates. Theirs is a reciprocal relationship of work, praise, and support from which both superior and subordinate benefit. The shelf-sitter, in contrast, aggressively tends to minimize the visiposure of all subordinates, especially those that threaten his security. High performance may shake his feelings of security as well as the high mobility of a subordinate.

Often a mobile executive may be assigned to work for a shelf-sitter because the responsibilities of such a position may call for exceptional talent at times, or the shelf-sitter's weaknesses may require the offsetting talents of a mobile executive. Shelf-sitters have little power of nomination; they must accept what is assigned to them. More than any other type of executive, they tend to look for themselves in their subordinates, who are usually supplementary types, although occasionally some may become crucial to the limited effectiveness of their superiors. It is seldom that they are without their favorites. Their deficiencies and weaknesses and those of their favorite subordinates may be offset by few, if any, balancing skills.

Mobile subordinates with complementary skills may be assigned to balance team effort, but their very strengths threaten the shelf-sitting superior and his favorite subordinates. They may consciously or unconsciously attempt to subvert the effectiveness of their mobile subordinate. Shelf-sitters may move concertedly against them, depriving them of the information and support necessary to do their assignments. Shelf-sitters may assign their mobile subordinates work that does not utilize their strengths. As a result of these antagonisms, a shelf-sitter and a mobile subordinate may clash either openly or covertly. When this happens, the shelf-sitter will attempt to seize upon the difficulty as evidence that the mobile subordinate is not qualified or willing to assume the role of a subordinate. The sponsor of the mobile subordinate may move him rather than move the shelf-sitter. If he does, the shelf-sitter has been successful and remains a block to any future mobile executive.

Sometimes a mobile subordinate may be assigned to a blocker to experience directly the ineffective style of a poor manager. Some of the most valuable experiences of mobile executives come from having to expose their talents to a shelf-sitter and from seeing the various forms of reaction. Sometimes a mobile subordinate may be assigned to help unblock a route that is occupied by a shelf-sitter. In such a case, the mobile subordinate must attempt to overcome the handicaps mentioned above and win the shelf-sitter over to him. This is a fine exercise in which the mobile executive has everything to gain and nothing to lose. If he is successful, he will replace the superior, open up a route, and gain invaluable experience besides. If he fails, he will learn what he did wrong, but because of sponsorship his mistakes will be underestimated. He will simply be moved to another job.

Seldom will he replace the shelf-sitter if it comes to open battle because the corporation sets a high priority on obedience to superior authority and will not allow even a shelf-sitter to be overthrown. Few palace revolts are successful for this reason. In rare cases will the battle between the mobile subordinate and the shelf-sitter result in the summary removal of the latter. When this does happen, the battle has not usually been overt and public, and the corporation can remove the loser without setting a bad precedent. One thing is certain, a battle between a shelf-sitter and a subordinate who has little or no sponsorship is never decided in favor of the latter. In fact, two shelf-sitters in over-under relationships can battle for extended periods of time before either one is hurt radically. The executive who stands to gain the most from a clash with a shelf-sitter is the one who has sponsorship, and he can best impress his sponsor by acting prudently. Essentially this means that he should not embarrass his sponsor by a public demonstration of his differences with his shelf-sitting superior.

Another reason a clash seldom results in summary removal of the superior is that, paradoxically, shelf-sitters are needed at all levels. Without shelf-sitters, there could be few mobile executives. All cannot be of the same sort. Moving shelf-sitters every time they have difficulty with mobile subordinates will destroy whatever dignity and effectiveness they may have. In addition, the mobile subordinate is given a means of dealing with his shelf-sitting superior if the latter is removed at the expense of the former's acquisition of the more mobile and organizationally useful skills. All of which tends to suggest that at any given time, many mobile executives are not crucial subordinates to their immediate superiors. They are temporarily engaged in a difficult struggle to enhance the overall effectiveness of a shelf-sitting superior and his team of subordinates. This is a developmental exercise which holds many potential advantages to the corporation, to the shelf-sitter, and to the mobile subordinate.

To become effective and mobile, the executive must have before him models of effective managerial behavior. He stands to gain immensely from trying out their ideas and techniques and judiciously rating them on the basis of results. There are superiors that represent models of corporate behavior, whose styles reflect the values and priorities of successful men. A representative model may be at any level in the corporation. He may exist at the lower-middle-management level because he has modeled himself after a superior. The executive who has high visiposure of both lateral and vertical types is more capable of spotting a genuine model from a superficial one. He can see that his model's behavior is achieving the kind of results that gain the highest rewards, one of which is mobility itself. The most mobile executives tend to gravitate toward representative behavior.

The modes of representative behavior are manifold. Contrary to many reports, there are a number of ways of behaving that are at the same time individual and still representative. Innovative behavior is what helps to give the executive positive exposure. Occasionally, his superior may be mobile and not representative and not a model. This superior is successfully innovating; he is acting differently yet keeping the support of his superiors. But the subordinate may not know that he can safely attempt to model himself after this superior, or he may be reluctant to do so because he has sufficiently high visiposure to see that this superior's behavior is unusual. Because it takes time to see a positive connection between his superior's behavior and high support, the subordinate may play it safe. If the executive does not have high visiposure, he may fail to see how unique and controversial is the behavior of his superior. He may develop into unrepresentative behavior and go the way of his superior. If the superior succeeds, the executive may also; if he fails, so may the subordinate.

In the early stages of his executive career, a subordinate needs to model himself after somebody. He may adopt the mode of a superior who, unknown to him, is actually a shelf-sitter. First-level men make this mistake quite often. They may become so useful to their superior that they become crucial to his effectiveness. It may be a while before the subordinates realize that they have become too much like shelf-sitters. Because a subordinate has learned essentially weak skills and unrepresentative behavior, his potential for development may be discounted by lateral and vertical superiors. This illustrates that blind conformity and imitation are dangerous.

Most corporations know that a young executive tends to become very impressed by his superior's qualities. To keep him from learning any one mode of managerial behavior, the alert company will give him, as a first-level manager, a chance to work with several superiors before he is discounted. Based upon this reasoning, laterals may occur commonly at lower levels. It is reasonable to expect that a first-level manager who fails dramatically will receive a demotion rather than a lateral transfer, regardless of the effectiveness of the superior. The presumption is that all superiors are effective enough for the subordinate who has sufficient managerial potential to avoid dramatic failure. On the other hand, that all superiors are effective enough to ensure the development of potential talent is never presumed.

In other words, if a new manager fails, it is because he is unsuited for managerial responsibility. If he is evaluated as marginal, it may be because he needs more development. This may include a different position or a new superior or both. If a first-level manager dramatically exceeds his superior's fondest expectations, it is because he has great talent and, hence, great potential. At this point, the manager may be exposed to positions and to superiors who know how to draw out his potential talent and develop it further. He may be given a lateral transfer or a promotion. The principle seems to be that dramatic success or failure is due to the individual, but marginal success or failure may be due to a poor superior. Subordination to several superiors will help to sharpen the distinction between the relative contribution of the subordinate and his superior to his performance.

During the early stages of his career, the future president does not reveal in his managerial behavior exceptional talent or dramatic results. He learns efficiently, however, from his mistakes, which are not of the kind usually ascribed to the lack of talent and potential but are simply entrance mistakes. There are errors that new managers can learn to avoid by exposure to the behavior of effective superiors.

It is a fact that some of the best superiors for instructing new executives are shelf-sitters of the kind represented by group D. They recognize that their advancement in the corporation has terminated, and they have become adjusted to their positions and levels. Often, they have the patience to impart their wisdom, the age to enjoy the coming and going of young men, and the security to do fairly well what they please. This includes singling out an occasional man who has high potential and putting an extraordinary amount of effort into his training and preparation. This kind of shelf-sitter is invaluable in the help that he can give to a young man who may as a result gain a permanent foothold on the corporate ladder. A shelf-sitter may be a developer even though he is not developmental himself. A corporation that knows its range of shelf-sitters may route developmental types through their departments.

The mobile executive has left behind several shelf-sitters who have helped him to become effective. There are few presidents who cannot point to a shelf-sitter and say, "He became a turning point in my career." To these men we may ascribe the term "crucial superiors." This includes both mobile and immobile types. The mobile executive leaves no stone unturned in his desire to gain experience and skill. He is often heard to say, "I have never worked for a superior from whom I have not learned much." In sum, shelf-sitters who either block or enhance development are critical figures in the world of the mobile executive. A shelf-sitter may not be a blocker. He may not be going anywhere, but he may help others to develop their talents and enhance their mobility. For that matter, all shelf-sitters, A, B, C, and D, have the opportunity to play the role of crucial superiors for developing talented subordinates. A lot of route blockage and imbalance would disappear overnight if shelf-sitters were to adopt the objective of developing men better than themselves. The acute shortage of executive talent is partly attributable to the uniform lack of a developmental attitude among shelf-sitting superiors. They fail to develop people as a strategy of survival. They fear that talented subordinates will place them in an unfavorable light. One way they can avoid negative exposure is to have subordinates whose talents match but do not exceed their own. There is sufficient flexibility and looseness in the ways by which work loads may be arranged between superiors and subordinates and among the latter that the work objective may be achieved without an aggressive developmental strategy. For this reason a corporate environment singularly dominated by the ethic of hard work and loyalty will almost guarantee the perpetuation of mediocrity. Because the formal objectives of work are being satisfied, the shelf-sitting superior feels invulnerable to the accusation that he is not doing his job.

Besides, it is hard work to develop talented people and get the formal job done as well. What incentive does a shelf-sitter have to exert the imagination and industry to do more than what is formally required of him? Seen in this light, the efforts of corporations to breed superior talent are precariously hinged upon shelf-sitters doing their part. The weakness in the breeding scheme is represented by shelf-sitters, who by far outnumber mobile types. They can suffocate talented people without the corporation knowing it. The powers that be may suspect that these shelf-sitters are suffocating talent because of the frequency with which young, well-educated men apply for transfer or leave the corporation. But this as an indicator is subject to error for the following reasons. First, the men who egress may not have the emotional maturity to sustain long-run endurance. They are not durable types and will leave sometime anyhow. Second, they may egress not because their superiors lack a developmental theme but because these superiors lack managerial skill in the traditional sense of the term. They are lousy superiors. Third, the superiors may be developing talent, but not that of the egressor. The men who leave are not considered by their superiors to be developmental, and they may be right in some or many instances. Fourth, they may work their subordinates too hard, expect too much, and get too much out of them. The egress rates among subordinates to Geneen at International Telephone & Telegraph and Tex Thornton at Litton Industries are very high. Yet they are known for getting men to walk the last mile for them and for developing many excellent executives. The products of Geneen's "president machine," as it is called at ITT, are among the most marketable executives in the industrial community. As does Tex Thornton at Litton Industries, Geneen has a strong developmental attitude; but unlike Thornton, he demands almost intolerable amounts of work effort, and his crucial subordinates give it.

For these reasons, a high egress rate may not be a reliable indicator of a poor attitude toward developing talent. But it is practically the only indicator available and, therefore, must be utilized prudently. Crafty superiors who are put under the gun to reduce their quit rates may do so without changing their attitudes toward developing talent. Furthermore, the efficiency whereby work objectives are achieved may decrease along with the work level itself. For any superior, maximizing work performance and talent development is terribly difficult. For shelf-sitters, particularly of the B, C, and D categories, it is well-nigh impossible. For example, several corporations that realized this predicament made explicit the norm that one of several necessary conditions for the superior's promotion was to have one or several subordinates of high capability ready to step into the superior's position. Practically no change in behavior occurred among shelf-sitters C and D because they did not want a promotion in the first place. If anything, making this norm implicit in the promotion program established for them minimum standards of performance. They knew better what not to do in order to survive on their shelves. They formulated their strategies of survival more wisely. The lack of a positive reaction was partly attributable to their disbelief that the norm would be enforced and partly to their knowledge that no sanctions were attached to violators. In other words, no one was to be demoted or fired if he did not find or develop highly capable replacements. Shelf-sitters fear demotion more than promotions and salary adjustments.

However, an unusual amount of superficial change proceeded from the offices of the B shelf-sitters. By means of the communication process, they talked a good game. They issued more memos and memoranda about their achievements and spoke more glowingly about their subordinates. Unfortunately, they attempted to impress their superiors about the capabilities of a few subordinates who, as their favorites, were more loyal than capable. The superiors who responded most affirmatively were mobile types or temporary immobiles of category A. The point to be made from knowing the dynamics of shelf-sitters is that they formulate strategies to maintain and enhance their self-descriptions and to reverse those of their superiors' evaluations that are nonsupportive of their self-descriptions. The utilization of a developmental policy with their subordinates must be consistent with the shelf-sitters' career strategy or it will not be accepted. For this reason, the executives who are most apt to develop talent are those most likely to desire mobility and to be mobile. Mobile executives need capable subordinates because the latter increase their effectiveness and, hence, their mobility opportunities. If executives do not have or do not want opportunity to improve, it is not logical to expect that they will produce capable replacements.

The answer to this dilemma lies partly in minimizing the production of shelf-sitters without ridiculing their contributions. Not all can be mobile, but not all immobility is a result of personal choice. Much immobility results from poor managing, faulty evaluation, too rapid mobility, and careless importing of outsiders. Many men sit on shelves because the corporation does not allow in-house recruiting. In the most confirmed shelf-sitter there resides a latent spark to do something different and a desire to be more effective.

He might want to practice self-nomination, but in all probability he is not aware of opportunities to move within the organization and needs to be encouraged to seek a transfer. Career day represents a technique of in-house recruiting. At least once a year the corporation formally declares a career day during which every boss becomes a potential headhunter and job hunter. Preceding this day a list of job openings and permanent reassignments is given to each individual. Anyone at any level may apply for a transfer with total immunity. Since both superiors and subordinates stand to gain from career day, each releases the other from his commitments and loyalties. Of course, the applicant may be judged not qualified, but the idea becomes quickly established that the individual as much as the corporation must assume responsibility for his career.

In corporations that have tried career days, the transfer lists show the kinds of moves that occur in place of quitting. Men made career relocation moves, career changes, and initiated career acceleration. Managers of technical personnel moved to other divisions, to other geographical locations, or to other laboratories. Managers returned to scientific research, executives of staff groups became functional individual contributors, sales executives assumed marketing roles, and lawyers were assigned to line responsibilities. Some made rather big jumps up and others made moves that gave them visiposure. Even those who moved down the ladder showed a high degree of pride. The key to their willingness to move to lower-level assignments was the fact that they chose to move and everyone knew it. In the vast majority of cases, only a slight loss of salary occurred because management figured the difference as part of the cost of recruiting. In all cases, the career-day mover was assured that he could always move back to a job comparable to the one he had left. In the course of five years, few chose to return but many opted for a second career-day move.

The long-range effect of this career-day program was to make legitimate the right to apply for transfer at any time the individual wanted to improve himself. He did not have to wait for career day to make his move. But more importantly, the increased emphasis upon becoming and remaining mobile elicited an enlightened attitude toward becoming effective and qualified. Many middle managers responded by utilizing better the talents of their subordinates. There were fewer shelf-sitters.

The producing of shelf-sitters largely comes from strategies of dealing with organizational reality. Men become what their limited opportunities require of them. Few shelf-sitters evolve from acts of free choice. The man who protests that he loves his work and desires no other challenge is more likely saying that he has learned to enjoy what has been given him or forced upon him.

The contriving of institutions such as career day to encourage individuals to step forward and practice self-nomination would not have to occur if corporations put more faith in the capacity of aspiring executives to determine what is best for them. Career day is not the starting point. Rather, self-nomination starts when individuals are allowed to say "no" with immunity to moves initiated by the corporation. In one corporation the author worked individually with twenty middle managers who were discovered by mobility auditing to have been geographically moved four times in five years. The division president was literally stunned by the extent to which geographical movement had gotten out of hand. So were the managers. He asked, "Why didn't they say 'no'?" The middle managers reported to the author that they did not think they could without jeopardizing their careers.

This corporation, which later adopted a form of career day, started first to correct this problem by allocating a specific number of geographical moves to each division on a per capita basis. But this policy was soon violated by requests upon requests for special dispensations. Then the corporation adopted the policy of allowing men to decline a corporation-initiated move and backed it up with strong measures of immunity from reprisal. An ombudsman with an open channel to every employee was charged with the responsibility of adjudicating violations of the immunity policy. The adoption of career day was a logical extension of the right to say "no." Individuals now had the right to initiate their own moves, a form of saying "yes," by self-nomination. Managers and executives became aware that they had a responsibility to themselves and to the corporation to say "no" to moves initiated by the corporation as much as the corporation had the responsibility to evaluate self-initiated moves. Such a practice served the mutual interest of both parties. Among shelf-sitters, then, is an untapped reservoir of talent. While corporations increasingly rely upon executive recruitment firms to fill their personnel voids, much of the needed talent reposes underneath their very noses.

In conclusion, men who enjoy the challenge of their work and want nothing better represent the stuff of which successful organizations are made. If out of free choice they decide to stay put, they must be given commensurate amounts of dignity. On the other hand, the corporations must not presume that all shelf-sitters have made free choices. They must be alert to the many ways that organizations induce more shelf-sitting than simple free choice alone would allow. To repeat, shelf-sitting grew surreptitiously as one of the many perversions of the loyalty ethic. In the corporation with an eye to acquiring, developing, and keeping talented men, loyalty to career becomes corporate loyalty.

CHAPTER ELEVEN

Success Chess

THE MOST IMPORTANT RULE for the person who sits down to plan his career is that he must comprehend the success game in its entirety. He must see things as they are. The proper term here is "reality-centered," and achieving such an attitude is a full-time effort in itself. It is all too human for men to perceive selectively, to allow their prejudices and biases to infiltrate their receiving apparatuses, to judge normatively before comprehending factually. Unfortunately, the opportunity to manage a career has increased at a greater pace than the awareness of what it involves. A little bit of success tends to produce easy generalizations that become overly binding upon future decisions. Actually, the successful executive acquires tentative rules that are subject to constant testing by experience or by the acquisition of information from more experienced people. The earmark of a future winner is this capacity to seek information that produces new prescriptions for action. In a sense, the executive objectifies his career and his career universe by, from time to time, stepping out of them mentally. This breaking of ego-

involving ties provides the perspective of a player in a game.[1] He
needs to know the rules of intelligent playing and the moves that
are available to him in any position. In other words, he needs to
know the constraints and opportunities that inhere in his game situation and the costs that accrue from any one move in terms of his
total set of options. These are his opportunity costs, which give him
a measure of what he is sacrificing by opting to move here or there.
In addition, he must understand trade-offs. These are personal
values that identify what is more and less important to him as he
visualizes his career program. Will he take less money for greater
challenge and, if so, how much less for how much more? In other
words, he perceives himself objectively as a subjective being by
identifying his private goals and interests. *He* becomes the essential
reality by which he will manage his many moves.

The study of mobile executives reveals this reality-centeredness.
The ultimate champion is one who, with a sweep of his critical eye,
visualizes the entire board before him and plans every move liable
to help him reach his career goals, taking into account at the same
time the likely moves of his opponents. Success in business relates to
success in chess. He must think ahead. The inability to plan his
moves far into the future restricts the executive to the superficial
strategy of making one move at a time. If the reader were to enter
any network of corporate beings, he would find endless numbers of
managers and executives working at the game rather than playing a
strategy to win. For the most part, they refuse to believe the reality
of their existence. They work for a living rather than manage their
careers. They have no choice but to be at the mercy of the corporations.

These immobiles would not be the tragical figures that they often
are if their decisions to stay behind while the winners pushed themselves to the top came from genuine choices based upon careful
readings of their goals and the manifold opportunities to achieve
them. In this way, some of the happiest people in a mobile society
that demands the mentality of a nomad could have the deepest
roots, and they should be respected for knowing their limitations

[1] The author is indebted to Hal Higdon for refining the concept of success
chess.

and real interests and wanting to settle down and stay put. This is their form of self-nomination. They "win" by "losing." At least one of every three aspirants to the top pulled himself out of the game of success because he realized that he was not equipped to continue his rapid pattern of mobility or simply did not want to. Others broke down because they had failed to recognize their thresholds of stress soon enough. Still others fell behind because they could not assimilate their experiences as fast as their next assignments required. They failed to perform effectively in their new positions.

On the other hand, our society does not have enough people who enjoy what they are doing and are content with what they have. They form the glue that keeps organizations together and they make mobility possible for others. But they may not be ready for the glue factory. They may be competent immobiles. Unfortunately for many others, their decisions to drop out of the success game are forced upon them by their employers or their wives and children. Such a decision may be based upon ignorance of the real choices even after he who makes it has lost out in one game, or it may be made from the lack of courage and independence. These immobiles represent the disadvantaged of the corporate world who are seldom recognized as such because of their lackluster personalities and their apparent high regard for citizenship and community involvement. But they are the real casualties of a mobile society. They are the alienated ones who may be seen going into their bars and taverns where they stop after work for a "belt" before they catch the subways and elevateds for suburbia. Or at home they engage in other rituals of relaxation and relief and escape before they find themselves involved after dinner in their many family and community activities. They may even be defined by neighbors as "big wheels," but while physically living they are psychologically dying because they are bored by the lack of challenge in the routines of their work. Because their community roles do not require the career risk and the mental verve and agility that go with more responsible positions, their minds slow down to an easy, comfortable pace. They are like idling reciprocating engines that are about to run out of fuel.

Still, these shelf-sitters get up at the same time every day and go to the same stultifying jobs which they do "out of their back pockets," and repeat the cycle day in and day out. For these managers and executives life is a veritable treadmill whose boredom is broken occasionally by the aggressive pursuit of activity off the job. But peace of mind remains beyond their reach. In a mobile society, few men can achieve self-satisfaction who must rationalize their boredom at work by appealing to their contributions to wife and family and community. The male ego is served most efficiently by the self-satisfaction generated from career achievements. No one is quite as old mentally as the executive who has been working twenty years for wife and children, and no figure is more tragic than the same man years later who faces retirement knowing in a final sense that he settled for less than he might have become. To mix metaphors, growing deep roots is, for him, digging his own grave. Career management is the ingredient today that teaches men how best to behave in order to succeed. It is a way of life that may overcome the fears and feelings of alienation, of being in the hands of an inhuman monster that paws young men into prematurely old men. In contrast to the alienated executive is the individual who practices overidentification with the corporation. This is the worst of all human relationships because it produces a fraudulant form of morality. He assiduously practices the theme, "my company right, never wrong." Insiders are particularly vulnerable to becoming company-centered. The corporation represents the sum total of their career universe. This identification produces a corporation with enormous power over the careers and destinies of its true believers for whom either alienation or overidentification becomes the apparent escape.

The larger, more powerful the organization, the more men must manage their careers in terms of their own coordinates and free choices. Success chess allows men to intelligently counteract the arbitrary decisions of their corporations, to address themselves as private persons, and to restore the balance between the needs of the individual and those of the organization. In short, the highest good accrues at that point where self and corporation intersect for mutually beneficial purposes. The final arbiter of this relationship must be the individual himself, since only he can commit himself to worthy goals and can experience the effects of self-condemnation or self-justification.

The mobile world offers freedom from the tyranny of working for a living. The opportunity to become mobile requires skill to make career events happen by design. The rules of the success game represent probabilities of the real world that the player must evaluate with judgment. They cannot be applied equally at any given time because some may be more relevant than others. A faithful reporting of the rules of success chess by men who have successfully managed their careers would initiate the following guidelines. All of these rules assume implicitly that whatever the move, both corporate and personal value will result. That is to say, if one is unhappy, he cannot be at his maximum best. If the corporation is unhappy with him, he cannot complacently sustain his illusion of security—not in a mobile world.

Rule No. 1.   Maintain the widest set of options possible. Options represent present or future opportunities to alter your behavior. It is less important to know where exactly you are going than to keep your options open. For example, what are you doing to your options when you accept a technical assignment that will diminish your opportunities to manage? What is the relationship between the time to be spent and experience to be gained from that technical assignment in terms of your opportunities to gain and show managerial expertise? Watch your 90:10 technical-managerial mix. Closing of your options may occur by remaining too long in technical work, be it accounting or engineering. Do not become stereotyped as an excellent technician in a company that wants both technical and managerial expertise or strictly the latter. When you see that you are becoming stereotyped, make a move within or without the company to break the stereotype. Be sure to maintain or enhance your options by joining a firm that values your interest in managing. As a second example, what are you doing to your options if you become stereotyped as a staff man? The fastest route to the top includes healthy doses of line experience. Then your staff expertise will be more beneficial in preparation for your line skill. It does not matter when you start as long as you maintain balance. Usually more line experience than staff will increase your options, and the reverse will diminish them. The higher you go the more influence and persuasion counts, rather than authority, and this can be best learned in staff. Hence, staff is the ace-in-the-hole card, but it is most powerful when played with a fine line reputation.

Rule No. 2. Observe the penalty of loss of career time. The most precious commodity is career time. Do not waste it by working for an immobile superior. The chances are that a shelf-sitter will stay—that he will not be replaced. Shelf-sitting is related to two phenomena that identify most corporations that have inside tracks to the top. They are route imbalance and route blockage. Route imbalance is a condition in which some routes that transport men to the top acquire more men at a given level in the corporation than can be promoted to higher positions. For example, suppose that in one company accountants move up rapidly and in large numbers into positions carrying middle-managerial responsibilities in finance and accounting. Suppose, also, that few men from the accounting channel go to the executive level in this corporation. The accounting channel has imbalance. Balance exists if the channel transports its per capita share of men to the top. Suppose in this same corporation that managers at the same levels in engineering processes move up more slowly and in smaller numbers, but a greater per capita share of them go into the top corporate levels. In fact, there are few future officers of the corporation who do not spend the major share of their middle-management careers in engineering and allied responsibilities. Thus, engineering and accounting functions are imbalanced. Another way to identify route imbalance is by looking at the mobility rates of divisions. For example, in this same corporation a particular division has three times the average number of managers at middle-managerial levels than the average number for all divisions, yet it produces less than one-third of its per capita share of executives. These kinds of imbalance are extremely common in the world of mobility.

Route blockage is a condition that occurs when the route to the top in any division or function is blocked by immobile men. Suppose in this same corporation that upper-middle managers in accounting functions and allied responsibilities are blocking the upward mobility of managers below them. This condition may be discovered by the number of managers in lower positions who either quit the company and attempt to leverage or apply to central personnel for a transfer. Because of this route blockage, men have their upward mobility rates severely curtailed and log jams pile up men on top of men. It must be noted that route blockage may be partly a route imbalance, but not all imbalance is a function of blockage. There are blockers even in highly mobile channels.

When the mobile executive runs up against a condition of route imbalance or route blockage, he has to extricate himself in order not to lose precious amounts of career time. But this maneuver is most difficult without using his option of quitting and going to another corporation that offers greater mobility to men of his functional identity. If he stays inside the company, he must let it be known to central personnel, to his superior, or to someone who has powers of nomination that he wants to get into another route. But watch to see how much the loyalty ethic is in vogue. This is a booby trap. Loyalty is essentially working hard with little overt display of desire to be mobile. The mobile executive may show his true colors under the flag of high achievement. It is presumed that if he works hard and diligently, that he wants to get ahead. He may ask for promotions, and few turn them down without arousing the distrust of superiors. The principle is that he who thinks more of himself than of his work and superior cannot be loyal. If he does, he is power-hungry—a climber. Watch this stereotype. As a general rule, mobile superiors move every three years. Determine how much time he has left before he will probably move and then make your decision whenever you become convinced that his upward mobility has become arrested. Be careful not to become his crucial subordinate or you may become equally arrested with him.

✓   *Rule No. 3.* Become a crucial subordinate to a mobile superior. Not just anyone will move when the superior moves. The crucial subordinate is as important to his boss as the boss is important to him. You will know how crucial you are to him by how much depends upon your performance, by the number and the quality of your special assignments and projects, and by how much your behavior produces consequences. Remember, in most corporations, power and authority are defined differently. Authority is the right to order behavior and expect compliance. As such, it is delegated by men in higher authority, belongs to a position, and is inherited by the managerial occupant. Authority is viewed as proper and legitimate, a product of a natural ordering of men and their endeavors. Superiors have to maintain their authority over subordinates at all costs. This is done by assigning work to them and delegating just enough authority so that they may be held accountable for the results. The principle is that authority should be commensurate with responsibility, and since this is a nebulous equation and hard to measure objectively, most superiors underdelegate to avoid the worse sin of overdelegating, which may reduce the authority differentials that must be maintained at all times. This asymmetry produces relationships in which the superior remains unquestioned. He, in turn, defers as a subordinate to *his* superior, so that the corporate ladder may be preserved as an authority structure.

Mobile executives usually work to gain the capacity to influence others, including superiors, more than they are influenced by them. A subordinate may have power to influence his superior, but he never has authority. He influences his superior by becoming an intelligent worker in his behalf. By means of his outstanding contribution to his superior's effectiveness, he can greatly determine the jobs and degrees of authority assigned to him.

Be sure you note the base of your power and be wary if your power with your boss is supplementary rather than complementary. When you add to your superior's strengths you have less chance of going with him than when you fill in his voids, especially his managerial rather than his technical voids. If your complementary relationship is technical, he may move up to where his void dissipates, and with it you go too. Remember, trust is more crucial than loyalty. If you have trust and are trustworthy, loyalty is unimportant, but without it, loyalty becomes all-important. Trust is to be accessible, available, predictable. Two evil men may trust each other and not be loyal. The same goes for two good men. Never put yourself ahead of your boss even if you are terribly crucial to him. Why flaunt power in front of his face?

Rule No. 4. Always favor increased exposure and visibility. Every corporation has strategies that determine routes and practices that maintain them even when strategies would change them. Make sure you know what kind of route you are in. If manufacturing men inherit the presidency along with an occasional finance man and you are in sales, determine if you have gone as far as you can in sales without inordinate amounts of effort. Remember, sales is a legitimate route. It will take you to the top but not, perhaps, in your company. But do not move if you are still mobile in sales. When the cue comes to you that you are immobile—your job is becoming routine and dull or new job titles are being used in lieu of promotion, salary raises are ordinary or very large to keep you there— leverage to a corporation that has a strong reputation for being sales oriented. Remember, a no move is a move just as "no decision" is a decision in today's fast-moving world. You have decreased your options and lost career time the more you do the job out of your back pocket. You are losing experience and competency and career time. Perhaps a lateral move is in order. A move to the side at the same level in another function, department, or division may increase your visibility and exposure. It can only be made with finesse if you have achieved noteworthy performance in the job from which you are seeking a transfer. Besides the fact that you will not be as likely to get a transfer if you have not performed well, a transfer without a good reputation merely brings negative exposure. You merely let others know about your lack of skill and effectiveness. A lateral move is most powerful when you need it least from your superior's limited point of view. You know that he is cutting down your experience and visibility, but you cannot say this to him or you will give the play away. Hence, the power of a lateral move lies in the apparent virtue. You want to better yourself after first having made a major contribution to the corporation. Also, the manager must realize that he can move backward by staying where he is. To avert negative mobility, the individual must entertain the possibility of moving backward to move forward. For example, laboratories usually carry low exposure and visibility. One may sacrifice a high position in a lab to a lower position in a priority function or division and move ahead faster. Never be proud, always be alert to opportunities, and the leveraging down in order to move up faster must be considered a real possibility as it increases options and avoids loss of career time.

Rule No. 5. Be prepared to practice self-nomination. The mobile executive constantly scans the job horizon inside the company and outside. Working hard and intelligently will, of course, maintain options more than diminish them unless, of course, you are in a nonpriority function, department, or division. But everything else being equal, a high performer who knows what options are opening up because of transfers, deaths, retirements, or newly created positions has the best chance of applying for them. Boldly but properly let it become known to men with power of nomination and sponsorship that you want the job or want to begin to qualify for it. It is amazing the numbers of important people that will become aware of you for the first time because you stepped forward to express your desire to improve yourself. If you avoid carefully the indictment of being power-hungry and a ladder climber, you can properly shed your anonymity. Even if you do not get the first job you applied for, you become exposed to the right people. The consequences may be very positive, and if they are not, then you have a very important piece of evidence that, together with other facts, may suggest that this is not the corporation for you anyhow. This information must be treated as part of the reality to which your career strategy must be sensitive. Remember, at least two moves in a typical career span will be by self-nomination. If your corporation practices only nomination by superior, you can waste career time and have your options restricted by the immediate superior. The most powerful attribute of this rule lies in not having anyone who is your immediate superior determine your options. There are always some superiors who take it upon themselves to determine all the options of their subordinates—to manage their careers for them. Self-nomination prevents anyone but the individual himself from restricting his options. If your superior will not give his consent to allow you to self-nominate, he probably does not respect competency and the urge of competent people to keep themselves mentally stimulated. He is the wrong superior for you. Hence, the practice of self-nomination will give you information about your company and superior that is terribly crucial to managing your career. Do not be surprised if it finally does succeed after you have tried several times.

/   *Rule No. 6.*   Egress from the company at your convenience, not that of another. Move about with a determination that elicits respect. You know what you want, where to get it, and how to get it efficiently. If you decide to egress, do not let others determine your time, mode, and speed of egression. Always leave on the best of terms. Never allow a face-off to occur. If you see that you are on a collision course with your corporation or a player of greater momentum and sponsorship, head it off by either reducing the risk or extricating yourself from the trap by egression. Forestall the inevitable, because otherwise it will be difficult for you to return in the future, should you choose to do so. Quit while you are ahead unless, of course, you believe morally in your cause and wish to fight to the end. Such causes should overrule career designs, for they represent the stuff of which character is made. But if you find that your confrontation or collision is less than moral, if it is something for which sacrificing options and career time is unnecessary, anticipate the worst and take to the hills. Career management under these conditions is the better part of valor. A distinction may be made between the informal organization and the formal. If the grapevine indicates that you have goofed, leave posthaste, before the formal organization gets around to mustering the evidence, formalizing the charges, and legitimizing the penalty. This advice is especially pertinent if your goofing becomes identified as a mistake rather than an error. The difference between incompetency (mistake) and error (human frailty) is enough to slow your momentum. The question concerns your degree of momentum. If you have a long string of high achievements and high-level sponsorship, treat the consequence as an error and go about your business as if nothing happened. But if you do not have strong momentum via high-level sponsorship nor the virtue of a moral cause, egress before the formal organization makes you into a mark. Once the formal organization speaks through your superior to mark you for extra sanctions and penalties, you can become a scapegoat for all kinds of trivial sins of omission and commission going as far back as several years. The spoken word may reduce your options for returning or going far more than the unspoken.

Rule No. 7. Quitting requires the benefit of a rehearsal. Quitting is leaving without a job in hand. It is more often than not a response to interpersonal conflict. As an emotional release, entirely legitimate to human beings, its satisfactions can be short-lived. The number of executives who have fired their corporations in the afternoon and rehired them the next day are too numerous to mention. A truer test of whether you can enforce your quitting desires is to write out your resignation, put it in a safe place in your desk, and give yourself a week before you hand it to the corporation. Go home and inform your family that you have quit and then handle the consequences. Later, after informing them that you were rehearsing, take the role of the individual who has actually quit. Proceed to take a well-deserved vacation for a week, think of what you need to do to get a better job, what you want that you do not have, how to present yourself before placement firms to garner a better job. You might even bring your biographical data sheet up to date and send it to an ethical headhunter. After one week of rehearsing, the answer will come to you. Then act with the vow that you will not rehearse the act again. Next time is "for real." A week or so of careful role-playing will cut through the emotions and bring a degree of objectivity to the scene of conflict. Remember, you are not going to restrict your options unnecessarily. To avoid becoming your own worst enemy, you are going to be honest about who is causing trouble for whom, what the constraints and opportunities are, and how they can best be removed short of firing your corporation. Many have quit because they deceived themselves about the true source of responsibility for their career difficulty. This may lie more with the individual than the corporation. If you suspect this and have the courage to break through your self-deception, you will quit quitting every other day because of the stress created by ambivalency. Never leave the board in a state of high emotion.

Rule No. 8. Define the corporation as a market. For purposes of mobility, the corporation must not be visualized as a place in which to work for a living. It does not buy hands like it used to. A distinction must be made between talent and skill. The corporation does not buy talent; it cannot be bought, nor can it readily be identified. The corporation buys skills, and one can lose his skill but not his talent. Skill is best determined by real achievements, performance. The corporation represents a marketplace for skill that yields high performance. Skills change with corporate and economic cycles. When you find a company that values your skill highly, maximum effort should be dedicated to grinding out as much mobility as is possible before the cycle changes to favor another. In the last five years financial skills have become highly valued. Not by all corporations, of course. Men have stayed in financial activities in corporations that do not have a high cycle of financial priority when they could have leveraged to corporations that have high demand for their skills. If you conceive of corporations as being markets for specific skills, then go to the market that will offer you the greatest value. It is important that you read the economic cycle of your industry and economy for an advance profiling of your future constraints and opportunities. As another example, international business is a priority area now in many companies. If you can market yourself in that division, you will gain higher returns on value received than if you stayed in the domestic side of corporate business. Many executives worked hard with their noses to the grindstone when they should have been interpreting carefully the *Wall Street Journal,* the business section of the *New York Times, Business Week,* or some other periodical that keeps tab of corporate and economic cycles. Care should be taken about deciding when and where to leverage. If you hear of a corporation changing its strategy to include finance and finance is your skill, be careful of the timing. You may be too late once the corporation has already moved the right people into the new priority route. This is especially true because of the concept of crucial subordination. If the new president is a financial man from the outside, he probably will practice parallel leveraging and bring several strong financial men with him. What is desirable is to go to an industry or a company that is just about ready to pop your way and join it at a high enough level to be discovered when the strategy changes. This is what Lynn Townsend did at Chrysler. He joined it just before it moved into a strong financial orientation. He literally fell into it. But did he? Success does not arrive quite as nonchalantly as may at times appear. Good timing prescribes that you get in before the action starts, and the action will give you inordinate amounts of exposure and visibility. This constitutes leveraging at its best. It only *appears* as luck, whereas the leverager has read the economic and industrial barometers carefully and made his move accordingly.

Rule No. 9.   Never allow success to preempt your future. If you can succeed in one thing you can probably succeed in another. If you fail in one area you can probably succeed in another. The laws of probability dictate that a very complex organism called the human being can span several if not many areas of activity with skill and dispatch, and one cannot attribute to accident success in any one area or endeavor, nor is there such a thing as a natural, single endowment. Men are not born to do just one thing well. If you can have fun doing one thing, you can have more fun doing something else. Hence, the repotter (who changes his career rather than merely his career location) is made from the stuff of which mobile executives are made. Why should not success mean making several careers in the span of a normal life? Today men can entertain the option of two and three career lives. The one career life that transforms executives into one-worlders is no longer necessary. For many it is not even desirable. A tour of duty in business, then education, then government or banks can create high challenge irrespective of the achievement opportunities in each assignment. One can be a success without climbing a single corporate ladder. For that matter, success can come to men who move horizontally, who try, for example, applying systems theory and design to an office products division of a corporation, then to an education organization, then to a hospital. Why should one always have to climb vertically when repotting can be a lively livelihood? One today can become a kind of consultant who moves as the challenges that befit his interests open up. All too often success goes to the executive's head. He tends to identify himself after a few years of success in a given area as being a "natural." His talents exceed his self-definitions. His success prevents him from reaching for new and different careers and goals. He becomes victimized by his past achievements and, hence, immobilized. The odd thing about this immobility is that a failure may be more likely to try another area than the winner. Given the winner's logic, the failure should give up. However, the rich supply of talent that belongs to each human being allows for the probabilities of second and third careers whether he has failed or succeeded. This is truly the mobile executive's faith.

Index

Index